Decade
of Crisis

Decade
of Crisis

America in the '60s

Edited by
Andrew Kopkind
and
James Ridgeway

A MERIDIAN BOOK
WORLD PUBLISHING
TIMES MIRROR
NEW YORK

A MERIDIAN BOOK

Published by The World Publishing Company
Published simultaneously in Canada
by Nelson, Foster & Scott Ltd.

First printing — 1972

WORLD PUBLISHING
TIMES MIRROR

Contents

Introduction

The temptation to fit history into customized categories leads writers into the murkiest level of journalistic hell; and the more momentous the times, the greater the temptation. Even at its best, categorization denies the contradictions which are at the bottom of any age, and forges neat narratives out of thin threads. History, after all, is more process than progress, more spatial in its dimensions than linear.

The decade of the 1960s in America was so full of change and so extraordinarily confusing, that journalists seemed to utter relieved sighs when the arbitrary ten years' span ended and they could attempt to make sense of it. So far, however, the attempt has largely failed. The only commonly accepted description for the period seems to be "crisis," which does not explain the decade's effect, but merely names it.

The chapters in this volume — all derived from articles in the weekly news paper *Hard Times* — are not meant to sum up an age but to present aspects of a historical process. The years in which *Hard Times* was published as an independent weekly — the last of the decade of the sixties — were ones of phenomenal social criticism. The critics were everywhere: in traditional institutions such as universities, the mass media, and political organizations; and in new and imaginative counterparts such as the underground press, rock music, antischools, and radical political groups. Most important, criticism began to be perceived directly from the example of action: in the streets, in communes, in political collectives.

Hard Times was something of an anomaly in that critical activity: at once traditional in form and style and radical in content and action. Increasingly, the writers and editors abandoned much of their roles as detached critics and observers and became part of the process they were describing. It could hardly have been otherwise; in one sense, detachment, privatism and professionalism were underpinning values which had to come under attack.

In the years these articles were written, the crises in American life had moved from a concern for elements of institutional forms, to the very institutions themselves, to the consciousness of people within those institutions. For example, the movement for Negro civil rights of the early sixties went from sit-ins against discriminatory restaurants, to an attack on the racist nature of capitalism, to a radical critique of racism as inherent in the mass — and individual — psychology of American society.

* * *

It seemed to us that the primary purpose of journalism in the years of *Hard Times'* weekly publication was radical criticism, and secondarily a projection of possibilities for a "new society." For it did not seem logical then to give concrete form to ideas that had no chance yet of developing from the processes still in motion. As the institutional and political crises moved into the realms of consciousness, that priority seemed to become more valid; the urge — and the pressures — to come up with "solutions" were avoided, and perhaps wisely, by radical critics: "game plans" were best left to the apologists and reformers. We saw "problem" and "solution" not as separate entities, but as aspects of one historical process. For instance, Woodstock Nation was hardly a solution to the problem of a degenerating plastic culture, but an oppositional form: an active attack on the older cultural values. To see "hip culture" of the last few years as an ideal, or nearly ideal, form of social behavior seems like jumping the gun—and missing the point. In the same way, Weatherman politics (such as it was) could not be a significant organizational form, but rather a terrifying way of criticizing traditional forms which had failed to satisfy new needs and new demands.

The reportage and journalistic essays in this book begin to lay out the extent of radical criticism in the last two years of the critical sixties, when there were still integrating forces holding new and old forms in some common context. Since then, it seems, much of those forces has been dissipated; at least, it is difficult to occupy intellectually middle grounds for the most energetic audiences. *Hard Times* was never meant to be a coffee table decoration or a reference work on musty racks. The paper's original name was *Mayday:* a call for help, a call to the streets, a call for rebirth. (The name had to be dropped for copyright reasons.) *Hard Times* evoked a face more dour, but a face in the same crowd; after all, energy and agony are the closest companions of our times.

ANDREW KOPKIND AND JAMES RIDGEWAY

Part One
The Crisis
of Politics

Politics in the late sixties was measured as much by rumbles and demonstrations as by Republicans and Democrats. After all, assassinations and rebellions had both symbolized and precipitated the crises of the decade, and electoral events seemed to effect only small change. The beginning of the Nixon administration, in 1969, seemed to be a watershed; but after Nixon's base, his program, and his personality were analyzed, not much new could be added. From there, the radical criticism and analysis concentrated on the anti-war movement, the development of white and black revolutionary forces, and the struggles of those forces to stay alive, in the face of external repression and internal fragmentation.

1

The Nixon Age Begins

Andrew Kopkind

The Age of Nixon: the phrase does not exactly seize the mind with a sense of historical moment. It looks to be a sober season. The long march of empire enters dull days after its late triumphs, and the approaching epoch looms comfortably small against the terrible time of god-kings and monster-men now receding. The Age of Johnson—inspiring mainly in its madness—gives place to a gentler reign: Caligula is succeeded by his horse.

No one supposes that the imperial parade will stop, or even slow its pace. What changes is its aspect. Gross relationships still hold: the leaders to the led, masters to servants, colonizers to colonized, owners to owned. But as the Nixon administration takes over, the smaller details of aspect seem more important, or at least more newsworthy: a cautious Kissinger for a fiendish Rostow, a moralistic John Mitchell for a humane Ramsey Clark, Billy Graham and Norman Vincent Peale for Marvin Watson and Abe Fortas, Brazil (or Venezuela, or wherever) for Vietnam—if it comes to that. In some

2

cases — Hoover and Helms leap to the eye — the faces will not change, much less the meanings.

Where it really counts — in the way the great corporations, the huge universities and the vast foundations operate among themselves and in relation to government — change is not worth mentioning. One platoon of managers leaves for the "private" sector as another comes into the "public" bureaucracy. For instance, Harold Brown, the Secretary of the Air Force, is leaving the Defense Department to become president of Cal Tech — whose current president, Lee DuBridge, will in turn come to Washington as Nixon's science adviser. The swinging doors between the aerospace industry and the Pentagon are in great motion, and the foundations and academic institutes are sucking in one lot of experts and spewing out another

The interchangeability of personnel merely reflects the identity of long-term interests which both the outgoing Democrats and the incoming Republicans share. When people (those few) said last fall that there was "no difference" between the major-party candidates, they were pointing to that similarity beneath the variety of styles; what persists is corporate capitalism, imperial expansion, the military imperative, racism, welfarism. Nixon's programs will certainly differ from Johnson's — as Johnson's own 1968 programs differed drastically from his 1965 models. But policy in the broadest sense keeps its continuity. A vote for Lyndon Johnson in 1964 turned into a vote for Nixon in 1968, and it could not have been otherwise.

It is not a bad idea to keep a sense of that sameness in mind while apprehending the Nixon era at its outset. When all the cabinet appointments are analyzed, the programs evaluated and the proposals explained, the monolith beneath the surface sand seems just as solid as ever. But given such immutables, the politics of the next four (or however many) years will be shaped by the surface drifts, and now is as good a time as any to begin finding distinctions among them. The crucial question may not be answered for some time: how directly can America's new administration affect America's mood — and movements?

Before Nixon ever takes office, his administration is "distinguishable" from its Kennedy-Johnson predecessor in four aspects: electoral base, financial support, top personnel, and programmatic platform.

Early enough on election night—when Connecticut's returns came in—the pattern of Nixon's vote emerged: it would be white, suburban, well-educated, trans-Appalachian, post-thirty, Protestant. Its "mandate" was quite obviously for law-and-order, a solution to the war, reduced inflation, continued business expansion, and retreat from foreign adventure. Nixon is bound to give at least rhetorical service on those demands, although in every instance his space for action is circumscribed by political and institutional barriers.

Across the range of Nixon's politics runs the general disadvantage of a non-consensus presidency. Though he may represent the "objective" interests of the most powerful establishments, not all of them see it that way. Myths overlay perceptions, and elites compete; it is their nature. For reasons of historical accident and personal incompetence, Nixon has failed to include large chunks of a modern president's natural constituency in his camp. An important part of the "invisible government" of liberal foundations, university intellectuals, urbanists, social activists, union hustlers and Kennedy-McCarthy "exiles" are even now creating a powerful programmatic opposition, of a kind unknown during the Democratic days. The extra-parliamentary (though decidedly un-radical) forces will be joined by liberal Democrats in Congress and around state government. And to make Nixon's problems worse, a sizable bloc of moderate Republicans—hostile for any number of reasons to the new president—seems already to have constituted itself as an "internal" opposition.

The new oppositions will dream up, develop and propose programs which the Nixon administration could not possibly use. That is the whole idea. In the Kennedy and Johnson terms, liberals thought that their musings on poverty, race or foreign policy had some chance of enactment under the friendly Democratic administrations. It was mostly illusion, of course, but now conditions have imposed a new realism on the oppositionists. Even after the exaggerated "breakup" of the Democratic coalition, the leaders of the centrifugation elements—Walter Reuther, Joseph Rauh, moderate Negroes —never gave up hope of reintegration with a chastened Humphrey. Now, not one of them is interested in playing games with Nixon.

But political opposition is not Nixon's only headache. In each of his "mandated" areas of action he seems stymied by internal structural contradictions. For law-and-order he may increase legal and physical repression, only to find more disorder in response. In trying to end the war, he could come up against his own anti-communist rhetoric or the ideology of his supporters, or so aggravate the Pentagon that a solution is effectively blocked. Cutbacks in government expenditures to reduce inflation could spiral into a recession, or produce more severe urban unrest (from unemployment), or sharp labor conflict. Efforts to keep the eight-year "boom" alive could be costly and counteract anti-inflation moves; at the same time, international monetary troubles may ruin all Nixon's plans for economic management. The slight tendencies now noticeable in favor of withdrawal from hyperactive "globalism" could be reversed by military crises in any number of US-protected countries: Brazil, Thailand, Israel, Iran. Finally, there is no evidence at all that Nixon has the foggiest idea about dealing with the "youth revolt," either in repressive or cooptative ways. That phenomenon is perhaps least affected by grownups' politics or normal political developments as Nixon conceives them.

The composition of Nixon's financial base suggests certain vague pushes and pulls away from Kennedy-Johnson positions. Where the Democrats got their heaviest support from the immense international corporate conglomerates, Nixon's financial center of gravity is in banking and finance. Kennedy and Johnson had "promised" the imperial corporatists a suitable foreign and domestic climate for expansion: the Democratic package included intervention in domestic economic affairs, welfare and education programs, foreign aid, counterinsurgency in the Third World, and heavy defense procurements—for war matériel and Great Society projects.

Nixon will not stop the flow of goods and goodies, but he

seems less generous, and conservative financiers – especially those with more domestic than international interests – are his biggest fans. Among his industrial friends, the strongest are in the rear-guard economic sectors – steel, oil and unsophisticated manufacturing. It is hard to make definite predictions about the programs dearest to such hearts, but in general they take an old-fashioned, traditionally "Republican" approach to the world: anti-Keynesian, isolationist, budget-minded, anti-union. Their enthusiasm for developing the Third World is marginal. Secretary McNamara was speaking for the Democrats' corporatists – not the Republicans' businessmen – when he said (in Montreal) that, for the United States, "development is security." Nixon may say something like that from time to time, but his heart cannot be in the words.

The men Nixon has appointed to cabinet and sub-cabinet posts so far are perfect personifications of his base of electoral and financial support. Perhaps that is partly coincidence: many of those Nixon asked to serve, including some Democrats, refused the offer (a fact which in itself foreshadows Nixon's political problems). What he ended up with on TV the other night was a good metaphor for the power realities of his administration.

Press and public have concentrated their attacks – mild or strong – on the uniformity and consistent dullness of the cabinet lineup. There's truth in that charge, as anyone can see, but what's wrong with the Nixon men is not exactly their dreary personalities. It would be better if the key of their activity were pitched as low as their public images, but in fact they are not passivists at all. What is most dangerous is the cabinet's capacity for mindless – or heartless – meddling.

The Nixon men represent the old 1950's breed of middle managers, a species of administrator produced by the lesser demand of corporate capitalism to "rationalize" itself. Efficiency is all. In the business world, the middle managers look at balance sheets, read computer print-outs, and reorganize ailing divisions when profits lag. When things go wrong, they install Muzak, fire a third of the work force, substitute oleo for the more expensive spread in the factory snack bar, and fix the lock on the time clock.

Such tricks work well to maximize profits and cut costs for small companies, but the greatest international corporations do not take them seriously any more. There, expansion counts more than efficiency, and damn the costs. Decentralized department heads are encouraged to exercise any number of options while the corporate planners at the top catch only a glimpse of the dynamic of expansion down below. The heart of the Nixon administration is in the company-management approach. It is the way of operation that Wall Street lawyers, such as the Attorney General–designate, John Mitchell, or the new Secretary of State, William P. Rogers, know best. It is the way of construction company executives (three are in the cabinet: Volpe, Hickel and Blount), who operate a one-service business on a strict contractual basis. It also informs the mentality of academic "business economists," who are nothing more than jumped-up efficiency experts: Labor's George P. Shultz (dean of Chicago's graduate business school) and Agriculture's Clifford Hardin (head of the University of Nebraska) are prime examples in that category. Maurice Stans, the new Commerce secretary, is a banker and CPA. Melvin Laird, on his way to the Pentagon, is a small-town, small-time politician with the dimmest sense of international corporate operations. Of the bunch, only HUD's George Romney is even vaguely in the Kennedy-Johnson mold, as the former head of a big conglomerate (although American Motors was hardly a giant in its field).

The Nixon administration's smallness of vision may turn out to be its ultimate undoing. If the American empire is really analogous to a superconglomerate, it must carry through in the same ways the corporations do: rapid expansion, deficit financing, high risk-taking, option creation. Budget-balancing can kill the whole thing. The Johnson people had no rational plans and no priorities, but they were content to throw around 435 social welfare programs and let people pretty much take care of themselves. Local bureaucrats squabbled, but the top men confessed confusion and stayed reasonably clear of involvement.

The Nixon people will have no more priorities or better plans, but they feel compelled to work as if they did. John

Mitchell will want to keep track of everybody who crosses the street against the light, but he will see that he can govern less effectively that way than by admitting the impossibility of tight management. In the real world of competitive corporatism, less control does make more sense than the opposite. Nixon's talk of "decentralization" is not meant to devolve authority on lower bureaucratic levels, but only to give out responsibility, while the lines are strengthened. Hierarchies will be built, not weakened.

Exactly what the implications of "middle management" will be may not come clear for some time. It is possible that the campaign to "rationalize" specific functions will produce resentful independent blocs, rather than smoothly working units. For example, Kennedy and Johnson gave agencies like the CIA the sense that they were into more than they really had — or at least, there was always the hope that bigger pieces of action were possible. If Nixon attempts to compartmentalize agency responsibilities along rigid, "businesslike" lines, he will find more hostility and less efficiency — even in traditional terms — than he thought likely. In the area of welfare programs, the Democrats threw money around under the more or less straightforward assumption that it would stop people from rioting. To "rationalize," as Robert Finch promises, an essentially irrational system, would be to kill even that function.

On purpose, Nixon has been keeping extraordinarily quiet about his programmatic ideas for the next four years. His appointees have been instructed to keep appropriately closedmouthed. It may be that they are all keeping surprises to themselves, but more probably, they have nothing much to say. In all but a few areas, Nixon will offer nothing that is new. In foreign affairs, he will rely heavily on career foreign service officers (Charles Yost, the new UN ambassador, signals that trend) and follow their institutional bias toward Europe and against romantic development schemes. Alianzatype projects will give way to honest, straight, military aid to whatever dictators seem most capable of suppressing insurgencies. (In such policy lies another possible reason for CIA "independence": the liberals of Langley rather fancy giving great wads of money to reformists who promise long-term stability rather than military control.)

In Vietnam, Nixon seems ready to seek a solution along the Kissinger "phased withdrawal" proposals, if he can keep a Saigon government lively, and the Pentagon people quiet. To pay off the military and the industrial halves of the old "complex," Nixon will have to keep the defense budget high, and perhaps make good on part of the $120 billion "shopping list" of new weapons being circulated by the Pentagon and the defense industries. The Russians could help with an arms-limitation summit, but results there, even in the best of circumstances, will be a long way off.

In domestic welfare programs, Nixon will push "black capitalism" projects as his major contribution to riot control, although his pet urbanist, Pat Moynihan, will be promoting expensive family allowances, job training, and other high-cost items that Nixon will find hard to allow. The black entrepreneur bit may cool ghettoes off for a while: enough hustlers may take their payoffs to dull the edge of militancy for a short time. But Nixon has no plans for dealing with black pressure on the majority institutions—police, education, health services, and so forth, and it is there that the first severe strains of his administration will develop.

At that point, he will have to decide how far to go with outright repression. And it is there, too, that the liberal "invisible government" will begin to frame the major issues of the Nixon years. Some foundation, for instance, will assemble liberal support for "modernization" of police forces (games-playing readers may bet among themselves which three U.S. cities will have the first foundation-funded "model police precincts"). Another institute will present brilliant and unusable proposals for chic decentralization projects.

In such a manner, the dialectic of issue creation will unfold. Liberals will campaign for recognition of China, more aid to Biafra, and reasonable reduction of the arms race—while Nixon holds out against such pressures. Already there are dozens of straws in those winds: Gene McCarthy wants to go to Peking, Richard Goodwin is raking defense-budget muck, and returned Peace Corps volunteers and McCarthy campaigners are fact-finding in Biafra. Walter Reuther—his hopes for one more White House dinner now dim—is putting together yet another coalition of SCLC organizers, grape strikers, Head Starters, Teamsters, Poverty Crusaders—you name it—with the express intention of framing the labor/liberal issues of the 1970s. His allies will be the Kennedy-Johnson civil rights and antipoverty bureaucrats who are fleeing to sanctuary at colleges and foundations, from where they will launch their campaigns for integration enforcement, increased welfare budgets, school decentralization, and conservation of natural resources.

Up until now, most of those fights have been waged within the Democratic administration, and for that reason, the lines were not always clearly drawn. Now there will be a public battleground of a kind. There is no indication at all that the liberals out of power will have any more success than they had inside their Washington offices, or from their lobby chairs. What they want is to build a platform of reform which can be used in 1972 or 1976 as the rhetorical basis of a new Democratic administration. At that point, we will be back in 1964 again. *Plus ça change. . . .*

January 3–10, 1969

To the
Comfort Station
Andrew Kopkind

There was something for everyone last weekend in Washington. North Vietnam and the NLF got their big, peaceful march. The white radical movement got its street fighting. The liberals got the speakers' platform. The Nixon-Mitchell administration got its rocks off gassing the kids. The plate-glassed banks, brokerage houses and stores down Connecticut Avenue got their comeuppance. And the New Mobilization Committee to End the War in Vietnam, after endless negotiations, rebuffs and delays, finally got its portable toilets.

The Mobe's arrival at the comfort stations on the grounds of the Washington Monument did not signal the start of the New American Revolution. To no one's surprise, the masses of workers and peasants who marched there from the tennis courts in front of the Capitol building were in a mood to do little more than raise a limp V sign or dance idly to plastic tunes from *Hair*. Scorpio was still in the house of Aquarius.

"Give peace a chance" was a lyric specifically appropriated by Mobe leaders in response to threats of repression by the

11

government and predictions of trouble in the press. What has come to be known as "Mobe politics" was infused in the weekend's events by a number of subtle (and not-so-subtle) means. First, the New Mobe reversed its 1968 policy of *apertura a la sinistra* and moved precipitously to its own right. It blended easily with the post-McCarthy shades of the Moratorium and foreshadowed the colors of the pre-McGovern (or whoever) campaigns of the seventies. By week's end, it had successfully internalized the consciousness of the Justice Department. Mobe marshals — under the direction of peace bureaucrats — were used by federal authorities in Washington much as African natives were used by British colonial police in, say, the Gold Coast: to carry the white man's burden. The "peace pigs" were freaky and friendly, but whom were they working for? Were they *us* or *them?* Late Saturday, when 10,000 or 15,000 people split from the Monument grounds to march on the Justice Department, they were met first by Mobe marshals, not city cops — although the Mobe had explicitly disavowed participation in that march. The Mobe's chief lawyer gabbed with police officials over his walkie-talkie, and at one point he was overheard describing the demonstrators as "the hard-core helmeted few."

There were other ways, too, by which the Mobe froze the politics of the day into a moderate mold. Eugene McCarthy was chosen as the kickoff speaker in front of the Capitol, and George McGovern was a principal speaker at the rally (he had asked that numbers of Moratorium kids sit near the platform so that he would not be pelted with stones). Except for one or two speakers, no one talked to the political consciousness of the crowd; rather, they spoke to defuse protest and drain it of militant energies. No one up there is likely to be charged with incitement — of any kind. Those few representatives of the radical movements which originated anti-war demonstrations in this decade and had given it its motive force through the years were drowned in the thick Mobe soup.

The use of groovy marshals to protect Washington, not the marchers; the eagerness of the Mobe to "negotiate" what should have been considered its right to parade; the glib ac-

ceptance of the Justice Department's deformed category of
"violence" as the major issue of the weekend; the careful
construction of the line of march to avoid even a glimpse of
the White House; the insistence on a narrow and selfish message—stop the killing of U.S. soldiers—rather than a broader
one: It all went to insure that the Left would act on its own to
express the real rage of everyone in this bitter season.

* * *

Few of the 300 or 400 thousand young marchers in town
for the actions have ever been exposed to a basic, definitive
national "political struggle." There may have been examples
in the past: the battle for control of the labor movement's future in the thirties, for instance, when socialists and communists fought with a "coalition" of New Dealers, middle-road-
ers, and the Right. (The brief contest in the late forties around
the Henry Wallace campaign never amounted to much more
than a capitulation by a Left at once too tired, settled and ter-
rified to put up a fight.) Since then all the contests have taken
place within the center ring of establishment politics: Republicans against Democrats, reformers against traditionalists,
New Politics against Old Politics. But the past is really no
guide; the conditions which have given rise to the movements
of the sixties have no parallels in other eras of this century.

Now, a major political struggle is shaping up, and it's an
extraordinary event in American history. While the mechan-
ics of the fight are byzantine to a fault, the lines of force are
relatively clean; Liberals who see political change coming
from a reformed or realigned Democratic party are battling
with radicals who see the need for deep, systemic reconstitu-
tion of American society. The object of struggle now is definition of the "peace movement" and the terms on which it will
develop.

At present, the thousands who stood in the cold in Washington last weekend (and the millions, perhaps, at home or at
provincial demonstrations) make up a more or less unself-
conscious assemblage—less than a movement, really, although more than a mass. Its level of political understanding
of the society from which it has tentatively turned is low indeed. The Right Wing of the movement would just as soon

leave that the way it is. To restrict the peace movement's politics to a condition of existential anguish and practical discomfort (napalm on the one hand, inflation on the other) allows large numbers of people to be drawn in quickly — and it keeps their temperature down. If the white, privileged marchers on Pennsylvania Avenue really grasped the connections between the war, the imperial system, racism, economic exploitation, cultural manipulation, consumerism and police power (the way the blacks and working-class people instinctively do), they wouldn't have turned so sheepishly away from the White House.

The Left wants to define the peace mass in anti-imperialist and anti-racist terms. "Give peace a chance" is nice but nowhere; why not "Give revolution a chance"? The Left emphasizes growth in understanding of society and action against the state, rather than the mindless collection of bodies. Both sides use symbolic action, but the symbols stand for totally different perspectives on political change. The liberals assemble crowds to petition a basically legitimate government (however stupid or unheeding) for a redress of grievances; the radicals fight in the street, tear up draft records, shut down militarized schools or blow up corporations' headquarters — to demand destruction of illegitimate authority. United on the issue of the war, the two sides to the struggle are actually poles apart on the meaning and quality of politics in America.

* * *

There are roots of the present struggle in the late forties (at least), but the immediate origins lie in the McCarthy campaign. In the fall of 1967, the liberal-Left coalition finally and permanently split, on the basic principle of support for the black liberation movement. Until that time, the coalition had been led by those in the process of becoming radicals — the civil rights workers, the SDS anti-war demonstrators, the community organizers. But a new set of social and political conditions was turning young people's heads around, and the papered-over splits began to widen. At the convulsive National Conference for New Politics convention in Chicago that September, the blacks and the white Left refused to realign the coalition with liberal leadership. Martin Peretz, a Harvard teacher who helped bankroll that convention, stalked out of the Palmer House ballroom and announced to the TV cameras, "the Movement is dead."

And so it was, on its old terms. But implicit in the political system was the need for a "liberal" front to mediate divisive political conflict, and it was not long before Peretz, Allard Lowenstein and several other dropouts from the old movements began putting together a New Politics coalition focused on capturing the reformist wing of the Democratic party. The form for their efforts became the McCarthy campaign (and to a lesser extent, the Bobby Kennedy campaign). But the effort did not end with Kennedy's assassination and McCarthy's collapse. It began again last spring with the formation (on Marty Peretz's bread, among other sources) of the Moratorium committee, directed by old McCarthy and Kennedy hands and organized by clean-for-Gene kids, according to their privileged perspective on politics. The October 15 Moratorium was their show (although it was open enough on the local level to allow others to do their various things).

After that, the Moratorium people were at a loss to know how to move. In one sense, they were trapped by their own weapons: They had been attacking "violence" on the left for so long that they did not know how to operate in a situation which might be "violent." But they also were not sure of where they stood politically in relation to the movement they were seeking to lead.

For a year or more now, the "moderates" in and around the peace movement have been "violence-baiting" the Left. But their attacks are more autobiographical than descriptive: They are clearly saying something about themselves as well as about their opponents. The "new liberals" of the late sixties gain respectability by agreeing with the categorical definition of violence used by press, politicians and government. Without analyzing the source of violence in the society and its near-monopoly within the power of the state, they accept the notion that it is the radicals who cause violence against a "neutral" social system. By rights, the issue of "violence" last weekend ought to have been the genocidal bombings of

Vietnam, the exploitation of the people of Latin America, the brutalization of the black community in the United States, and all the institutionalized forms of violence perpetrated against ordinary people every day. Against that, a pop bottle thrown at the Justice Department is as a bird dropping against an atom bomb.

Still, the Moratorium people were stuck with their definitions and their categories, and it wasn't easy for them to know what to do when the saw the peace movement, for all its docility, moving on to Washington against their own wishes.

Not to be cut out, a delegation of McCarthy-Kennedy men fell upon Washington to heighten the struggle for control of the terms on which the November actions would be projected. John Kenneth Galbraith, Adam Walinsky, Peter Edelman, Richard Goodwin and Jeremy Larner helped Moratorium leaders Sam Brown and David Hawk write a response to President Nixon's November 3 speech on Vietnam. (Larner used his Moratorium cover to get into meetings so that he could write an article on the events for *Life* magazine; or did he use *Life* as a cover for operating in Moratorium politics?) Walinsky tried to get the Rev. Richard Fernandez, a member of the Mobe steering committee, to kick the Communist party's delegate, Arnold Johnson, off the Mobe board. Then, having failed, he began working on Senators Goodell and McGovern to stay off the Mobe rally platform: "Do we want American students to follow Dave Dellinger or Sam Brown?" he asked his fellows at one meeting.

When it was obvious that the march would be a numerical success despite their own predictions of violence, the Moratorium people abruptly changed tactics and began taking over Mobe logistics. Moratorium leaders frankly stated that their own people were going to act as marshals. Senators and congressmen were convinced to join the action because, as one of Senator McGovern's assistants said, "If you don't join in, you leave the demonstration to people outside the system."

The more the Mobe grew bland and unoffensive, the more the politicians joined in. Rep. Allard K. Lowenstein announced at a meeting of the Council on Foreign Relations in Los Angeles that he was on board. At a meeting at the Ethical Culture Society in New York on November 9, Reps. Farbstein, Scheuer, and Reid, former Commerce Undersecretary Howard Samuels, and former Bobbymen Walinsky and William Vanden Heuvel announced their support (only Rep. Edward Koch, the Manhattan Reform Democrat, held out). Then, Reps. John Conyers and William Fitz Ryan moved into an active role. They tried to get Attorney General Mitchell to grant the Mobe a parade permit for Pennsylvania Avenue. Conyers tried—and failed—to see Nixon. With Rep. Ben Rosenthal, they asked the Justice Department to open Washington public schools to out-of-towners for sleeping space (permission denied). Rep. Richard Ottinger also asked for a meeting with Nixon about the permit.

All the time, the government was playing an elaborate game of chicken with the march organizers. The trouble was that the Administration wanted contradictory things: violence and peacefulness. Violence would (in Nixon's terms) discredit the entire peace movement and remove pressure on Vietnam policy; it would also allow the White House to crack down on radicals and make a show of force for law 'n order, against disruption. At the same time, Nixon hardly wanted a massive riot in Washington on his hands—or on his record. The image of armed struggle going on in his own front yard was quite properly terrifying.

The tactic the Administration used to deal with both objectives was negotiation—of every aspect of the march, from route to toilet. Issuance of a permit was purposely delayed until the last minute, so that the Mobe could make no firm plans until a few days before the action was scheduled to begin. At the same time, various governmental agencies worked to keep people away from Washington. The Justice Department kept the schools from opening up to the public. The FBI checked with bus companies across the country, ostensibly to determine the size of the crowd coming to Washington; predictably, many companies backed out of their commitments to travelers after the FBI came around: In Binghamton, N.Y., for instance, several buses scheduled to take Harper College kids were pulled out. The Interstate Commerce Commission called a bus company in Stony Brook, L.I., and said that it did not have the proper interstate papers to make the Washington run; another bus company in New York was similarly threatened, but its papers were in order, and it made the trip. So it was clear that at least part of the Administration was looking for trouble: the Mitchells, if not the Finches. Deputy Attorney General Richard Kleindienst (who talks about locking up "ideological criminals") recently told a staffer for a Republican House member that "we can't wait to beat up those motherfucking kids. If you thought Chicago was bad, wait till you see D.C."

As it happened, Chicago was worse. The Washington police were about as "restrained" as police can be these days— not because they were groovy or sympathetic, but because they were disciplined according to the political strategy of the weekend. Already, Mayor Daley had given pigs a bad name; Washington police did not want to stimulate the kind of national resistance to police power that last year's "police riot" in Chicago had done. So when the police wanted to clear the crowds Friday night near the Saigon embassy and Saturday at the Justice Department, they used a great deal of CS gas and a minimum of public clubbing.

What the police, the Justice Department and the Mobe marshals failed to do was break the Left, as they all, in their own ways, had hoped to do. Their use of fear, force and cooptation produced its own contradictions in militant actions Friday and Saturday. If no one spoke to the consciousness of the crowd at the Mobe rally, there were other means of expression, and now it is certain that those means are to be found in the streets.

As the weekend approached, there was a feeling in Washington that perplexing questions about political alignment, the future of the Movement and the course of U.S. policy in Vietnam might be answered. But when the revels were ended the questions remained. The "new liberalism," swinging desperately from Woodstock to redwoods to MIRV, is torn apart as surely as the "revolutionary contingent," and it is feeling Nixon's repressive wrath as much as the radicals. It's hard to believe another mass march can soon be mounted, and "local actions" cannot be successfully channeled into a liberal frame. And the war drags on. Interest seems to be focusing now on GI organizing; revolt is rife at Army bases all over the country, of a tougher kind than people have seen on college campuses. If the "peace" coalition attacks the Army system, the Movement, rather than the right-of-the-Left, could once more assume the leadership role.

The Left may have a real chance now, but its tactics and its organization are so fragmented that it still provides small threat. Friday's and Saturday's street actions were truly anarchic—spontaneous in the worst sense. The "organizers" organized nothing but the time and site of launch. A disciplined force as large as those seen at either action (the size and heaviness were curiously understated in the otherwise sensationalist press) could have played havoc with Washington. There was no want of revolutionary fantasies as people surveyed the targets and possibilities, but there was a total lack of tactical and organizational leadership. And that, obviously, cannot develop until new Left political institutions mature.

No one was interested in speeches Friday night when a crowd of about 4,000 young people gathered in Dupont Circle—locus of Washington's small street culture—to begin a march "in solidarity with the Provisional Revolutionary Government of South Vietnam." An anomalous thunderstorm that had drenched the city was just ending, and the night was wet-cold in the worst Washington way. Someone started to speak from the white marble fountain in the Circle's park center, and then people were streaming into Massachusetts Avenue, up "embassy row" four blocks to the Saigon embassy at Sheridan Circle. Just before the far circle, a line of helmeted, gas-masked police in full riot gear stood firm, guarding the Saigon embassy in the United States just as they have to guard the U.S. embassy in Saigon. In back of the police, searchlights went on and blinded the oncoming crowd. For a few minutes there was the familiar face-off: cops and kids, with a narrow DMZ in between. Then one bottle flew from the crowd toward the police line, and the gas grenades started popping. The marchers freaked for a moment, then marched back down the street and regrouped. A second assault was mounted, but this time the grenades came more quickly, and it was the atrocious CS gas, which cuts like a million knives in back of your throat and makes you move out fast. But people were more orderly in their retreat this time, and then small groups broke out of the main march and began "trashing" the windows of the banks and stores in the posh neighborhood nearby.

Friday night's action clearly sparked the militance Saturday at the Justice Department. People seemed up for it: "affinity groups" of sixes and dozens were getting together through the night and day. For many thousands, the rally was a bummer: not really Woodstock, not at all a campus insurrection—just a cold day with a little music and not much dope. People began drifting off soon after they arrived at the Monument, and by 4:30 it was time to move on out. The "organizers" of the march—called to protest the "conspiracy" trial in Chicago and other political trials—handed out flags and banners, and four 12-foot puppets of Nixon, Agnew, Mitchell and Judge Julius Hoffman were raised to guide the march.

The tone and tempo were drastically different than that of the Pennsylvania Avenue march earlier in the day. The red banners and the NLF flags were streaming and the chants were quick and loud: "Free Bobby Seale!" "Off the Pig!" "Stop the Trial!" "Power to the People!" The line swung around the Justice building, then came up against the Mobe marshals "protecting" the Constitution Avenue entrances. In seconds, the marshals were knocked aside, and people filled the streets for blocks in front of the building. Someone ran an NLF flag up the flagpole, and everyone cheered. Then a pretty pink smoke bomb went off in the bushes in front of the building. And then the gas attack began. This time, few people panicked, and when the first barrage had settled they came back, in close. Then there was another wave of gas, and another, and the whole building and the streets in the heart of the Federal Triangle were thick with smoke. When it was clearly overwhelming, the crowds began moving back toward the Monument. And then a strange thing happened. In the middle of all that gas, with the rockets going off in front of us as well as behind, people joined arms and began chanting: "Free Bobby Seale! Free Bobby Seale! Free Bobby Seale!"

People were together in a way they hadn't been all weekend, for some maybe never before, and in the thick of the gas we were laughing and cheering and not yet done.

November 24 – December 1, 1969

Going Down in Chicago

Andrew Kopkind

I prefer the philanthropy of Captain John Brown to that philanthropy which neither shoots me nor liberates me. . . . I do not wish to kill nor to be killed, but I can foresee circumstances in which both these things would be by me unavoidable. We preserve the so-called peace of our community by deeds of petty violence every day. Look at the policeman's billy and handcuffs! Look at the jail! . . . We are hoping only to live safely on the outskirts of this provisional army. So we defend ourselves and our hen-roosts, and maintain slavery. I know that the mass of my countrymen think that the only righteous use that can be made by Sharpe's rifles and revolvers is to fight duels with them when we are insulted by other nations, or to hunt Indians, or shoot fugitive slaves with them, or the like. I think that for once the Sharpe's rifles and the revolvers were employed in a righteous cause. The tools were in the hands of one who could use them. . . . The same indignation that is said to have

*cleared the temple once will clear it again. The question
is not about the weapon, but the spirit in which you use it.*
— HENRY DAVID THOREAU, 1859

There were twelve people in our two-man cell at the Chicago
police headquarters last Saturday after the SDS "Weatherman" march through the Loop. Our charges ran from disorderly conduct (my own) through possession of explosives to
attempted murder. The styles and situations of the dozen
were as widely disparate as the charges: A black student
(explosives) in boutique bell-bottoms stretched out coolly on
one of the two wooden benches, surveying the rest of us with
amusement as well as attachment. A long-haired New York
Weatherman, who said he had written and produced a musi-
cal version of the Columbia University insurrection, skillfully
sang both the instrumental and vocal parts of the Cream's "I
Feel Free." A very young, very rich kid (mob action) spouted
heroic slogans intermittently during a compulsive, anxious
monologue about himself. An uncommonly tender gang type
from a Michigan Weatherman collective washed a cellmate's
wounds with wet toilet paper and went to sleep on the crowded cement floor. Brian Flanagan, a bright and sensitive upper-
middle "moderate" who found his way inside a Columbia
building last year, and had now come to be charged with attempted murder (of Chicago's toughest judicial figure), rested
in another corner, dealing quietly with his own fear and a
large still-bleeding gash in his head.

The events of the afternoon were common to us all, whether we had been busted in the La Salle Street melee, or a mile
away (as I and two friends were). Solidarity and spirit grew
easily from the experience of fear and force; it was expressed
through the long first night in jail with songs and chants and
good talking. But beyond the fellow-feeling and gallows humor, much more drastic changes were running down within
us, and they could not be expressed at all, at least not then
and there. That protean rebellion which was born ten years
ago in the South; that found forms to fit the Mississippi Delta,
the Cleveland slums, the Berkeley campus, the hundred colleges and parks and Army posts; that appeared bloody last

summer in Grant Park and stoned this summer at Wood-stock: it ran that day in the Loop. Almost everyone else now thinks that that spirit of the sixties has found its end. But at night in the cellblock, we believed that it had found a new beginning.

* * *

Weatherman demands the willing suspension of disbelief. As an ideology of communism and a strategy of revolution, it shatters the reliable categories of thought and modes of action which white radicals have developed in the last ten years. It challenges the validity of an intellectual Left, which functions as a comfortable culture of opposition; instead, it asks that radicals become revolutionaries, completely collectivize their lives, and struggle to death if necessary. Nothing could be more threatening to the investments of thought and action which Movement people have made. Weatherman asks them to leap — in life expectations as well as political ideas — over a distance fully as wide as that which they crossed from liberalism (or whatever) into the Movement.

Since the civil rights movement moved North in 1964, white radicals have been working within a politics that was defined in the SDS "ERAP" community-organizing projects in Newark, Cleveland, Uptown Chicago, and a half-dozen other urban centers. Although the organizers used some revolutionary rhetoric, they were never able to find a strategy for mobilizing masses of people to restructure "the institutions which control their lives." Marches, sit-ins, tenant strikes and election campaigns inconvenienced but did not seriously threaten the welfare departments, housing agencies and city administrations against which they were directed. At length, the project workers — mostly white college kids — realized that those institutions could not be overhauled without wholesale shifts in power inside the "system" itself.

Since ERAP began to dissolve in 1966 and 1967, radical organizers have used basically the same strategy in other areas: campus strikes, draft resistance, Army base movements. The common principle was the organization of people in one locale (or in various branches of the same essential locale) to change the immediate institution which most oppressed them.

For example, students were organized to change "the university"; young men were organized to "stop the draft"; basic trainees were organized to "fuck the Army." It was hoped that such action might lead, in an always undefined way, to a chain reaction of structural changes throughout the whole system. But, of course, nothing like that ever happened.

Taken together, at least, that effort can hardly be counted a political failure, even if it did not accomplish its rhetorical objectives. What did happen was the creation of a race of radical organizers who are extraordinarily competent to do the work which their strategy defines. But there are obvious limits to the strategy, and after years of operational failures, a feeling of frustration and even desperation has set in. Many of the early organizers went off to the peripheries of politics: journalism, the academy, legal aid, teaching or even "liberal" government welfare jobs. And others went completely into personal "life-style" retreats in one or another wooded groves in New England, California or the Southwest.

As the repository of the political forms in the Movement, SDS has been struggling to break out of the frustration of repeated failure—or at least dispiriting un-success. The factionalism which has now become rampant is a direct result of that situation; politics without promise rapidly loses its coherence. The various factions within and around SDS accurately represent the political alternatives that now seem available. Progressive Labor, the "Maoist" party that was expelled from SDS last June but still holds on in an ambiguous role, expresses the conviction that revolutionary conditions already exist in the United States, and it requires only the organization of the industrial proletariat to set the revolution in motion. Revolutionary Youth Movement II (RYM-II) agrees in part with Progressive Labor, that workers organized "at the point of production" can become a revolutionary force in America, but it goes on to emphasize the paramountcy of subordinating white efforts to the "vanguard" of blacks and Latin movements. Despite their expansive theoretical flights, both PL and RYM-II work inside the framework of the community-organizing strategy. They try to get factory workers to demand "power" within their factories, or hospital workers — and users — within the hospitals, or soldiers within their bases.

Weatherman is something else. It is, in theory and practice, a revolutionary "army," and it flaunts that notion: "Come to Chicago. Join the Red Army," the leaflets called out. At this point — only a few months after it was born — Weatherman presents this schema: The fight against the American empire, at home in the black "colony" and abroad in the Third World, is the center ring of world politics today, within which the American system will eventually come to grief. The colonized peoples — black Americans and Third World guerrillas — can "do it alone"; but white Americans can both deepen and extend the fight if they disregard the position of "privilege" their white skins automatically provide, and learn to live and die like unprivileged guerrillas. In Weatherman's book, it is "racist" to accept white privilege in any way.

From that ideology flows a set of shattering implications. First of all, Weatherman action has to be directed at "material" aid (not just rhetorical support) to the anti-imperialist fights. It isn't enough to march or leaflet in support of the Vietnamese or the Black Panthers; there has to be an active effort to pull the machinery of empire off their backs.

Next, Weathermen have to understand the necessity of risking death, in terms of the historical necessity of revolution. It is the custom of intellectual Lefts around the world to sit sipping coffee (or its current moral equivalent, smoking dope), grooving on other people's revolutions, staring at posters of other revolutionaries, and waiting for one's own revolution to start tomorrow. Weatherman says that tomorrow is forever, and the time is always now. To the widespread charge of "adventurism" on that account, Weatherman insists that nothing that hinders the empire from carrying out its "business as usual" against the colonies can be a worthless adventure — although, of course, some actions are of more strategic value than others, and that there is a time for up-front fighting and a time for background organizing.

The life arrangements which have been built to deal with both the personal and political consequences of Weatherman are collectives—numbering now about a dozen in Ohio, Michigan, Illinois, New York, Maryland, Washington State, and Colorado. The intensity with which they work is almost indescribable; they are crucibles of theory and practice, action and self-criticism, loving and working. They are widely experimental: some now are considering rules against men and women living as "couples"—a form of privatism which inhibits total collectivization. In a few, women talk of intensifying their personal relationships with other women—as a way of getting over the problem of "women-hating women," which derives from female self-hate—akin to the self-hatred people in oppressed groups, such as Negroes and Jews, seem to contain. Often, members of collectives are revving at such high speed and intensity that they sleep only every other night; the rest of the time they are working—reading, criticizing, writing, traveling, pushing out the problems of the collective, and out talking to other people.

The Weatherman perspective treats collectives as "pre-party" organizations, building eventually to a fighting Communist party. A structure of leadership is developing with the "Weather Bureau" at the top, regional staffs under that, and the collectives providing local cadre. The principle of authority is a form of "democratic centralism," with as much self-criticism thrown in as anyone can bear—probably *more* than anyone can bear.

But despite that formal plan, Weatherman is still primarily an organizing strategy, not a fighting force. Heavy actions in the streets and schools are undertaken more for their "exemplary" effect on potential Weatherpeople than for their "material" aid to the Viet Cong. Weatherman wants to get at high school and community-college dropouts—not middle-class university kids—and it believes that the way to do it is to convince them that they can fight the authorities who daily oppress them: cops, principals, bosses. Weatherman as a strategy was born last April at Kent State University in Ohio, when a small group of SDS activists broke first through a line of "jocks" and then a phalanx of police to occupy a building where a hearing was being conducted on disciplinary and student-power issues. The attack so galvanized the campus that 5,000 students came out the next day in support of the SDS fighters.

* * *

There's no denying the antagonism to Weatherman within the radical Left—not to mention the sheer horror with which liberals and conservatives view it. In some places—Detroit, for instance—un-Weatherized radicals have tried to form coalitions specifically aimed at destroying Weatherman. Some of the best New Left radicals believe that Weatherman is destroying (or has destroyed) the Movement. Movement spokesmen, such as the *Guardian* and Liberation News Service, are almost viciously anti-Weatherman; the underground press, for the most part, thinks Weatherman is positively insane. Such hostility is more than mere factionalism. It represents total rejection of Weatherman's revolutionary form.

Weatherman itself doesn't help matters. Perhaps because of the intensity of their own lives, the members cannot accept the relative lethargy of other radicals. More than that, Weathermen have built such elaborate political and emotional defenses against their fears of death and imprisonment that any challenge to the meaning of their work directly threatens their identities. It is obvious that Weatherman is quasi-religious and "fanatic" in a way; they see those who stand apart as the early Christians must have seen the pagans. It is difficult to die for a cause that their peers reject.

The Movement's antagonism is particularly wounding because Weatherman has so far failed to attract the large numbers of people it hoped would follow "up-front" fighting. All summer and in the early fall, Weatherman tried to organize its dropout constituency by running through schoolrooms yelling "Jail break!", fighting with hostile kids, and carrying NLF flags down beaches literally looking for trouble. When trouble came, the Weatherman fought, and in many instances "won"; but the actions did not mobilize the hordes of kids the organizers had expected. There were famous Weatherman horror shows: in Pittsburgh, where members ran through a school and were arrested, with no organizing effect; and in Detroit, where a group of Weatherwomen (now called the Motor City

9) entered an examination room in a community college, locked the doors, subdued the teacher, and then took two hostile male students out of action with karate blows.

It's hard, too, for many outsiders to grasp the dramatic—often comic—aspects of Weatherman's political style. I first saw Weatherman as the "Action Faction" of SDS at the national convention in Chicago last June. It surfaced the first afternoon; during a particularly dreary maneuver by Progressive Labor, the Action Faction people leaped up on their chairs waving Red Books and chanting, "Ho, Ho, Ho Chi Minh. . . ." They succeeded in breaking up PL's silly obstructions by an essentially dramatic move, which had elements of both parody and instruction.

That element has carried through into all aspects of Weathering, so that at times it is difficult to tell whether the entire phenomenon may not be a gigantic psychodrama. Most Weathermen, in their own self-criticism sessions, are aware of the dangers of the emotional "trip" that revolutionism entails. At a meeting one night during the Chicago weekend, speaker after speaker warned against the "death trip" or the "machismo trip" or the "violence trip." "We act not out of our private emotions, but in accordance with our political understanding," one Weatherman said.

Because Weatherman is still so young, it would be fatuous to condemn it as worthless or elevate it to heroic proportions. Its contradictions are apparent, even to most Weathermen, who are defensive outside their collectives but truly self-exploring within. What seems most troublesome right now is Weatherman's simplemindedness about the varieties of political experience in America; as revolutionaries usually discover, violent struggle and less intense organizing are not mutually exclusive. RYM-II and independent radicals are still producing organizers who can serve a variety of functions; to put all radical eggs in a Weatherbasket would be unutterably foolish.

Nor is there much evidence that violence can mobilize thousands of kids, even in Weatherman's chosen dropout pool. Real revolutionaries have a contempt for violence, not an adoration of it; it is used only as a last resort, as a response to specific oppression. As yet, most people do not comprehend the relationship of the police in America to the B-52s in Vietnam. A revolutionary party finds its moral authority in leading an oppressed people in retaliation against their intolerable oppressors: That's how the Viet Cong did it in Vietnam and how People's Democracy is doing it in Northern Ireland. To most people outside, Weatherman is a vanguard floating free of a mass base.

But there's more to it than that. What appeal Weatherman has comes in part from its integration of the two basic streams of the movements of the sixties — political mobilization and personal liberation. Since the breakup of the ERAP projects, few radical organizations have been able to contain and combine both streams. Those in the "liberation" stream have gone off on private trips; those in the political stream have been reduced to Old Left sloganeering and dreary demonstrations. Weatherman does break through, with its liberating collective sensibility and its active mobilization. However disastrous or brilliant its strategy may turn out to be, its spirit, purposefulness and integrity ought to command respect.

* * *

I had come to Chicago last week to see the range of actions planned in and around the trial of the "conspiracy" — the eight men charged with conspiring to incite a riot at last year's Democratic convention. The trial itself is a depressing affair, as political trials almost have to be — played as they are on hostile turf with no real chance of gaining the offensive. Slogans such as "Stop the Trial" seem too inflated even to shout, and except for a spirited action on opening day staged by the Panthers outside the Federal Building (Bobby Seale is one of the "conspirators"), radicals have stayed away in droves. Meanwhile, the defendants are picking up support from *Life* and *Time* magazines and liberal civil libertarians — all of which may be helpful to them, but does not seem to move the radical movements this year.

The RYM-II actions were not particularly enlivening, either. One afternoon, a few hundred people stood in a muddy park outside the Cook County Hospital and listened to uninspired speeches (some of them directed against Weatherman), but the prospects for organizing a "Revolutionary Youth Movement" out of it all seemed remote indeed. Reports of the Young Lords' (a young Latin community organization) march on Saturday were encouraging, but RYM-II's role in that was admittedly secondary.

The Weatherman march was political psychodrama of the best and worst kind. It began dully at the site of the statue of the Chicago policeman, a singular symbol of power, in Haymarket Square, which had been blown up at the beginning of the week. It was hard not to fear that Weatherman's history might be as tragic as the Knights of Labor or the Wobblies; that it would never have even the trigger effect of John Brown's raid; that before it developed, death or long prison sentences would cut off the experiment at its inception.

The crowd was small and the weather was cold and wet. Just after noon, a posse of plainclothes detectives fell upon the small crowd of marchers and arrested Mark Rudd and several other Weatherman leaders. No one was at all sure that the march would ever happen. Then from around a corner came the sound of shouts and cheers, and a brigade of about a hundred Weathermen burst into the street, fists raised, chanting and laughing: "Ho, Ho, Ho Chi Minh. . . ." Then there was a send-off speech, and people joined arms and stepped quickly down the street into the deserted Loop. After a mile of marching, the column suddenly lurched, and there was fighting and rock throwing and wailing sirens and the paddy-wagons were soon filled to overflowing. For an hour afterward, police picked up Weathertypes on the streets and brought them in on various minor and serious charges.

Now some say that the police attacked first, and others say the Weathermen took the offensive; but it is true that the Weathermen did not shrink from the fight, and we all thought in the cellblock that night that simply not to fear fighting is a kind of winning.

October 20–27, 1969

Weekend

Andrew Kopkind

The first time I was in the streets in New Haven was twenty-six years ago, when I marched alongside my father in the Civil Defense contingent of a Fourth of July parade, during World War II. My father was a divisional leader of the Air Raid Wardens, and he kept a small stockpile of gas masks in the attic of our house, for use in the event of enemy attack. The masks were objects of wonder and pride to me, and I carried one in its canvas case, tied around my waist, in the parade. Much to my disappointment, the war ended without an enemy attack. The German Spy who carried on extensive clandestine operations in the wooded lot across from our house disappeared without a trace in May 1945. He was replaced only briefly by a Japanese Spy assigned similar duties. After the war, my friends and I played out our fantasies with the surplus gas masks, with large galvanized metal hand-pumped fire extinguishers, and the rest of the disaster-control paraphernalia left in the attic and made obsolete by peace. Then the wooded lot was leveled and "developed" with one-family brick or wood houses. Our fantasies took other turns.

My next demonstration in New Haven came nine years later, on a mild May afternoon at the end of my senior year in high school. An argument had erupted between the Good Humor ice cream man and the Jack and Jill ice cream man over trading rights for a choice corner in the middle of the Yale campus. Student partisans of each side argued boisterously among themselves for a while, and then joined in a united front against the university, moving vehicles, and the downtown business establishment. I came upon the scene after school let out that afternoon, at the point that the squabbling around the ice cream issue was turning into a general insurrection. The riot lasted well into the evening. The mayor, a lugubrious undertaker named William C. Celentano, arrived at one corner of the Green on board a fire engine and read the Riot Act to the unruly crowd through a bullhorn. I had never heard the Riot Act read before that afternoon, nor since. Undeterred, the rioting students assaulted the Hotel Taft, ran through its rooms, and streamed toilet paper from its windows onto the streets below. At length, we were pushed back into the Old Campus, doused with water from fire hoses, and locked in the quad. No one took it very seriously. My father was the New Haven D.A. at the time, and I believe he was in charge of prosecuting those few students who were arrested. I doubt that any of them served a day in jail.

There have been other riots in New Haven since then: panty raids gave way to ghetto uprisings; but I have kept my distance. I chose to leave town when I went away to college, and except for brief family visits over the years, I have not wanted to return. From those infrequent trips home I realized that the city was undergoing drastic changes in its physique and its politics, but my nostalgic curiosity in the new New Haven was hardly equal to my sense of alienation from the whole scene. My father, a Republican, was removed from the prosecutor's office by a Democratic administration which seized state power in the fifties, and has maintained its hold to this day. Richard Lee, the reformist Democratic mayor, bulldozed much of the city to the ground and, after a decade of delays, built rows of glassy office blocks, lyrical parking garages and chic townhouses atop the rubble. Inhabitants of the "slums" torn down were left to shift for themselves. The mindless "community action" programs which Lee laid on the blacks provided new careers for the upwardly mobile, and very little else. Nothing he did in his years of rule could prevent the full-blown black revolt which convulsed the city in 1967.

Yale's rulers embarked on a similarly wasteful building and expansion program of their own, in so close a relationship to Lee's as to invite indictment for incest. Lee was a Yale PR man before he assumed the mayoralty, but that was only the most up-front connection between the university and New Haven. Town and gown political and economic interests are inextricably tied. According to the excellent pamphlet "Go to School, Learn to Rule," published this month by two radical research and political groups, Yale holds almost $100 million worth of tax-free property in New Haven: one-third of all untaxed real estate in the city. Such depletion of the Grand List impoverishes the city's finances. Yale is far and away the major economic, political and social power in New Haven. Yale controls the principal health and psychiatric services for the community; it commands the important cultural institutions; it constitutes the social elite; it instigates or vetoes public works that touch its extended interests. Moreover, it hardly pays lip service to the rhetoric of "community involvement" which other great universities now feel compelled to produce. All in all, it is the dominating force in a wide New Haven community of almost half a million people, which Yale treats as a kind of support population for its 8,000 students.

* * *

When I was growing up in New Haven, Yale provided the models and set the standards for acceptable values and behavior. Sons and daughters of the white middle class in New Haven were showered with Shetland sweaters, bathed in buttoned-downs, inundated with natural shoulders from the tweedy boutiques of York Street. We went to all the Yale sports events, the Yale concerts, the Yale museums, the Yale libraries, the Yale movies. New Haven's only three high schools (in those days) were clustered in one compound in a corner of the campus. (They all fell under Yale's expansion program, and were replaced by high-art university dorms.) As high school students, we competed with Yale underclassmen for dates with the more desirable local girls. The Yalies always won.

The attributes of a Yale man—snobbish, super-cool, careerist—were transmitted through all Yale's contacts to the community around, and if those values were always resented on some level, they were respected on another. Sub-cultures of New Haven society—particularly New Haven youth—might react to Yale with hostility or affection, but it was to the overwhelming fact of Yale's presence that they were reacting.

But until very recently, there was no understanding by Yale's students of Yale's power role in New Haven: and certainly no interest in changing it. Yale's rulers—the Corporation*—set or influenced social policy for the local population in the general interests of a few thousand, and specific interests of a few dozen: those at the top of the power pyramid. That whole system was categorically denied, of course; an alternative model of "pluralistic" interaction of community interests was provided by Yale Professor (of course!) Robert Dahl, whose "study" of New Haven's political institutions "Who Governs?" became the classic document used to avoid discussion of Yale's real role. Dahl's description of the decisionmaking process elevated PTA meetings and aldermanic hearings to a station of commanding and exclusive influence. (Lately, Dahl tells his students he's dreadfully sorry he ever wrote that book.)

Pluralism dies hard in New Haven, just as it does elsewhere, long after Wright Mills' body moldered in its grave. It serves Yale's elites so well as an ideology that few are so foolish as to abandon it. For if it died, Yale would be vulnerable to pressures from all those it so coolly exploits: its em-

---

*Frederick B. Adams Jr., Edwin F. Blair, William P. Bundy, J. Richardson Dilworth, Caryl P. Haskins, William Horowitz, Harold Howe II, John V. Lindsay, William McChesney Martin Jr., Joseph I. Miller, Right Rev. Paul Moore Jr., Spencer D. Moseley, William W. Scranton, Cyrus R. Vance, Arthur K. Watson, John Hay Whitney.

ployees, the "consumers" of its health facilities, those displaced by its land expansion, and all those who suffer and despise its integration with and support of the national imperial machine. Yale commits its share of substantive acts of oppression; but its functional role in American society in the primary production of elite cadre — unaccountable to ordinary people and unresponsive to their needs — makes it much more than a run-of-the-sty Pig.

In a real way, Yale denies "power to the people," for it organizes and keeps power unto itself. Yale is complicit in imperial expansion not only because it recruits students for the CIA, trains men for ROTC, and delivers social science research to spy agencies; more important, it fills the great corporate boardrooms, the State Department seventh floor, and the international lawyers' offices with men trained to express Yale's imperial values in their life's work. Yale perpetuates racism not only because it pays black employees (when it hires them at all) low wages or takes in too few black students, but, surpassingly, because its standards of intellectuality are culturally lily-white. Yale did not put Bobby Seale in the New Haven County jail; but it is a designer, supporter and executor of the system of society that led him to that place.

* * *

In the fifties, there was a lively institution practiced by the gentlemen of Yale called the "pig party." In this instance, the animal metaphor had nothing to do with an oppressor in the police force or the ruling class, but referred rather to an ugly and promiscuous girl — usually of local origin and with few educational credentials. On certain occasions in the school year, Yalemen in a fraternity or secret society would invite a bevy of such women to a party in whatever Gothic chapel they called home. The men alone knew the "key" to the affair; the women were delighted to attend such a toney function, and did not recognize that which they had in common with each other. Invariably, the evenings ended in drunken orgy, and the Yalies dined out for weeks afterwards on stories of the party.

Of course, that was Yale at its very worst, but it symbolized what I thought was the universal corruption and hypocrisy of the Yale spirit. It never surprised me, in the mid-sixties, that there was no big radical movement on the Yale campus. Long after Berkeley blew and Columbia collapsed, Yale's cathedral towers stood unstained on New Haven's Green. Conventional wisdom attributed the absence of movement to President Kingman Brewster's liberal reign, but New Havveners knew that there was a lot less to Brewster than met the eye. More than anything else, Yale was quiet because Yalies didn't care.

Now that has all changed; and again, it is not because of Brewster, but in spite of him. The anger of a generation finally reached the ivied tombs, blew away the pig parties, discredited J. Press, and last weekend filled the Green with shouting, fist-waving freaks. No need to exaggerate: God, Country and Yale still stand, and the majority of the students do not see themselves leading revolutionary lives. But the student strike and the weekend rally in support of the Black Panthers are the biggest thing to hit Yale since Dink Stover, and in its own way it constitutes as important an event in the radicalization of elite education in America as the uprisings at Berkeley or Columbia.

The route to the Green is marked with milestones familiar enough in this age. In 1966, the "peace" campaign of Yale Prof. Robert Cook for Congress developed into an independent "Movement" organization, AIM. Cook did poorly in the election, but he and his organizers kept AIM alive as a center for political activity, in closer or looser coalition (as those things will be) with a militant black group called the Hill Parents Association. Those few "New Left" students at Yale who wanted to do political work in New Haven naturally gravitated to AIM and HPA.

AIM (and its black ally) went through all the changes common to Movement organizations in the late sixties, but unlike many, it managed to stay alive and active. AIM people published a newsletter, started a coffeehouse, took jobs at community colleges, formed communes and collectives, focused on Yale and New Haven issues with a radical approach. AIM's visibility was high in the liberal Left, low elsewhere. At Yale, there was a proper SDS organization for a brief time, but it was completely taken over by the sectarian Progressive Labor faction, and the non-PL people had little to do except work around AIM or drift off into smaller ad hoc groups.

Because Yale had not been polarized by radical actions, there was a predictably large McCarthy/Moratorium constituency; predictable, too, was its vocal anti-radicalism. But by 1969, connections were being made between people and movements at various points, and it all came together one night last spring in the Ingalls Skating Rink, a soaring Saarinen structure on the edge of the Yale campus. The issue that night was ROTC at Yale, and there was a multi-party struggle to decide its future and, by extension, the political temper of the student body. SDS members, Moratorium types, "moderates," faculty and administrators battled it out at the podium, while the Corporation sat in the bleachers in back, looking more like a Greek junta than a Greek chorus. The result was a "compromise" of some sort, the dimensions of which are lost in my memory. "King" Brewster emerged as a liberal hero that night, not so much for what he did as for what he didn't; "Brewster," someone said later to a reporter, "is a charismatic listener." I was in New Haven that night, for my father had died a few weeks before, and I wandered into the rally to see what was happening at Yale. It was not a very revolutionary affair; I had seen more struggle over the issue of ice cream. But in a back row I saw four young blacks—a woman and three men—who alone in the vast hall appeared not to be Yale students. I watched them for a moment, and heard them shout "Right on!" at an appropriate juncture in the debate. After an hour or so, they rose and left. "The Panthers," a friend said to me with a nod. "The woman's Ericka Huggins."

* * *

I can remember having only one black friend at high school in New Haven. He had light skin, spoke posh, and went on to Williams or Amherst, I think, after graduation. I had one Gentile friend, too. Everyone else I knew was a middle-class Jew. *Gentlemen's Agreement* was the defining movie of my childhood. Ericka Huggins' husband grew up in New Haven, also; but I would have known him, or his brothers and sisters, only if we were in the same room at the same school. Hillhouse High School was "integrated" in that way.

I don't know exactly how Ericka got back to a jail in New Haven, but now she is one of the nine Black Panthers charged with murdering Alex Rackley a year ago this month. The police say the Panthers believed Rackley was an informer and murdered him—on Bobby Seale's orders—after a lengthy interrogation and a torture session. The interrogation was presumably recorded on tape to be used as instructional material for other Panther chapters.

The Panthers say that Rackley was a member in good standing of the party, and that he was murdered by undercover agents in order to set Bobby up for a murder rap. They say that Seale was brought to New Haven by a Yale administration official to speak at the University; the official has vanished. George Sams, the "Panther" who supplied police with details of the alleged murder, is thought to be an agent, or crazy, or both. Warren Kimbro, another member of the New Haven Panther chapter, has confessed to participation in the crime, in exchange for which his murder charge was reduced by one degree. Kimbro pleaded guilty after his brother, a Florida policeman, was flown to the New Haven jail by the D.A., and closeted for a long talk with Warren.

Such "evidence," if it is that, will be pored over when the trial begins, probably at the end of the summer (the court hearings so far have been preliminary, concerned with bail and so forth). But although the popular press insists that the question of who killed Alex Rackley is all that really counts, that is at bottom not the issue at all. "The facts," Tom Hayden said at the rally on the Green last Saturday, "are irrelevant." For crime, after all, is definitional, and punishment is problematic. Murder is a category defined by the interests of those with weapons. No one was punished for executing Benedict Arnold, no one stands accused of the murder of Che Guevara, no trial will be held for the guardsmen who shot the four Kent State students. In all those cases, like so many others, the murders were acts of war, outside the concern of a judicial system. Seen one way (at least), the killing of Alex Rackley was an act of war, whether committed by Panthers or pigs, and if Bobby Seale pulled the very trigger (an act not even the police accuse him of; he never saw Rackley) and were convicted of murder, he would be neither a criminal nor a political prisoner: He is a prisoner of war.

Despite the fatuous talk of "fair trial," the people who came to New Haven for May Day were drawn by the perception of a war game, not a civil liberties issue. They were on the Panthers' side. The Panthers had organized the event—primarily through the genius of Douglas Miranda, the 19-year-old Panther who directs the support campaign in New Haven—and the whites who helped were struggling to submit to Panther discipline. It was not always easy. Internally, Panther politics is every bit as disputatious as other Movement examples, and for weeks before the rally it was never clear what the Panthers wanted whites to do in New Haven. In the May 2 issue of *The Black Panther*, the official party newspaper, New York Panther leader Afeni Shakur excoriated the "so-called revolutionaries of Babylon" for "jiving, pimping . . . but not waging revolution." Afeni continued:

"You have not delivered one political consequence to the planned execution of a humanitarian. And to further your laziness, your cowardice, you allowed David Hilliard and Emory Douglas to be kidnapped. There isn't enough firepower being heard or felt in Babylon. Demonstrations have got to be on an even-steven basis. You start demonstrating with .357s on your hips."

It hardly matters that Afeni was wrong (white kids in New Haven were so active that they forced Judge Mulvey to release Hilliard and Douglas, who had been sentenced to six months for contempt). Her anger at the white Movement springs from all the disappointments Panthers have had with whites; all the broken promises; all the failures of support when it would have been crucial. Last summer, the Panthers tried to make an alliance with SDS and other white radicals in the United Front Against Fascism conference in Oakland. It came to nothing. Eldridge Cleaver had issued a "manifesto" from Algiers, warning of an impending "race war" if Bobby Seale were executed. But until New Haven, whites had not committed themselves to the Panthers' struggle.

* * *

Nixon was giving his Cambodia invasion speech on the radio as I turned off the Connecticut Turnpike into New Haven. The President was denouncing "anarchy" as I pulled up in front of a house where one of the radical collectives was billeted. The building was elegantly reconstructed from a dilapidated townhouse in what was long ago the richest section of town. From under a streetlight across the way, three or four fat, middle-aged men watched me and a few friends approach the house. After a round of suspicious self-identifications, a young man opened the door. He had short blond hair and wore wire-rim granny glasses and work clothes. He carried a shotgun in his hand, and as we entered he pointed it rather awkwardly at his own chin. Three young white women sat doing paperwork at a desk in the front room. A shotgun rested in a window bay. The windows were covered by bedsheets. The women raised their fists in greeting and said, "Power to the people." The interior of the house was glass and brick and white wall and indirect lighting. I flashed on Godard, and then felt mildly disgusted with myself for succumbing so quickly to allusion.

We drove around the city in the night. Most of the stores and public buildings were boarded up with plywood. Police cars prowled the streets. Everyone we met told us how tense they were, and how uptight the city was. Later that night, Kingman Brewster held a little meeting with some of the Chicago "conspirators" who were in town for the weekend. Cyrus Vance, a leading member of the Yale Corporation, sat quietly through the meeting; he had had ample experience with civil insurrection in Cyprus, Detroit and Vietnam. The Rev. William Sloane Coffin sauntered into the meeting and invited himself to stay. ("Brewster is Sihanouk," Hayden said in his rally speech Saturday: not much of a ruler but committed to a "progressive" role so long as those above and below keep him in power. Sooner or later, of course, he will be de-

posed by those who feel he is selling out or by those who feel
he is cashing in. But for now, Hayden said, he will protect us
and he should be supported.)

* * *

I suppose that other demonstrations last week could be
described in just as dramatic terms as the Yale action, or that
as much importance could be placed on any one of a dozen
other college uprisings. New Haven had seemed critical at
first because it had been building for weeks as a media as well
as a Movement event. By chance, it was the first college
demonstration after the invasion of Cambodia. In fact, the
renewed bombardment of North Vietnam was taking place as
the rallies were going on, and the announcement came while
ten thousand people were still sitting on the Green. The
Panthers and the white organizers quickly decided not to
broadcast it to the crowds, and instead sent people home
abruptly to avoid the "violence" that might be expected if
word of the bombing went out. The events of the next week—
the convulsive collegiate twitch against the war, the murders at
Kent State, the calls for national actions—seemed almost to
erase memories of New Haven. But that weekend was no
minor meeting. If the elements on the Green were already
old, still the mix was new. The crowd was freaky, dopey, and
rocky, but it was beyond Woodstock; or perhaps it was
Woodstock Nation, Marxist-Leninist, the revolutionary part
of the whole.

It was not so much the events of the New Haven weekend
as the context which gave it meaning. The Panthers finally
settled on a strict rule of non-violence (urged by Attorney
Charles Garry), not because it would lead to a better deal for
the defendants, but rather as a way to ensure bigger and heavier actions in New Haven when the trial begins. The combination of Panther discipline, press hysteria and the presence
of Army and National Guard troops enforced the rule. The
days were bright and warm, and there was just enough dope
and good feeling to keep spirits high. The speeches, for the
most part, did not mar the fine days; the best of the lot were
made by Miranda and Hayden. They defined the terms of
radical coalition, set goals for the developing revloutionary

movement, and generally encouraged Long Marching. There were suggestions for further actions this summer—and hopes were raised for enormous rallies in New Haven and at the UN in the fall. Abbie Hoffman got the biggest response with his usual Woodstock rap, and if it was devoid of much logic, it still made sense as a connection on-the-spot.

Yale loved every minute of it. Those students, teachers and administrators who were not into the revolutionary aspects of the action maintained a proper Lord and Lady Bountiful attitude and dispensed services with almost obsessive zeal. Everywhere you looked there was someone with a sandwich, an apple, information, a toilet or a bottle of eyewash. Signs were printed with symbols for various services: a little house for housing, a cup and saucer for refreshment, a plate and fork for food, a toilet, a red cross, and so on. It was like an autobahn somewhere.

New Haven weathered it all with only mild hysteria. Much to my disappointment—once again—the city did suffer enemy attack. A peaceful demonstration marred an otherwise promising holocaust. The tweedy haberdashers boarded up their windows against Alaric and the Visigoths; but the most Gothic thing about the weekend was the flying buttresses on Dwight Chapel. There was sporadic tear-gassing on the Green at night, but no one got very alarmed. The mayor did not read the Riot Act. I looked in my attic for a gas mask, but found only an old saxophone and an album of 78 rpm records.

May 11–18, 1970

The Trial

Andrew Kopkind

Chicago

It was said of the 1945 World Series that both the Detroit Tigers and the Chicago Cubs were so war-weakened that neither team could win. Something like that judgment has been applied in these closing weeks of the trial of the Conspiracy 7 (or 8, 9, or 10, according to whichever of the available calculi is preferred). The certain fate of the defendants and their lawyers — regardless of verdict — and the expense of energy and leadership suffered by the radical movements is balanced against the months of insult to the judicial system: "A loss for all," mourns *Time* magazine this week. But neither politics nor baseball is a zero-sum game. The Tigers, after all, won the 1945 Series. And although the scoring is obscure in the current contest, it seems clear that the orderly administration of justice — as she is practiced now in America — has lost the most. For that is what the trial was all about.

The Nixon Administration — not the defendants — chose to make the trial a political event. As former Attorney General Ramsey Clark had predicted, the Justice Department's invocation of the conspiracy law against the anti-war movement signaled the imposition of general political repression such as the United States has not seen since Nixon's earlier involvement with McCarthyism.

Attorney General Mitchell and Chicago's U.S. Attorney Thomas Foran selected the original eight defendants much as Frank Capra used to cast his war movies ("I want six volunteers—Smith, Cohen, Garibaldi, Sluckiwicz, Murphy, and Thomas Jefferson Roosevelt Jones"). The Chicago all-stars were picked for their symbolic value and their leadership roles: Bobby Seale, the black man and the Panther; Tom Hayden and Rennie Davis, the SDS veterans; Abbie Hoffman and Jerry Rubin, the anarcho-Yippies; Dave Dellinger, the Mobilization coalitionist; John Froines, the activist professor, and Lee Weiner, the street organizer and second-level cadre. It was important to have as much of the Movement's spectrum represented as possible (next time there will be women, too) in order for the effect to be truly chilling. In political trials final dispositions are of secondary importance: the act of prosecution is primarily intimidating and decapitating. Who remembers whether Eugene Dennis ever went to jail? Ramsey Clark and the Justice Department "liberals" who brought the Spock indictments in 1967 may have sincerely (if secretly) hoped for ultimate acquittal, but the damage they did in bringing the case could never be undone by verdict or higher-court reversal.

To mean anything at all, the defense must also be political. To accept the convention and conceit of common criminality consigns the defendants to defeat in the real terms of the trial. The government may contend that Doctor Spock or Dave Dellinger are no different from car thieves or wife beaters, but everything about its conduct of the cases confirms the pretense of that contention. The several "conspirators" are seen by the government as "ideological criminals," in Deputy Attorney General Kleindienst's ominous phrase, and their political positions prove them guilty as charged.

Short of seizing judicial power, there is no foolproof way for radicals to conduct a political defense against political prosecution. The courtroom is the government's turf and it commands the range of options. It has informers and agents willing to testify to anything. It controls the selection of a jury and it can keep tabs on the feelings of jurors as the trial progresses. The judge is not an impartial arbiter but a member of the government team only thinly disguised (whether he knows it or not). The Justice Department has immense resources; the defense is impoverished in every way inside the court. Most important of all, the government can define the issues at hand; the defense has either to accept them and hope for a lucky break ar attack the definitions at their roots.

The Chicago defendants tried hard to politicize their trial: that is, to expose the meaning of their prosecution and present it to the jury and the country. And in a sense they succeeded almost in spite of themselves. There was never a clear strategy for the eight. The government assured confusion at the defense table by bundling widely disagreeing fellows in one bed. Dellinger's militant pacifism, Abbie Hoffman's theatrical anarchism, Hayden's visionary pan-radicalism and Bobby Seale's black Leninism defied neat packaging.

Certainly the eight, or most of them, expected some amount of "confrontation" to go on at the trial. If there were to be real politics presented, they would have to reflect the sensibilities of the radical generation that arrived in Chicago in August 1968. The demonstrations of that month could make no sense now—to the jury or the people outside—without re-creation of their moods as well as a recitation of their ideologies. How could Abbie explain the Yippies' call for "public fornication" (in their 1968 manifesto) in that sterile glass courthouse before a judge so uptight that he had to spell out b-a-l-l-s and b-i-t-c-h when reading the record of contempt? How could the jury understand the deep-rooted rage of radicals in the streets when the defendants and their lawyers had to sit listening to informers' lies and a judge's obtuseness? It may have been unwise for Dellinger to say "bullshit" or William Kunstler to embrace Ralph Abernathy, but it was necessary and it was true.

After all, it was Judge Julius Hoffman—not the defendants—who set the terms of the courtroom confrontations, just as Mayor Richard Daley had set the terms of the actions in the streets. The Judge could have cooled it in court as Daley could have cooled it in the streets; both men chose violence. Hoffman was an extension of Daley, by other means: as the laws of the rulers are extensions of their politics.

* * *

Judge Hoffman's conduct of the trial contained elements of both *Grand Guignol* and *petit mal.* At times, it was hard to tell whether he was punchy or apoplectic. Variously characterized as Mr. Magoo and Adolf Eichmann, he was rather a character wholly unto himself, an original: shrewd, cruel, stubborn, arbitrary, bizarre — and not without a certain wit and an amount of perverse compassion. He understood his part in the drama he made: a foil too perfect for the desperate hijinks below his bench; an eleventh Marx Brother in a hysterical *Night at the Opera* in which he turned up as the Phantom. If Julius did not exist, Abbie would have had to invent him.

There's no doubt that Judge Hoffman enjoyed it all immensely — his power over the defendants and their lawyers, his dramatic notices (even the bad ones), even his place in the history of the revolution. He postured, grimaced, nodded, dozed, cackled and wisecracked with maximum effect. The outbursts he created by outrageous rulings were merely scenes in which he could get back to center stage. And all along he knew that he alone would deliver the curtain line — and *exeunt omnes*, in tears.

A large part of the defense consisted of responses to the judge's antics. He baited the culture heroes the defendants called as witnesses and even feigned a mild bemusement to Ginsberg's "Om." He fiddled while Ramsey Clark burned, and then slapped contempt citations on the lawyers for answering with anger his refusal to let Clark testify. He prohibited a delay of less than two months in the trial's commencement, so that Bobby Seale's lawyer, Charles Garry, could not join the defense. When Seale demanded his right of self-defense, the judge bound and gagged him to encourage the spectacle. The other defendants and the other lawyers behaved just as they had to — and just as Judge Hoffman knew they would.

The defendants' basic problem was making the events of

1968 understandable a year and a half later. It was not
enough for them to insist that they had done nothing wrong;
obviously, they had done *something*, but its definition could
not be isolated from the political context of that dreadful
year: the war, Johnson's retirement, political assassinations,
the riots of April, Daley's "shoot to kill" order, the hippie
"cultural revolution," the military defense of Chicago, and
the Convention itself. If the jury understood all that, it just
might be sympathetic; if people outside understood, the
meaning of a whole generation might come a little clearer.

The judge, of course, tried to block contextual testimony at
every turn. Ramsey Clark was not allowed on the stand because, the judge ruled, nothing he would say could possibly
be relevant to the case. Ralph Abernathy was barred because
he arrived a few minutes late in court. Those who made it
into the witness box were silenced at the merest mention of
testimony which might explain the defendants' actions. And
all the time the government built its case against them by
exploiting the atmospherics of radical protest. What acts of
contempt that occurred in the courtroom—certainly the most
serious ones—flowed from that essential imbalance. In a
contemptible court, only the contemptuous are just.

During the trial, however, the meaning of the disruptions
was not always so clear as it seems now in retrospect. Early
on, differences developed among the defendants. The first
major point of departure was the removal of Bobby Seale
from the other seven; then, there was talk of a general refusal
to continue, as a protest against the inherent racism of Judge
Hoffman's decision to call a mistrial for the one black man
among the eight. Seale asked the others to go ahead with their
trials, but even so, they felt impotent and trapped. Later,
when Dellinger's bail was revoked for saying "bullshit," several of the defendants wanted to disrupt the trial so ferocious-
ly that the judge would have to revoke their bail too.

But the remaining six stayed out of jail until the end. One
model for their behavior seemed to be Jerry Rubin's famous
appearance before the House Un-American Activities Committee in 1966, when he appeared in Revolutionary War cos-
tume and generally acted so outlandishly that the hearings

dissolved in the farce. But the contrary model was Tom Hayden's appearance before the same committee in 1968, when he seemed to play along with the rules but in effect succeeded in turning the hearing on its head—so that he controlled and directed the show. But there was no good way to integrate Hayden's subtlety with Rubin's directness, and the total effect did not synthesize the two styles but merely mixed them.

* * *

If the trial were to have any significance outside the courtroom, the defense would have to organize a campaign not only for support but for attack. The government sought to discredit and decapitate the Movement by indicting its leaders; it was the defendants' responsibility to connect themselves to a popular base and legitimate the Movement's objectives.

At least that was the theory. In practice it was a difficult duty to discharge, not only because of the essential disparities among the defendants, but because of the utter fragmentation of the Movement as the sixties ended. Abbie and Jerry had a considerable following in freak nation (and a lot of media visibility) but "Yippie!" was admittedly a put-on party, and neither Simon and Schuster nor Random House seemed to be the agents of revolution. Tom Hayden and Rennie Davis had some attachments with active radical organizations, but they had also accumulated a decade's natural resentment, here and there, and they were floating on the edges of current organizational politics. Dave Dellinger is universally respected in the Movement as an avuncular Ho, but it would be hard to find three other people who share his particular brand of politics. Alone among the defendants, Bobby Seale was connected to a real base—the Black Panther party—but its heavier problems elsewhere (and his, too) made it unlikely that much organizing would go on around his conspiracy indictment.

The Panthers staged the best demonstration in Chicago during the trial—on opening day in September—and there were dozens of good rallies around the country when the defendants flew out to speak after the daily court adjournments or on weekends. Abbie and Jerry, in particular, hoped that the Justice Department demonstrations during the Washington Mobilization March on November 15 would lead to a national movement around the Conspiracy; but although the action was exhilarating, the movement did not really materialize. In too large a part, support action was organized through the old boys' net of early SDS people, Mobe functionaries and personal friends of the defendants. If there were a large national radical organization, it might have made the Conspiracy its winter project: action would be undertaken by chapters on campuses, in communities, or wherever. But, of course, nothing like that organization now exists.

A logical (if not necessary) consequence of radical untogetherness was the inch-by-inch drift of the Conspiracy toward the liberal Left. It was certainly more comfy in that bag, and while impeccable radicals were baiting the defendants for this or that political error, the liberals were outraged at Judge Hoffman's desrespect for civil liberties and the government's general nastiness about peaceful dissent.

In Chicago, the defendants made attempts to relate (as they say) to Weatherman, RYM-II, the Panthers and other radical groupings, but the ambience of the Conspiracy office was much milder. In the nature of things, the defendants assumed the aura of media stars, and as the real performers trooped in to testify or express their support, the social whirl quickened. Morale in the office was shaky at best.

As the trial drew to a close, spirits seemed to pick up. The press, which had been treating the case perfunctorily for months, suddenly regained interest. In the long middle of the case, reporters were satisfied simply to fill the requirements of their editors for a daily story. They fixed on a set of conventional categories into which each session's events were placed: the "antics" of the defendants, the weirdness of the judge, the freak-outs of the spectators and the frustration of the defense lawyers. Bobby Seale's moments made the front page, and the silenced songs of Phil Ochs, Country Joe and Judy Collins were good for a few laughs, but most of the time the stories were buried. It was hard for the real importance of the trial to be broadcast.

Toward the end of January the jury realized that the end of the trial was upon them. Full-time spectators and participants say that an entirely different feeling was projected from the jury box (seeing those fourteen stone-cold faces, it is a bit strange to imagine any feeling at all). By then, everyone knew that both defendants and lawyers would be packed away for contempt whatever the actual verdict in the case; the judge practically said as much himself. Still, no one could have been prepared for the final week.

* * *

MONDAY: Judge Hoffman accepts 86 of 88 instructions suggested by the government for his charge to the jury—and 34 of 79 offered by the defense. Chuckles. The judge turns angrily to the defendants' table: "The conduct is continuing right down to the last observation." He then turns down a defense motion to show films of the 1968 demonstrations—already entered and used in evidence—in its summation. (The films would probably show the unprovoked, brutal police attacks on demonstrators.)

TUESDAY: Assistant U.S. Attorney Richard Schultz, the dogged and somewhat prissy prosecutor on the government's legal team, begins his summation. The August 1968 demonstrations, he says, were to signal "the start of the revolution" and establish "a National Liberation Front—the political arm of the Viet Cong—in the United States." The government's police and informers and intelligence agents were "impartial observers"; the defense's big-name witnesses (Jesse Jackson, Dick Gregory, Julian Bond, Judy Collins, Allen Ginsberg, Terry Southern, Norman Mailer, Arlo Guthrie, Phil Ochs, Richard Goodwin, etc.) were "duped." The defendants were like "Lenin and Mao Tse-tung."

WEDNESDAY: Leonard Weinglass begins summarizing the defense case. The government's witnesses could not be trusted as "honest men," he says, because they were paid informers and agents. (*Objection. Sustained.*) "Violent statements are not violent," he says; the trial is "an act of vengeance" by Chicago authorities.

THURSDAY: Weinglass finishes his portion of the summation; he says that in the sixties people such as Martin Luther King took their protests into the streets. "There is no proof" that King would have had anything to do with the 1968 demonstrations in Chicago, the government says in objection. Weinglass argues that the events of August can't be understandable outside of the larger context. (*Objection sustained.*) Weinglass tries to quote from Clarence Darrow's defense of Communists in a famous Chicago case fifty years earlier, but the government and prosecution won't let him explain. He does manage to get in a line from the Passion (according to St. Matthew).

Kunstler begins his summation—the defense's last word. It doesn't work: He's too rhetorical, somehow inauthentic (as Weinglass had been movingly honest). He gets bogged down in a detailed recitation of the events of an alleged "bomb plot" by one of the defendants in an underground garage; people feel he may have raised new doubts about his own client, rather than quelled them.

FRIDAY: Kunstler recoups. He slips out of the garage incident, then moves on to his final flourishes:

"The hangman's rope never solved a single problem, except that of one man. You can crucify Jesus, poison a Socrates, hang a John Brown or a Nathan Hale, jail a Eugene Debs or a Bobby Seale, kill a Che Guevara, assassinate a John F. Kennedy or a Martin Luther King. But the problems remain." "Look what happened to all of them," one of the defendants remarks mournfully.

U.S. Attorney Foran winds it up. The defendants lured innocents to Chicago with promises of sex in the streets. The defendants are "evil men"; Jerry Rubin worked best at night "like most predators." He appeals to the jury's philistinism and tells the members (ten men and two women) not to be swayed by intellectual arguments but rely on the evidence of their senses—that is, how the defendants looked and acted in the courtroom. The defendants, he says, "corrupted" innocent children: "We can't let people do that to our kids. The lights of Camelot that kids believe needn't go out." He finishes with a quote from Jefferson: "Obedience to the law is the major part of patriotism."

SATURDAY: Judge Hoffman gives his two hours' worth of "instructions" to the jury. He begins by quoting the long indictments in full (he has done it before before in the trial) so that the jurymen can see just how guilty the defendants are. The jury leaves at noon, and the rest of the people in the courtroom are about to file out when the judge says he has a few other "matters" to take up. Then he begins reading the contempt citations. Dellinger gets thirty-two counts. Before sentencing, he asks Dellinger if he has anything to say: "There are two issues the country refuses to take seriously and refuses to solve — the war in Vietnam and racism," Dellinger answers.

"I don't want to talk politics with you," the judge says angrily, cutting him off. Dellinger continues:

"You want us to be like good Jews going quietly to the concentration camps while the court suppresses the truth. It's a travesty on justice. The record condemns you, not us."

Dellinger's two teenage daughters applaud and shout approval. Marshals fall upon them; a woman cop tackles the elder daughter and drags her out. Kunstler stands before the bench, sobbing, his arms outstretched: "My God! What are you doing to us? My life is nothing. Put me in jail now, I beg of you." Dellinger is led away. "Right on, beautiful people," he says softly, smiling. As the door shuts, Rennie Davis approaches the bench: "You have just jailed one of the most beautiful and courageous men in the country."

"You're next," the judge snaps to Davis. He gets twenty-three citations, then is allowed to make a statement. "You represent all that is old, ugly, repressive and bigoted in this country," he tells the judge, who cuts him off and sentences him to two years, one month and nineteen days in jail.

Then Hayden. This time, the defendant works his way brilliantly through an hour of "argument" and explanation, and the judge seems confused, apologetic and self-justifying. Hayden tells how two Justice Department gooks tried to convince Ramsey Clark not to testify, and one of them followed Clark to Chicago and right into the courtroom. Hayden's argument is so skillful that the judge is impressed: "A fellow as smart as you can do awfully well under this system." Abbie shoots back: "He doesn't want a place in the business, Julie."

Finally Hayden is asked if he has anything to say in mitigation of punishment. He stands motionless by the defense table, his arms at his sides. His eyes are red and wet and his mouth is trembling. "I would like to have a child. . . ." He can't finish the sentence. The judge is crueler than he has ever been. He cracks: "That's where the federal judicial system can't help you." (*No laughter.*) Hayden answers fiercely: "And the federal judicial system can't help you prevent the birth of a new world." Hayden picks up his papers and his coat and walks toward the lockup, the marshals following.

Abbie is next. He ends defiantly, then walks to the spectators' section, gently kisses his wife, and smiles: "Water the plant."

SUNDAY: Weiner and Froines get theirs. Then Kunstler's citations are read. When told he can reply, the lawyer approaches the bench and leans on the lectern. He reads from a prepared statement:

"Yesterday, for the first time in my career, I completely lost my composure in court. I felt such a deep sense of utter futility that I could not keep from crying, something I had not done publicly since childhood. I am sorry if I disturbed the decorum of the courtroom, but I am not ashamed of my tears.

"Neither am I ashamed of my conduct in this court for which I am about to be punished. I have tried with all of my heart faithfully to represent my clients in the face of what I considered and still consider repressive and unjust conduct toward them. If I have to pay with my liberty for such representation, then that is the price of my beliefs and sensibilities.

"I can only hope that my fate does not deter other lawyers throughout the country who, in the difficult days that lie ahead, will be asked to defend clients against a steadily increasing governmental encroachment upon their most fundamental liberties."

Kunstler gets four years and thirteen days. Judge Hoffman finishes off his contempt extravaganza with Weinglass, whose name he misstates for the umpteenth time during the trial. Weinglass never raised his voice or uttered a discourteous word during the trial, and he does not begin to do so at the end; his crimes consist mainly in attempting to get important testimony before the jury against the prosecution's wishes and the judge's unheeding rulings. Weinglass gets a year, eight months and five days. All told, the eight defendants (including Seale, who is at present serving his four-year contempt sentence) got nineteen years, one month and three days for contempt, before any verdict was rendered.

* * *

The jury took four days to reach a verdict, and when it was in there was more a sense of anticlimax than surprise or dismay. A "compromise" was what the defendants had always thought would be most debilitating; it would split the coherence of the Conspiracy, confuse the public and make hardline organizing that much more difficult. The government and the judge would look a bit better than if there had been a straight conviction—or a total acquittal. As it is, the defendants face long prison terms on the contempt charges and—except for Weiner and Froines—sentences on that part of the indictment on which they were convicted.

But the trial wasn't just about winning acquittal, which was always thought unlikely for the six chief political actors among the conspirators. Its purpose was to expose the unlawfulness of the new law, the disorderliness of the old order. If the trial had taken place in one or another of those countries that Americans dismiss as "totalitarian," it would be universally recognized as an outrage. It's a little more difficult for people to make the same judgments about Chicago.

But there's no substantial difference between other repressive regimes and ours. American tones may be softer and the colors more muted, but underneath the effects are the same. Repression is real, and if the politics necessary to fight it are not always so clear, at least they are available. There's energy now to wage a heavy campaign against repression around the issue of the trial, and the events of the last week—from Congressional speeches to marches in the streets—suggest that more will happen in the days after. For the issue isn't the freedom of "the ten"; at last, it is the freedom of us all, and those who think that they are neither in conspiracy nor in contempt will have to fight to prove their innocence, or their right.

February 23–March 2, 1970

To Off
a Panther

Andrew Kopkind

The Black Panther Party has found more sympathy in its moment of extermination than it ever did in its whole tragic life. But such brutal irony fills the history of black people in white America: A black man must be a victim before he is a hero. Black challenges to white power are always denied; it is only when a black man is defeated that the white tears flow.

The decapitation — at least — of the Panthers appears now to be complete. The killing of Fred Hampton in Chicago, the siege of the Panthers' headquarters in Los Angeles, and the arrests of David Hilliard and Bobby Rush just about finished the ability of Panther leaders to move freely — or at all. Since an Oakland Panther named Bobby Hutton was killed in April 1968, more than twenty-five party members have died in violent combat, most frequently at the hands of policemen or police agents. Hundreds have been arrested and uncounted scores are in exile or underground. The party's work continues in some aspects; the newspaper, *The Black Panther*, appears weekly and provides the main source of revenue. A breakfasts-for-children program operates in several cities, and there are a few free medical clinics run by Panther chapters. Political education classes are held for Panther members, and some high school organizing is going on. But it's obvious that the forward motion of the Panthers has been seriously slowed.

Whether the Black Panther Party — in its present form — can thrive again is problematic; but in the aftermath of the events of December, it has been consigned by whites and many blacks to a certain grave. Upon Fred Hampton's tomb, liberals of both races sing funeral songs with words full of great pity but little praise. Like palefaces who wrote heroic ballads about the redskins they slew, the "civil rights establishment" has bestowed upon the Panthers a folkloric role, the while denying its own part in the slaughter. There are already nine separate investigations of the Panther's troubles. The great corporate foundations are fairly falling over themselves trying to get into the act. Ford has granted the Arthur Goldberg/ Roy Wilkins "Commission of Inquiry" a cool quarter-million to confirm the obvious fact that the Panthers are being repressed.

The twenty-eight commission members,* individually and with their organizations, have spent the last three years condemning the Panthers' "violence," and thus helping to create the climate in which revolutionary blacks could be easily repressed. Even a cursory glance through the newspaper clippings shows how the anti-militants have used their standing in the white political system to illegitimize militancy.

Roy Wilkins, for example, has condemned black power, ghetto insurgencies, black studies programs, reparations to the black community, separate black labor organizing, and just about everything that is up-front in the black liberation movement. He has indulged in sly red-baiting: "If you ask me

---

*Arthur Goldberg, Roy Wilkins, Clifford Alexander, Julian Bond, Sam Brown, W. Haywood Burns, Kenneth Clark, Ramsey Clark, John Conyers, William T. ("Bumps") Coleman, John Douglas, Melvin Dymally, Marion Wright Edelman, Jean Fairfax, Jack Greenberg, Richard Hatcher, Philip Hoffman, Jesse Jackson, Arthur J. Lelyveld, Morris Abram, John de J. Pemberton, Louis Pollack, Joseph Porter, Charles Palmer, A. Philip Randolph, Cynthia Wedel, George Wylie, Whitney Young.

whether Mr. Carmichael is his own man, I am sorry I don't know Mr. Carmichael and his connections well enough to guess. . . ." Wilkins, Whitney Young and the others have continually belittled the significance of militancy: "Carmichael's following amounts to about 50 Negroes and about 5,000 white reporters," Young wrote in a Right-wing magazine in the month that Bobby Hutton (and Martin Luther King) were murdered. Dr. Kenneth B. Clark, the academic establishment's favorite "militant" Negro, used to say things like "black power is a shoddy moral product disguised in the gaudy package of racial militance," and he warned Negroes not to be "cowed into silence by unrealistic Negro racists." When black students occupied a building at Cornell last year, Clark—a member of the New York State Board of Regents, which has partial jurisdiction over Cornell—said, "The spectacle of American college students concluding their armed occupation of a campus student union building by a victorious exit with sixteen rifles and three shotguns at the ready restimulates the feelings of revulsion and sadness one felt when viewing the Birmingham police use of cattle prods on human beings. . . ."

It's hardly hot news that Wilkins, Clark, Young and the rest have come down hard on black militancy. What's crucially important is that such positions have led directly to the extreme forms of state violence against blacks which they now condemn. By excluding the militants from the "masses" of the black movement, the liberals gave the necessary assurance to government and police that repression would not seriously be opposed. And so, except in words, it has not.

At best, the various commissions may provide a margin of "cover" for Panthers and their brothers. It is conceivable that enough exposés of unnecessary police brutality may restrict police to merely "necessary" forms. But the history of such liberal efforts is hardly encouraging, even in that ambiguous regard.

The liberal politicians (in one manner of speaking or another) who put together the commission have their own fishes to fry. Liberals in office are primarily concerned with social control; liberals out of office want nothing more than to get back in. They see the major hindrance to that goal coming from the far right: Agnew, Mitchell and the Chicago police, they fear, may destroy them if given a free hand. And so the point of liberal politics is to oppose the Right. (Radicals, on the other hand, conceive of a system which is still basically centrist, with Agnewism playing a role of functional support: to help Nixon fend off an independent Right-wing attack.) In any case, liberal politics in these times serve the interests of those who play them, and only tangentially may help others to stay alive.

The likely result of the commissions' to-ing and fro-ing are reports that condemn the use of "illegal" or brutal repression against Hampton and the Panthers by the police, while chiding the Panthers for "provocation." Given the current mood of Mitchell-baiting, the non-governmental reports will doubtless slap at the Justice Department, too. But even the "best" possible report will accept the police and court definition of "violence," and will anchor that usage in the assumption that there's nothing so wrong about American society that it can't be changed by non-violent dissent, federal programs, and the good will of the liberal elites: in other words, another "report," such as the ones which have done nothing to interrupt the steady descent of the iron boot on those in the forefront of change. And then the sad songs will cease.

* * *

It was only three years ago that the Black Panther Party slid into public consciousness. The mood of those days was most evocatively recalled by Eldridge Cleaver, who wrote that he "fell in love" with the Panthers at his first sight of them—at a meeting of black militants in San Francisco:

"Suddenly the room fell silent. . . . There was only the sound of the lock clicking as the front door opened. . . . From the tension showing on the faces of the people before me, I thought the cops were invading the meeting, but there was a deep female gleam leaping out of one of the women's eyes that no cop who ever lived could elicit. I recognized that gleam out of the recesses of my soul, even though I had never seen it before: the total admiration of a black woman for a black man.

"I spun around in my seat and saw the most beautiful sight I had ever seen: four black men wearing black berets, powder blue shirts, black leather jackets, black trousers, shiny black shoes—and each with a gun; in front was Huey P. Newton with a riot pump shotgun in his right hand, barrel pointed down to the floor. Beside him was Bobby Seale, the handle of a .45 caliber automatic showing from its holster on his right hip, just below the hem of his jacket. A few steps behind Seale was Bobby Hutton, the barrel of his shotgun at his feet. . . ."

The party had been formed a few months before by Newton and Seale, who had begun organizing "black power" action in Oakland's Merritt College. The name Newton chose reflected his affinity with Stokely Carmichael's Black Panther organization in Lowndes County, Ala., where a late SNCC project was underway to win electoral control of one of the hardest-core Black Belt districts.

Like the Lowndes project, the Black Panther Party has its historical roots in the transitional period between the breakup of the integrated civil rights movement in the rural South and the white North, and the development of a black liberation movement in the urban ghettoes. Newton and Seale drew more on the revolutionary thrust in the black streets than on the reformist ideals of the white universities. "What we are doing," a California Panther once remarked in those early days, "is putting Malcolm and Mao together."

The Panthers dug the *Little Red Book* (and made money from selling it), but they never went completely "chinois." The material of their politics conveyed the authentic weight of the black experience in America. Newton's program, which is still the party's basic platform (it is printed each week in the newspaper), put traditional demands of Negroes in the United States in a revolutionary context:

1. We want freedom. We want power to determine the destiny of our Black Community.

2. We want full employment for our people.

3. We want an end to the robbery by the white man [later changed to "capitalist"] of our Black Community.

4. We want decent housing, fit for shelter of human beings.

5. We want education for our people that exposes the true nature of this decadent American society. We want education that teaches us our true history and our role in the present-day society.

6. We want all black men to be exempt from military service.

7. We want an immediate end to police brutality and murder of black people.

8. We want freedom for all black men held in federal, state, county and city prisons and jails.

9. We want all black people when brought to trial to be tried in court by a jury of their peer group or people from their black communities, as defined by the Constitution of the United States.

10. We want land, bread, housing, education, clothing, justice and peace. And as our major political objective, a United Nations–supervised plebiscite to be held throughout the black colony, in which only black colonial subjects will be allowed to participate, for the purpose of determining the will of black people as to their national destiny.

The statement of demands ended with a quotation from the American Declaration of Independence.

Explicit in the points was the conception of a "black colony" within imperial America, similar to—but functionally distinct from—the colonies of the empire in the Third World. That notion had been hanging around for a number of years; but what was different was the Panthers' implicit Marxist analysis of the imperial system. The racism which permeated everything was not a self-contained and self-supporting phenomenon, but a consequence of imperialism. Because of their colonial history, black people had to struggle against the system as blacks; but liberation could not come until the entire imperial machine was destroyed.

From that ideology flowed a number of crucial implications. First, the enemy wasn't simply "whitey," but specifically the white ruling class, and the final struggle was not between races but between classes. Second, black people should organize for that struggle as blacks, and not—as "orthodox" Marxist-Leninists insisted—as members of an integrated working class. Third, liberation did not depend on the establishment of a separate territorial black state but on the defeat of U.S. imperialism. Fourth, white revolutionaries had a valid role in the whole process—as allies of black revolutionaries, at work "behind the lines" of the Mother Country. Finally, the Panthers' demands could not be coopted by corporate or federal handouts and cash-ins; only a revolution could satisfy them.

* * *

It took some time for whites—even white radicals—to dig the Panthers. At first, the Panthers were objects of amusement: Posters of Huey in his cobra chair, flanked by spear and gun and African artifacts, had an appeal that was more pop than political. But then Eldridge Cleaver began writing and speaking, and his words weren't funny at all.

Inevitably, the Panthers became a media event. *Ramparts* magazine built circulation on Cleaver's writing; television and the mass-circulation press inflated the Panther image and marketed it along with nudity, drugs and rock music. Cleaver became the paradigm native revolutionary hero, an American Che. Pressures grew on the Panthers to move out of their base in Oakland; soon, black hustlers as well as black political activists were calling themselves "Panthers" whether they were actually in the party or not. Any dude who wanted a little money or excitement could pass himself off as a real live Black Panther and hijack a plane to Havana or raise funds from willing white Leftists.

It is doubtful if there have ever been more than several hundred bona fide Black Panther Party cadre in the country, or more than several thousand who identified themselves in any specific way with the party organization. But the Panther myth was so outsized that it must have seemed as if there were a hundred thousand of them. Local and federal police agents began to infiltrate Panther organizations—as thoroughly as they had done in Communist party cells a generation earlier.

The real Panther leadership was hard put to deal with the overblown national image. At the same time that key figures were feeling the first predictable blows of repression, pressures to expand were mounting. Even the development of the solid Oakland "foco" was stunted as the party began to think of itself as a powerful national organization.

At that point, the contradictions were formed which led at last to the Panthers' extreme distress. The emergence of a nationwide Panther presence aroused the authorities before the Panthers were really ready for defense, and before they had organized a wide enough circle of support for political protection.

Panthers would shout "Off the pig," and while it may have been a promise or a metaphor to ghetto people, uptight whites took it literally. As a matter of fact, the Panthers never formulated — or practiced — an aggressive strategy against the cops. For all the reported "gun battles" between Panthers and police, there are no cases of armed forays by Panthers, or even sniping. Huey had said at the start: "It is not in the panther's nature to attack anyone first, but when he is attacked and backed into a corner, he will respond viciously."

The Panthers' primary strategy was to organize people in the ghettos around their demands — and even to begin implementing the easier ones, such as black education and food, medical and clothing services. Because those demands carried a revolutionary force — they could not be granted by the system as presently constituted — the Panthers expected repression, and armed themselves for it. Huey said:

"Without protection from the Army, the police, and the military, the institutions could not go on in their racism and exploitation. Whenever you attack the system, the first thing that the administrators do is to send out their strongmen. If it's a rent strike, because of the indecent housing we have, they will send out the police to throw the furniture out the window. They don't come themselves. They send their protectors. So to deal with the corrupt exploiter, you are going to have to deal with his protector, which is the police, who take orders from him. This is a must."

The attacks began early enough. Cleaver was warned that his prison parole (from a pre-Panther conviction) would be revoked if he continued to engage in political activity. The police began following the Panthers around Oakland, and the Panthers began counterpatrolling the police. To a certain extent, the Panther patrols were effective in keeping cops off the backs of ghetto people. But the police counterattacked by harassing and arresting the Panthers, and in one "routine check" of a Panther car, Huey Newton was arrested. In a flash there was gunfire: Huey and one policeman were wounded and a second policeman was killed. Huey, of course, was charged with the murder. For several days afterward, Panther members in the San Francisco Bay area were rounded up and arrested on irrelevant charges.

Six months later, Cleaver and several other Panthers in three cars were stopped by police in Oakland; they were out getting provisions for a big barbecue picnic to be held in a park the next day. Again, there was an "argument" and shooting — at the Panthers. Cleaver wrote about it in his cell at Vacaville:

"Common sense told me that I'd best have my hands up by the time I cleared the front of my car. But before I cleared, the cop on the passenger side of his car started shouting and firing his gun, and then the other cop started shooting. . . . The explosions from their guns sounded right in my face and so, startled, I dove for cover in front of my car. . . . It took only a split second to see that they had us in a crossfire, so I shouted to the brothers, 'Scatter!'. . . . As we started across the street, one of the Panthers, Warren Wells, got hit and let out an agonized yelp of pain. . . . A cop with a shotgun was running after me, shooting. I didn't have a gun but I wished that I had! (O, how I wish that I had!). . . ."

Cleaver and Little Bobby Hutton made it into the basement of a nearby house. The cops shot into it: "We lay down flat against the floor while the bullets ripped through the walls. . . . The pigs started lobbing in tear gas. . . . I took the opportunity to fortify the walls with whatever we could

lay our hands on: furniture, tin cans, cardboard boxes. . . .
We decided to stay in there and choke to death if necessary
rather than walk out into a hail of bullets. . . . One of the
shots found my leg and my foot with an impact so painful and
heavy that I was sure I no longer had two legs. . . ."

Then the police shot firebombs into the basement, and
Cleaver decided to surrender. "I called out to the pigs and
told them that we were coming out. . . . There were pigs in
the windows above us in the house next door, with guns
pointed at us. They told us not to move, to raise our hands.
This we did. . . . The pigs pointed to a squad car parked in
the middle of the street and told us to run to it. . . . Then
they snatched Little Bobby away from me and shoved him
forward. . . . After he had traveled about 10 yards the pigs
cut loose on him with their guns."

* * *

The crackdown in the Bay area was met by mass demonstrations and solid support by blacks and white radicals. The
Panthers had done the essential work of base-building. Huey
Newton's trial was the political event of the year, and "Free
Huey" was the leading slogan; and Huey's amazingly light
sentence—two to fifteen years—attests to the Panthers' success. But outside of Oakland, the repression was more successful, and the arrests and murders mounted with only weak
protests in their wake. At length, the total effect of the nationwide anti-Panther campaign weakened the Oakland base, too,
and the whole organization entered a nightmare period of
siege.

As their troubles deepened, the Panthers began to redirect
their activities and emphasize different aspects of their strategy. There was less talk of armed struggle and more work to
"serve the people." The breakfasts-for-children program was
successful in many cities. But the liberal approval of the project did not allay fears that there was a bit of politics being
served with the cornflakes. The crackdown continued.

At the same time, the Panthers were intensifying their fra-
ternal relations with white radicals. "Coalitions" were formed
with the Peace and Freedom Party (Cleaver ran for President
of the United States), with the Oakland Seven (white youths

charged—and acquitted—of conspiracy in anti-draft demonstrations), and most important, with SDS.

What followed was the organization of a white base to support the Black Panthers, and although it was an attractive idea
to many whites, it had the effect of eroding the Panthers'
black following. Many black militants had always opposed
the Panthers' openness with white radicals. Cleaver was
widely criticized for writing for whites, speaking to white college audiences, and generally "relating to white reality." Non-
Marxist black militants and black "cultural nationalists,"
whom the Panthers consistently bad-mouthed, treated Newton and Seale as "traitors to their race."

Last summer, the Panthers called a national conference in
Oakland to build a "United Front Against Fascism." By all
accounts it was a dispiriting affair. Most of the participants
were white Leftists, and it ended in destructive factional argument. The program that was supposed to come out of that
UFAF conference—a petition campaign for community control of police—never came off the ground. The Panthers were
understandably bitter—bitter—both at the lack of black support for UFAF and the disputes among the whites. In the
next months, the Panthers began violent rhetorical attacks
against the white radicals who did not singlemindedly follow
them: in particular, the Weatherman element of SDS.

* * *

The difficulties which the Panthers have endured have as
much to do with the fragmentation of the Left as a whole as
they do with the un-togetherness of the black movements.
The groups with whom the Panthers coalesced are for the
most part weak and struggling. The celebrated "Rainbow
Coalition" in Chicago—the Black Panthers, the Young Lords
(Latinos), and the Young Patriots ("hillbilly" greasers)—
sounded glorious but has yet to make much sense as a coalition, although both the Lords and the Panthers have a certain
strength on their own turfs. The alliance with SDS—which
consists now of a relationship with the RYM-II faction
only—has not been noticeably effective in recent months.

The Panthers may in theory be the "vanguard" of the new
American Revolution, but in practice they have yet to win

legitimacy—especially in the black community. There, a hundred parties contend; in almost every city there are black organizations across a range of politics of almost indescribable complexity. In terms of national consciousness, the Panthers' supremacy is being challenged by two groups in particular: the Republic of New Africa and the League of Revolutionary Black Workers.

RNA was the home base of Robert Williams during his long years in exile, but once home, he seems to have abandoned it. He has resigned the presidency and has fired the vice-president as his lawyer (in favor of a white liberal Democratic Michigan state senator). RNA demands a separate black nation, made up of five Southern states; how it will pry them loose from the Union is not yet clear. RNA is doing low-level organizing of high school kids in a few cities (Detroit, Brooklyn, New Orleans), generally on the basis of anti-white black nationalism.

The League seems to be moving much faster. Organized at first in Detroit as an insurgent campaign within the United Auto Workers, it has now expanded into a citywide black movement. It publishes a weekly paper, *The Inner City Voice*, and has just about taken control of the West Central Organization, an old Saul Alinsky project. The League is tight with the Black Manifesto reparations committee (as both the Panthers and RNA are not), and it is training high school cadre in "freedom schools," readying candidates for UAW leadership, and struggling for union power inside various factories. For the time being, the League seeks to avoid the pitfalls of national expansion; it chooses to concentrate its effort in Detroit, but its example is widely watched.

The Black Panther Party is still in the forefront of black liberation, even if it is not universally acknowledged as the vanguard. It played a heroic role at a moment of historical necessity: It stepped out front and raised a revolutionary banner. Its tragedy is that the ranks behind were thin and disorganized.

Fred Hampton was murdered because he was a black man: and because he was a revolutionary. He was born black; he chose revolution. So the persecution of the Black Panther

Party is part of two grim American traditions: the casual extermination of black people and the repression of real radicalism. But the determination of the assault against black revolution only underlines its seriousness. Huey Newton saw it: "As long as there are black people, there will be Black Panthers."

January 12 – 19, 1970

Part Two
The Crisis of Resources

What began as a minor concern about the quality of consumer goods grew into a vast social movement to protect and improve the environment. The "ecology" movement—in numbers, range, and legitimacy—surpassed the anti-war movement by the end of the sixties. At last there was a cause of social action that most of white, middle-class American could espouse because it meant something directly for their own lives. But there was no direct line from ecological concern to effective action; and because most of the activists were typologically prone to shrink from a fight with authority, the movement could be easily diverted, evaded, or simply bought off.

A Screeching Halt

James Ridgeway

While there is a publicity barrage about the national drive to stop air pollution, the federal government's program is in chaos, and Nixon's proposed reforms will only make it worse.

Motor vehicles cause about two-thirds of all air pollution in the country. There are two obvious ways of dealing with this situation: One is to build non-polluting automobile engines; the other, to develop non-polluting rapid transit systems, which could ease congestion in large cities as well as reduce the amount of filth in the air. Unfortunately, very little progress has been made in either direction, and future prospects are dim.

It is technically possible to make engines which would greatly reduce pollution. In such circumstances the usual course would be for the government to contract with industry to make non-polluting engines, as it did in contracting for design and construction of the SST. But the auto and petroleum industries and the maze of construction interests which make up the highway lobby are dead set against a new kind of engine. Rather than face off squarely against industry on this issue, the government has basically dropped whatever opposition it ever had to the internal combustion engine and instead set out on a dubious program to control the engine by setting emission standards. That means making new kinds of mufflers which will somehow do away with the pollutants after they have been produced. Detroit claims it can make such mufflers. But so far the technology does not seem very advanced: The emission system now installed in automobiles is the same one developed by the industry in 1962.

The emissions standards only apply to new automobiles, which make up a tiny fraction of all the cars on the roads. Thus, even if the new kinds of mufflers work, they are not likely to have much influence on air pollution. Moreover, emission controls will cost a great deal in maintenance; some estimates run as high as $6 billion a year.

Carbon monoxide, oxides of nitrogen, leads and oxidants are the primary components of vehicle air pollution. The government first set emission standards for January 1968. Progressively stiffer standards have been proposed for 1973 and 1975. According to a report by the Senate Commerce Committee, "The present emission standards will not stabilize, much less reduce, vehicular air pollution. Studies indicate that, under existing controls, automobile air pollution in the United States will more than double in the next thirty years because of the projected increase in both the number of vehicles and miles driven by such vehicles. Ironically under the present emission standards, oxides of nitrogen emissions, the main villains in the photochemical smog production, will be higher than they would be if no standards existed." That is because current standards regulate hydrocarbons and carbon monoxide only. The best way to reduce these pollutants is to raise the combustion temperature, which, in turn, increases oxides of nitrogen production. Even if devices were effective, there would be no assurances that they would be maintained through the life of the car. Beginning in 1973 the government intends to establish standards for oxides of nitrogen. There is no indication whether or not the automakers will abide by this standard.

In 1967 the Senate Commerce Committee began an inquiry into the feasibility of alternative engine systems with a look at electric automobiles. They did not seem a sensible alternative because batteries were too bulky and expensive. Eventually the committee recommended development of a steam car, driven by a Rankine-type engine. In a Rankine engine fuel is ignited outside the engine in a burner. The heat produced by burning heats a fluid — water or some other neutral fluid — and is thereby converted to a vapor. The vapor becomes the power source for the engine. Valves are opened and shut to control entry of the fuel into a shaft where it turns the pistons which drive the wheels. The Rankine engine car runs on a variety of fuels. It can burn regular gasoline or operate on low-grade white kerosene. Rankine fuel is less refined, less costly and less polluting than fuels which go into internal combustion engines.

After the Commerce Committee study was made, William Lear, the inventor, showed some interest in building prototype steam cars, and he is said to have put $6 million of his own money into a development program. But recently Lear said he became convinced it was impossible for an independent company to compete with the auto manufacturers. He now argues for building a prototype gas turbine engine, which he believes Detroit might be persuaded to adopt. Gas turbines also are low in pollutants.

Because of Detroit's opposition, the government's research program aimed at developing alternative engines is small. In 1970 Congress appropriated $108 million for the National Air Pollution Control Center. Of that total $38 million went for research and development. Only $9 million of that was committed to research on vehicles. In the past few years, the government has spent no more than $500,000 a year for research on alternative engines. Thus, only a tiny percentage of an admittedly small budget goes into motor vehicle research although motor vehicles cause the great bulk of pollution. For 1971 Nixon requested a reduction in research funds, down from $38 million to $27 million.

Every year the government buys 60,000 motor vehicles, Recently, Sen. Warren Magnuson sponsored legislation establishing a $50 million fund which could be used by the government to purchase vehicles powered by alternative, pollutionless engines, thereby creating a sort of test market for industry. Under the terms of the legislation, which has passed the Senate, the government would pay more for non-polluting vehicles than it does for ordinary vehicles.

One of the ideas behind Magnuson's scheme is to entice Lear into building a prototype gas turbine car. Some senators hope they can bring Lear together with the management at American Motors. They think American Motors would jump at the chance to build an economical gas turbine car, as a way to get the company out of the dumps.

* * *

The alternative to replacing the internal combustion engine is to ease the pollution in large metropolitan areas through development of mass transit systems. The Senate already has passed a mass transit bill, and it now awaits clearance in the House Banking Committee. The bill nominally calls for spending $10 billion over twelve years. Actually, however, it would enable the government to spend only $1.8 billion in the first five years, and because the funds are to come from the general revenues and must be appropriated each year by the rural, predominantly Southern members of appropriations committees, they are not likely to reach even that level. (The appropriations committees routinely kill funds for public works, such as public housing, which don't appeal to the members.) The House Appropriations Committee already has put Congress on notice it does not care for the mass transit bill's approach. One way around this would be to establish a special trust fund, which might be replenished by excise taxes from automobile sales. That would have assured the program a certain independence and continuity. However, the trust fund idea was opposed by the Bureau of the Budget and by Nixon's aides in the White House.

* * *

The other primary causes of air pollution are the so-called "stationary" sources: electric generation plants, oil refineries, chemical plants, and other industrial apparatus. While there has been a widening publicity campaign aimed at cleaning up this sort of pollution, very little real progress has been made. The recent study by John Esposito and a group of Nader's Raiders makes clear what an utter mess this whole business has become.

The air pollution laws were written in imitation of the water pollution legislation. Thus, the Clean Air Act of 1963 sets out a cumbersome procedure by which the federal government can pressure the states into making plans for pollution abatement. Under that law, if the Secretary of HEW believes the soot, smoke, etc., from one state endangers the health and welfare of people living in another, he can call a conference of pollution control agencies of all affected states and municipalities. As with the water pollution conferences, the air pollution conferences are coffee klatches where federal officials berate state and local officials and try to persuade them to agree to some abatement plan. There are no rules of evidence, discovery proceedings, etc., and the polluting industries are not party to the proceedings. Following the conference, the Secretary of HEW writes a report, and if there is no sign of agreement on an abatement plan, he can suggest "necessary remedial action." If after six months nothing happens, then the secretary can call formal hearings, and if after that there is still no improvement, he can give the case to the Justice Department for prosecution.

In the history of the Clean Air Act there have been but a handful of enforcement actions, only one of them involving a large metropolitan area. That case, which concerned New York City, simply stopped after two sessions of the conference; nothing ever happened. Plans for conferences in Philadelphia and Chicago have been shelved. Funds for abatement actions have been cut from $500,000 in fiscal 1968 to $390,000 in fiscal 1971. Officials employed to enforce the abatement provisions of the law were shifted out of their jobs. Finally, in February of this year, Sen. Hugh Scott, speaking for the Nixon Administration, introduced legislation which would delete the federal abatement provisions from the law, thereby effectively withdrawing the federal government from air pollution control.

The person largely responsible for turning the Clean Air

Act into a dead letter was Sen. Muskie, the pollution champion. In 1967, at the urging of industrial groups, Muskie decided it was time to legislate the government out of the pollution business. That was accomplished through passage of the Air Quality Act. LBJ and the liberal Democrats were very high on "creative federalism" at the time and the Air Quality Act was considered a modern example of "creative federalism" and embodied the "regional approach." Actually the law was pretty much written by Jennings Randolph, the West Virginia senator who represents the coal industry, and the Manufacturing Chemists Association. It is mumbo jumbo: Under the legislation, the National Air Pollution Control Administration designates certain "air quality regions." A region is an imaginary line drawn around an urban area and its environs. The communities lying within the boundaries of the line generally share common topographical meteorological and industrial patterns. The theory is that these common features will facilitate the eventual establishment of air pollution control standards. Unfortunately, since the "region" is not a unit of government, it is a meaningless designation. The Air Pollution Control Administration then issues "air quality criteria" and "control techniques." These documents assist the states in establishing "ambient air standards" for the different regions. Instead of measuring smoke from a stack to determine, say, whether its sulfur dioxide content is above or below a national uniform emissions standard, pollution officials instead sample the "ambient air" throughout a region to find the sulfur dioxide levels. Then they work out "plans" for controlling the sulfur dioxide. The act is obvious hokum, and since 1967, the year it was enacted, not one state has established a complete set of standards. Nixon now wants to make this situation even more chaotic by establishing national ambient air quality standards which the states are to enforce.

Last week the House passed a clean air bill which essentially implements Nixon's "reforms." It requires the federal government to establish national air quality standards which would be enforced by the different states. The legislation would also require the government to establish standards for stationary sources of pollution if the Secretary of HEW found the situation was "extremely hazardous" or where the pollution contributed "substantially" to the endangerment of public health. Standards for stationary sources, however, would only apply to future installations, and not to plants already in operation. The Senate bill is expected to extend such standards to any hazardous emissions, whether from new or old installations. Even so, the wording is vague and action can only be taken at the discretion of the secretary. Basically, the thrust of the legislation is to further the already unworkable scheme for air pollution control based on ambient air standards.

The air pollution laws are literal nonsense. But they serve a useful function from industry's point of view by making pollution legal and by creating a publicity smokescreen behind which pollution can increase. The trick in the pollution game has always been to write laws which legitimize pollution, and which at all costs prevent the government from discovering and disclosing levels of pollutants of the different industries. For years the Bureau of the Budget has blocked every effort by the Federal Water Quality Administration to find out how much pollution is put into the water by different industries. The same process has been true with air pollution. In 1967 when Congress had the Air Quality legislation under consideration, industry witnesses testified against an Administration proposal which, if adopted, would have given HEW authority to require polluters to disclose what they were putting into the atmosphere. As a result Congress dropped compulsory disclosure, and instead directed the government to gather that information by securing the "cooperation" of industry. Shortly after the Air Quality Act was passed, the pollution people drew up a questionnaire as part of their Air Contaminant Emissions Survey, and sent it along to the Bureau of the Budget for clearance. (Under the law, federal agencies may not issue questionnaires to the public without first securing clearance from the Budget Bureau). The Budget Bureau then got in touch with the Advisory Council on Federal Reports, a group of businessmen who act as a liaison between the federal government and the business community. The Council asked for a meeting with Budget. According to the Budget Bureau minutes of that meeting, held on May 23, 1968, "industry asked if company data could be and should be released to the press. . . . Industry did not object to aggregate figures but objected to scare headlines pinpointing a particular plant as the cause of air pollution." At that point representatives from the NAM, American Petroleum Institute, Manufacturing Chemists, and National Coal Association badgered the Budget Bureau, which in turn pressured the pollution agency. The air pollution agency eventually backed down and agreed to an innocuous questionnaire which assured industry total confidentiality. It also agreed not to use the data establishing criteria for standards, one of the original purposes of sending out the questionnaire.

* * *

Amidst the current heavy publicity barrage, it is sometimes difficult to understand the utter arrogance with which businessmen view the air pollution issue. In making its report Esposito's group of students sought information firsthand from businessmen. One student was granted an appointment with Harry Jackson, public relations expert for Lubrizol, the Cleveland, Ohio, additives manufacturer.

"I'd like to talk to you about Lubrizol's problem and program for air pollution control," the student began.

"What are you going to do with the information?" Jackson asked.

"Well, I worked for Ralph Nader last summer on air pollution. We've heard a lot about Lubrizol and its pollution."

"Do you work for Nader now?"

"No, I'm in medical school at Case Western Reserve."

"Oh, we give a lot of money to that school."

"Do you mind if I take notes?"

"No, I don't mind, because I'm not going to tell you anything."

[*Taking notes*] "Why is that?"

"Because you have no authority to ask these questions."

"Of course, I have no legal authority, but you are the public relations man, aren't you?"

"That doesn't make any difference."

"Why won't you answer any questions? Is this the company's official policy?"

"Yes, I've talked this over with our officials and our legal counsel, and we've decided that we don't have to answer your questions. You don't have the right to ask us these questions."

"Well, I wanted to talk to you about the episode in August 1968, which resulted in a breakdown of your plant's equipment."

"Lubrizol made an official statement to the press. Have you seen it?"

"No, could you tell me what it said?"

"I'm not at liberty to say."

"But if it's a press release, it's obviously public information."

"You'll have to find it yourself. I'm not at liberty to tell you anything."

June 15–22, 1970

Masters of Waste

James Ridgeway

In imitation of the War on Poverty, the Nixon people are now pushing the War on Pollution. "A major goal for the next 10 years for this country must be to restore the cleanliness of the air, the water and that, of course, means moving also on the broader problems of population congestion, transport and the like," Nixon declared recently. He went on to say, "Unless we move on it now, believe me, we will not have an opportunity to do it later, because then the people will have millions more automobiles and, of course, the waters and so forth developing the way that they do without plants for purification, once the damage is done, it is much harder to turn it around. It is going to be hard as it is."

But while Nixon says he's keen for ecology, the Administration is busy behind the scenes gutting measures aimed at halting destruction of the environment. Here are a few examples:

Nixon opposed congressional attempts to raise appropriations for sewage works from $200 million to $800 million because of inflationary impact. Congress passed the $800 million appropriation against Administration protests, and the President signed the bill. The Administration now indicates it will not spend the extra money. Instead, it proposes to junk the existing federal sewage grants program altogether and institute another financing scheme which experts predict will inflate the bond markets and possibly result in reducing the already pitiful number of sewage works now planned or under construction.

HEW Secretary Robert Finch recently testified against Sen. Edmund Muskie's bill, which would create a pilot program to test means of recovering and recycling solid wastes such as plastic, paper, tin cans and bottles. The bill would authorize a research program and make available some money for experimental projects. Finch said it was too costly.

Although Congress passed water pollution legislation in 1965 which directed the government to establish national water quality standards by 1967, those standards still have not been set. This is an embarrassing situation, and last October, David Dominick, water pollution commissioner, promised to resolve the outstanding exceptions by states to the standards by January 1, 1970. However, it is now mid-January and the government has approved complete sets of standards for only four states — Arizona, Minnesota, Nebraska and Utah — and two territories — Virgin Islands and Guam.

Over the years, Congress has pressured both Democratic and Republican administrations to be more aggressive in requiring industries and municipalities to abate pollution. But Carl Klein, Assistant Secretary of the Interior in charge of water pollution programs, takes a more relaxed attitude. He favors negotiation rather than bringing action in court. Thus, in October, the Federal Water Pollution Control Administration served "180-day notices" on U.S. Steel, Jones & Laughlin, Republic Steel and the city of Toledo — charging them with violation of the water quality standards. Among other things, the government said Jones & Laughlin discharges cyanide into the Cuyahoga River, which drains into Lake Erie, already a ghastly cesspool. Typically, instead of moving promptly in court to halt the discharges, the government gave the companies until April of this year to come forward with their "plans."

Meanwhile, Klein and Commissioner Dominick have announced a reorganization of the water pollution administration so that it may become more efficient. The reorganization involves a scheme to rotate regional directors of the administration. The pollution people have been reorganized so many times they are punch-drunk. But this reorganization has its purposes. It allows "Clean Water" Klein, as he's known to friends, to get rid of H. W. Poston, the regional pollution director for Chicago. Poston takes a very hard line against industry in the Chicago area, and since "Clean Water" Klein doesn't agree with tough enforcement and his home town is Chicago, he wants Poston out.

One of the most difficult pollution problems is industrial waste. Industry puts different sorts of stuff into rivers and lakes. The government doesn't know what kind of stuff or how much stuff because it has steadfastly refused to ask the companies what they discharge. For years the Congress has been asking the government to make an industrial waste inventory, but the Budget Bureau kills the idea so as not to embarrass industry. And again this year, reports are that the proposed industrial waste inventory has been put off.

While oil pollution poses a growing threat, Congress can't decide on laws for controlling oil spills.

Meanwhile "Clean Water" Klein races around the country, staging gimmicky teach-ins on ecology and creating student groups called SCOPE (Student Council on Pollution and the Environment) to counteract Gaylord Nelson's planned teach-ins this spring. More important, "Clean Water" and everyone else in Congress and the Administration wants to somehow defuse the eco-freaks before they go berserk and perform some barbaric anarchist act.

* * *

Oil spills are becoming a major source of pollution. In part this is because tankers are losing their oil cargo at sea. In November, *Environment* magazine included a run-down on some of the better-known oil spills. It is pretty staggering how much petroleum goes overboard. Here are some of the most recent accidents: In 1966, the tanker *Seestern* pumped 1,700 tons of oil into the Medway Estuary, Kent, England, killing thousands of birds. The next year, the *Desert Chief* spilled 1,200 barrels in the York River, Virginia, again killing thousands of waterfowl. The same year, heavy oil slicks hit thirty miles of Cape Cod, killing waterfowl. (Ships often jettison cargo at night.) And during 1967, federal authorities reported seventy-five different incidents of oil pollution in Cook Inlet, Alaska. In 1968, the *Ocean Eagle* split up off Puerto Rico, flooding the coast with one million gallons of oil. The same year, the *World Glory* broke in two off South Africa, spilling 46,000 tons of oil onto the coast. In 1969, the *Hamilton Trader* collided with another vessel, spilling oil all over the North Wales coast. The Louisiana coast got drenched with oil that year when an oil rig was damaged. Then, also in 1969, the French tanker *Gironde* collided with an Israeli ship and spilled 1,000 tons of oil onto the Brittany coast.

This list of accidents doesn't include the *Torrey Canyon*, which broke up in 1967 off Land's End, England, dumping 118,000 tons of oil into coastal waters. Nor does it include the Santa Barbara catastrophe last year. That was caused because Stewart Udall signed leases in an area he knew contained geological faults. Santa Barbara is a clear case of the Interior Department's buckling to the oil companies, with no consideration whatever to protecting the environment.

These accidents at sea reflect a general trend. According to *Environment*'s survey, 200,000 tons of cargo were lost in 1948 — compared with 550,000 tons in 1963. The dangers of pollution increase as the size of the tankers grows larger. The *Torrey Canyon* carried 118,000 tons. It is now common for supertankers to carry 200,000 tons of oil. Tankers of 500,000-ton capacity are being designed. The loss of one of these mammoth tankers would equal the loss of all the oil spilled overboard in the last ten years.

The situation is made all the more hazardous because of the growth of the tanker fleet. A group of British experts who surveyed the *Torrey Canyon*, said, "The risk of accident is a very real one. In the three years preceding the wreck of the *Torrey Canyon*, 91 tankers were stranded in various parts of the world, while 238 were involved in collisions either with tankers or other vessels. Over the world at large, tankers have thus been involved in potentially serious accidents on an average of about twice a week for the past three years [prior to 1967]. Sixteen of the 329 ships which were concerned became total losses; and in 39 cases cargo spillage or leakage occurred."

Because of the growing fleet of supertankers, small ports are anxious to dredge their harbors to accommodate the big ships. The interest is especially keen on the East Coast, where there has been a concerted move to bring in Middle Eastern or Alaskan oil to foreign trade zones, such as the one planned for Machiasport, Maine. Cheap oil is viewed as a way of creating work for the depressed Northeast, reducing fuel prices, and as a way of revitalizing the intercoastal shipping business. It also means increasing heavy shipping traffic in densely populated areas and areas where there is a real demand for saving what is left of the beaches and shoreline. If, for instance, a ship the size of the supertanker *Manhattan* were to collide in the fog off Long Island Sound and begin spilling oil, Santa Barbara would seem like a small stain.

Many oil spills originate on shore. The Corps of Engineers estimates that 40 percent of the 2,000 oil spills during 1966 were from land-based facilities. The oil pipelines which run up the East Coast from the oil fields are often poorly marked and in poor condition. It is not at all uncommon for bulldozer operators working on housing developments to lose their minds and begin nudging pipelines, causing them to burst and start gushing.

Any sort of control over oil pollution, like most other matters involving pollution, relates to the fuels industry. Congress is not willing to grapple with fuels policies, and instead it passes piecemeal legislation aimed at penalizing individual polluters. Even when it comes to this, there is argument. The operative law now says the government must prove "wanton and willful negligence" by a polluter (an oil tanker, say), and if it succeeds in doing so, then levy a small fine. In the case of pollution emanating from the shore, the federal government has no power at all. In the Senate version of a new bill, spilling oil into navigable waters is made illegal. To escape liability under this new legislation, an offender would have to prove the spillage was caused by war, an act of God or by a third party. He would be liable for up to $14 million. The House bill, on the other hand, insists the government prove the discharge is "willful or negligent." These may seem like technical details; but in effect, the Senate places the burden of proof on the shipping company or oil combine, whereas the House leaves the burden of proof on the government. The different versions are now stuck in conference, and it is likely they'll never emerge.

Neither bill provides any protection for citizens, communities, business or other types of enterprise which are injured because of an oil spill. The oil combines have no responsibility to communities which become unlivable because of oil spills. In fact, an oil spill remains a handy, relatively inexpensive way of killing off shore communities, ruining business, running the people out and taking over the coast for more oil exploration.

The oil industry hopes the bills will die in conference, and that instead the Senate will ratify the so-called Brussels Treaty, which concerns liability for spilling hazardous materials overboard. The U.S. negotiating team at Brussels included people from the State Department and the oil companies. The treaty represents the interests of the maritime countries and the oil firms, and the industry hopes it can be sneaked through the Senate to pre-empt the field of international law for spillage.

* * *

Since 1956, the government has made available limited amounts of money in the form of grants to local governments to help them pay for the construction of sewage treatment plants. The total spent is now $200 million a year, and the money is spread around the nation according to a complicated formula which takes into account geography and population. In practice, the formula works against big cities, where sewage disposal problems are most acute. Since the projected costs for pollution abatement in New York state alone are over $1 billion, the program is a joke. While Sen. Muskie and

Rep. John Dingell have pushed hard to increase the money for sewage treatment facilities, the Nixon Administration opposed the increases. Nonetheless, Congress passed an $800 million appropriations bill. The President signed it, but the Administration now indicates it won't spend the money.

Among the reasons for not spending the money is the President's determination to junk the sewage grants program entirely and substitute a new financing scheme in its place. The new scheme has come to be known as the Hickel Plan after the Secretary of the Interior floated it in the press a couple of months ago. The Hickel Plan would work as follows: The government would junk the grants program, and instead, local communities would be encouraged to sell bonds to pay for sewage treatment facilities. These bonds would be popular, according to Hickel, because the government would pay the principal, leaving the communities to pay the interest. In effect, the communities and government would split the total cost. That's pretty much how the current grants program works. The hitch is that in a period of high interest rates, a community would get stuck for much more than half the cost. In fact, if the scheme worked as planned, communities would flood the bond markets, driving up interest rates. Needless to say, there is considerable enthusiasm for the Hickel Plan in Wall Street, where it is viewed as a boon to the tax-exempt municipal bond market.

The Hickel scheme involves a behind-the-scenes battle between the Treasury and the municipal bond men. In recent years the Treasury has lobbied within the Administration to do away with tax-exempt municipal bonds. The municipal bond market offers a huge tax shelter for wealthy individuals and institutional investors. In the past the Treasury has insisted that sewer bonds should be made taxable. During the tax reform debates, the Treasury proposed to cut out tax-exempt bonds altogether. But John Mitchell, who in private life was highly regarded as a municipal bond attorney, persuaded the President to save the tax-exempt municipal bonds. Now the business is to be expanded.

The effect of the Hickel Plan may be to curtail the development of sewer projects. Local communities, hard pressed to build new schools, pay for police, etc., will hesitate to sell bonds, and thus there will be fewer sewers built, not more.

* * *

LBJ liked the "quality of life" slogan, and now Nixon is copying him. Both administrations pursue the same policies, a piecemeal approach through public works: handing out a project here or there, running an experiment, tightening a law. In doing so, they create the image of slowly correcting these complicated environmental problems. Meanwhile, the oil industry does what it pleases.

The central issue in pollution is the strategy of the fuels industry (i.e., the oil companies) — how it plans to monopolize the energy business — and the ecology slogan has become a cover for this enterprise.

January 19–26, 1970

Dying
of Consumption

James Ridgeway

During the Johnson administration Congress passed a series of laws to protect consumers. The measures were eagerly accepted, since they cost no money but gave the Democrats an image of reforming the industries. It is not surprising that they never came to much, even in terms of the minor technical alterations which were meant to substitute for a radical restructuring of the industrial economy.

One of these measures was the so-called "truth-in-packaging" law. It was supposed to make life easier for consumers by requiring manufacturers to package goods in uniform sizes. Actually, the law does not do that. It requires the Commerce Department to reduce the variety of package sizes. With a handful of exceptions, the department has ignored the law. The law also requires the Federal Trade Commission and the Food and Drug Administration to issue regulations governing the so-called "cents off" come-ons which companies use to lure customers. However, these regulations have never been issued.

About the same time Congress voted truth-in-packaging, it passed truth-in-lending. That law requires banks and credit companies to state simple interest on the loan. The idea was that the consumer could shop around for cheap credit, a ludicrous notion since interest rates are usually the same and because money is made available to people on the basis of class and occupation. In Washington, department stores turned truth-in-lending into a sales pitch. When they announced their lending policies, they also urged consumers to buy more by reducing the amount of money required on accounts each month.

While the truth-in-lending and packaging laws are bizarre examples of what is meant by "consumer protection," there are other more serious ways in which this slogan is used to bolster industry.

Each year automobile manufacturers raise the price of new cars, often citing the cost of government-imposed "safety features" as a reason. But that's not the real reason. The Bureau of Labor Statistics, which collects price data from the manufacturers, reported in 1968 that average prices of new cars went up by $40. The manufacturers said changes made in response to federal safety standards cost $4 per car. In a report on 1970 models, issued last month, the BLS said the average price per car climbed $107. Of that total, safety items required by the government cost $7.50.

Auto safety laws have worked to the advantage of the manufacturers in other ways. The carmakers are required under the law to alert owners when they detect a safety defect. The manufacturers are citing such warnings as a defense in damage suits brought against them by people injured in crashes caused by unsafe design. Large insurance companies insure the automakers against product liability; because of the safety laws, their rates to the manufacturers have increased. Those rates are passed along to the consumer in the form of higher prices. That way the car buyer pays for corrupt pricing systems in two industries. In addition, the auto companies are now believed to be passing on the cost of anticipated recalls of autos with safety defects. If this is so, they are charging people for fixing unsafe autos before they are even made. All of this means that "safety" has been built into the marketing system so that the stockholders will be protected, and the consumer will be further exploited.

At the same time, the Highway Safety Bureau, the office created to administer the car safety laws within the Department of Transportation, is beginning to resemble yet another Detroit annex in Washington. A recent case suggests what is going on there:

Last year engineers in the bureau discovered a serious flaw in the manufacture of a 15-inch wheel made by GM for use on certain GMC and Chevrolet trucks, made between 1961 and 1965. The flaw in the wheel meant it was likely to break apart, resulting in a crash. There are some three-hundred instances in which the wheel has gone to pieces. The bureau engineers regarded this as a dangerous situation. Last spring they argued within the bureau and the Transportation Department for the government to move against GM and require the company to send out warning letters to owners and replace the wheels. There was general agreement within the government on this matter, and it was decided to take action against the company. At that point, Transportation Secretary Volpe stepped into the picture. He called James Roche, head of GM and told him about the proposed action; Roche talked Volpe out of moving against GM. Immediately, GM sent teams of engineers and lawyers to Washington for meetings with the Highway Safety Bureau officials. The meetings resulted in a victory for GM. The company sent out weak letters to truck owners suggesting to them that there might be something wrong with their trucks. The technical people in the bureau still felt the case against GM was strong and they continued to build up supporting evidence. A second try was made to attack GM this fall, but again the company representatives came in, met in behind-the scenes sessions with bureau personnel, and the case was dropped. Now, different groups of "public interest" lawyers are discussing possible suits against GM.

Apparently, the creation of the Highway Safety Bureau

proves what Ralph Nader, among others, has always contended: that regulatory agencies end by being tools of the industries they set out to control.

People who concern themselves with "consumer protection" in autos seldom push beyond the narrow matter of safety design. They don't question basic concepts underlying the transportation system. Instead, they work to make the existing system "efficient." However, there has been one attempt to deal with the problem of transportation at a more fundamental level, and it is interesting to see how that turned out. Three years ago there was widespread dismay over the air pollution situation. The Johnson administration had refused to pressure the automakers into installing emission control devices on their cars, and there was serious interest in the Congress in developing alternative types of engines. Sen. Magnuson's Commerce Committee began hearings on developing the electric car. This was a shocking idea to the automakers, who hate the electric car. At first they laughed at the notion, but then as the Commerce Committee began to turn up people who had made their own electric cars, the automakers rushed to Washington, called a press conference and announced they were soon to introduce their own electric cars. (But that never happened.) The Commerce Committee's interest in the matter began to subside; then a special technical study group of industrialists and scientists was created in the Commerce Department. This group studied the situation, then issued a report which was skeptical of the electric car, but proposed instead to develop a steam car. William Lear, the businessman-inventor, announced he was building a steam car. Last fall, consumer lobbyists in Washington were touting Lear sky high. Newspapers blew up articles about his car. There were stories about how Lear's steam car was fast, efficient, cheap. He would go into business himself, taking on the automakers. But first Lear was to capture the imagination of the American public through a daring publicity stunt. He would enter the car at the Indianapolis 500 and beat the hot models from Detroit. According to the stories, automakers were so worried that they were trying to keep the steam car from running, citing technical grounds. Government officials, congressmen and even Ralph Nader expressed enthusiasm for steam cars and Lear's work. It was something of a shock when William Lear recently arrived in Detroit and declared, "I've thrown in the sponge on steam."

"I've been billed as the great champion of the steam car and I've got 5,500,000 reasons why I'm not," Lear said. "No matter what you do [with steam] you'll never come up with something that's good for the public." Lear then said he had concluded the idea of such a system "is ridiculous — no one's going to do it."

The steam car charade went according to American myth. First there was the dispassionate, scholarly, objective research which found it all possible. Then there was the tough-minded, hard-driving Horatio Alger inventor in his Nevada shop. The end result has been to give the automakers an even firmer hold on the monopoly for internal combustion engines.

Pretty much the same approach is being used in the efforts to "reform" the automobile insurance industry. Automobile insurance rates have steadily climbed over the past ten years. The companies all claim the prices must go up because they are suffering such heavy losses due to drunks, crazed teenagers and dumb blacks smashing up cars. The companies have narrowed the insurance market to the so-called preferred risks, those people who have not had accidents, forcing other drivers to buy insurance from fly-by-night high-risk companies. However, the high-risk operators go bankrupt and sometimes are crooked: The managements disappear, or money is siphoned off into other enterprises. All of this is an embarrassment to the industry, and several years ago Sen. Thomas Dodd, an insurance yo-yo, introduced legislation to provide public money to guarantee these little high-risk companies. In essence Dodd was asking the public to sponsor a fringe insurance pool into which the big companies could dump the people they didn't care to insure. The bill never passed, and instead the stink over auto insurance rates has now mounted to such an extent that the Transportation Department has begun a two-year study on the insurance system.

In all likelihood this study will not be especially relevant because the automobile insurance companies are not really in the insurance business. They are investment trusts and make their money in real estate, banking, small loans. The facade is insurance. The business is investments. It works like this: The companies claim they are losing money because of sleight-of-hand accounting methods which enable them to disguise certain income, namely, the income from their investments. They cite the underwriting losses shown on their books as evidence to persuade state insurance commissions to let them raise rates. They then concentrate on selling to preferred risk customers, at the same time cutting off people who have had accidents and those the companies think might have accidents. The object is to build a steady flow of cash for investments, while at the same time reducing the loss record in order to protect the investments. Recently auto insurance companies have turned themselves into holding companies and from that vantage point moved directly into conglomerate style operations, owning banks, small loan companies, credit firms, airlines, real estate and film companies. Thus far, the study of auto insurance rates in the Transportation Department has succeeded in keeping the Congress off the industry's back and providing a cover while the companies change themselves into holding companies and conglomerates. It's hard to see how the study of auto insurance rates can ever have much relevance, since it concerns insurance companies and not investment trusts.

* * *

The "consumer movement," as it is sometimes called, isn't really a movement, and has never really caught on among ordinary people — perhaps because of the muddy politics involved. When politicians or lawyers thunder about protecting the "public interest" in these matters, they often are defining the public in terms of their own interests and constituencies. Almost inevitably, consumer protection becomes a game among elite groups.

The recent interest in consumer legislation has come from two directions. On the one hand, there are the last of the Populist radicals in the Congress. Chief among them is Wright Patman, who is well known for his attacks on money. From time to time Russell Long attacks the drug patent provision with an old-time Populist fervor. L. H. Fountain, a North Carolina Congressman, runs some tough investigations of the drug companies. Kenneth Roberts, a former congressman from Alabama, laid down the basic groundwork for all the auto safety legislation. The late Estes Kefauver of Tennessee sponsored the only serious reform of the drug industry. These men are all Southerners or from border states, and the work they have done really has come closest to affecting ordinary people, saving them from some exploitation in the markets and keeping unsafe and ineffective products off the shelves. Others who have been interested in consumer protection include Sen. Gaylord Nelson of Wisconsin, Rep. Benjamin Rosenthal of New York and the late Sen. Robert Kennedy.

The most important advocates of consumer protection are the trial lawyers, who are loosely organized through the American Trial Lawyers Association. This is a maverick group with occasional populist-progressive tendencies.

In recent years, the trial lawyers have mounted a devastating attack on American corporations. Their suits begin as simple damage claims, then broaden into attacks on the conduct of the corporation, tracing in the most fundamental, radical manner the injury of individuals back through the corporation hierarchy. They show in great detail how corporate officials engage in calculated plunder and injury of the populace. Discovery procedures of the court enable the lawyers to obtain and introduce into court records documents revealing precise details of corporation activity. Juries are convinced and damages running into the millions have been set against companies. Congressional committees spend time assembling and reprinting documents from these cases.

The effects of this legal attack are profound. Not only do the courtroom victories enhance the power and prestige of the trial lawyer within the legal fraternity as well as amongst the general public, but they turn the court into a legislature. As in so many other fields, litigation has become a principal avenue for correcting corporate abuses. Even members of Congress, despairing of writing laws, sue in court to accomplish their reforms.

Since the court has become the arena where the post-industrial economy is adjusted, every citizen needs a lawyer — not a legislator — to look after his interests. Perhaps this helps explain the keen interest by Ralph Nader and many other young lawyers in restructuring legal education, "improving" law schools, developing centers for the practice of law in the "public interest," and so on. In reality, they are working toward a new definition of a governmental system, in which "lawyers" are a commanding elite. Nader's fundamental task is not so much to protect consumers as it is to organize his own constituency, the legal profession, for the assumption of power in a post-industrial society. In that process, he must mediate between seemingly opposing lawyers, in order that they function as a single power elite — as Republican and Democratic legislators have learned to do. At the same time, the legal establishment has to deal operationally with the corps of technicians who can — according to this model — patch up social faults.

* * *

Fundamentally, consumer protection is a way to make the existing economic and social system perform more efficiently for the benefit of large industries. In a narrow sense the large business organizations need an expanding market for their products and services, and it is therefore imperative for them to persuade people that goods are safe and beneficial. Over the long run, safety is part of the sales mechanism.

The evils of the business system, so well revealed by the trial lawyers, are its values — exploitation of masses of people in the interests of the very few. Consumer protection begins by understanding that one must fight the idea of consumption which is essential to exploitation. On the simplest level, it is not necessary to buy a car every year, to eat plastic food, to have clean-smelling breath and perfumed genitalia. Babies need not be fed food that is made to taste pleasant for their mother's benefit. Stores don't have to color oranges and lemons, and so on. As war is the method of extending empire abroad, mindless consumption is the method for colonizing us at home.

December 1 – 8, 1969

Mountain Revolt

T. N. Bethell

Charleston, West Virginia

The focus of the Appalachian revolt has shifted for the moment from Kentucky, where ordinary people have been engaged in sporadic guerrilla warfare against the strip miners, to West Virginia. Beginning in mid-February thousands of miners left their jobs and refused to go back until the state legislature passed a bill awarding miners workmen's compensation for black lung disease—a gradual, incurable, ultimately fatal clogging of the lungs from the inhalation of coal dust. It was no ordinary strike: the United Mine Workers union opposed it, and it was aimed not so much at the coal operators as at the state government. Eventually 43,000 men joined the walkout, and coal production in the state come to a halt. The legislature passed a bill this month.

The miners' protest was part of a pattern that had begun to emerge in Appalachia. Two years ago, OEO-financed Appalachian Volunteers organized a Citizens Fair Tax Committee, which startled the West Virginia legislature by lobbying en masse, although without much success. Last year a similar election reform group shook up some of the state's feudal county governments, which traditionally maintain voting rolls mostly of the deceased. In Kentucky, citizens' groups succeeded in preventing the Army Corps of Engineers from pork-barreling them out of their homes with an unnecessary dam. Others successfully blocked strip mine bulldozers with the combination of the threat of civil disobedience and the threat of guerrilla warfare. None of these acts of protest stopped the exploitation of Appalachia, but they have resulted in a spreading awareness among the people of just how powerless they are in the hands of the colonial government.

In West Virginia the striking miners were up against an overpowering array of strength. About a dozen companies determine the state's destiny; without their support nothing much happens in the legislature. Consolidation Coal Co., which produces about one-fourth of the state's coal, heads the list. Other large coal producers — Island Creek and Eastern Fuel & Gas — are allied with Consol. The state's other major powers include Union Carbide, Dupont, American Electric Power, Columbia Gas, Weirton Steel, and three railroads — Chesapeake & Ohio, Norfolk & Western, and Penn Central. This group is backed up by a line of coal, steel, and chemical firms. Generally the powers operate behind a facade of trade associations, so it is hard to know who is pulling which strings. Typically, during the black lung battle full-page newspaper ads belaboring the miners were signed by The Southern Coal Producers Association, Greenbrier Coal Operators Association, Kanawha Coal Operators Association, and Smokeless Operators Association. The average reader would not have known that these are all part of the Bituminous Coal Operators Association (BCOA), the industry's national pressure group set up and controlled by Consol.

Empires and colonies are complex affairs, of course, and there is more than one facade at work in West Virginia. Over the past two years, for example, most of the giant coal companies have been absorbed by even bigger oil companies. Consol is a subsidiary of Continental Oil; Occidental Oil owns Island Creek. Behind the oil companies are a handful of large banks. Four in particular dominate West Virginia: Morgan Guaranty Trust, Chase Manhattan, Mellon National, and Continental Illinois National. One or more of these banks is closely connected to every company on the master list of industry. And finally, behind the banks, power in West Virginia traces to a few of America's ruling families.

For example, look who controls Consol: The principal stockholders are the Mellons of Pittsburgh through their bank, and George Humphrey, Eisenhower's Treasury Secretary and head man of the Hanna mining combine. (Humphrey is in favor of increasing unemployment as a way to curb inflation, a view shared by the current Treasury Secretary, David Kennedy.) Kennedy's old bank Continental Illinois sits on the board of Consolidation Coal, and Morgan Guaranty has two director interlocks with Continental Oil. The Rockefeller family's Chase Manhattan Bank doesn't show up in the open as a power in the Continental Consol combine, but the Rockefeller Foundation owns 350,000 shares of Continental Oil, and since Morgan Guaranty and Chase Manhattan own stock in each other, the Rockefellers are very present in West Virginia.

This has recently become a source of some embarrassment to John D. Rockefeller IV, who at thirty-one has just been elected West Virginia's secretary of state on a Mr. Clean campaign designed to take him eventually to the White House. During the long black lung battle Rockefeller was conspicuously silent, and the reform forces attacked him for it. To the *Washington Post* he explained, "I can't go everywhere and do everything, so I have to choose where I go and what I do—but I sure blew this one." Dr. I. E. Buff, the Charleston doctor who led the black lung fight, said it wasn't that simple; Rockefeller was too close to the coal industry, he said. Rockefeller denied it: "Neither myself nor my family have any financial interest whatsoever in any coal mine in West Virginia."

Last week Sen. Percy, whose daughter is married to the young Rockefeller, was making calls to New York publishers searching for an author who could be sent down to West Virginia for two weeks of quick research on black lung in order that the young Rockefeller might be informed. West Virginians are beginning to think that Jay Rockefeller is the local pro-consul for the empire.

But the empire appears to have many proconsuls, some of them nominally hostile to each other. For example, there is the United Mine Workers of America, self-styled foe of the coal barons. Curiously, however, the UMW and Consol were recently tried and found guilty in federal court of conspiring together since 1950 to create a monopoly of the coal business for a few heavily mechanized giants. That partly explains why there are only one-third as many men working in the mines now as there were in 1950. For the past ten years, moreover, the UMW and Consol have been allied in the National Coal Policy Conference, a superlobby where big business and big labor work together to assault congress.

During the 1960s the union built a chain of first-rate hospitals in Appalachia, then a few years later withdrew thousands of cards entitling miners to free medical care and finally in 1963 sold the hospitals. Since that time the union's welfare fund has developed a $180 million cash surplus, $67 million of which is kept in the union's own bank, The National Bank of Washington. The UMW membership is down to a fraction of what it used to be, but the men at the top are doing very well indeed.

Some of the younger miners in West Virginia are cynical about the union leadership. But there is no real rebellion yet; the older miners still think of John L. Lewis as God and can't believe that his successor might be trying to screw them.

The federal government, even more than the UMW, is doing its part to preserve West Virginia as a colony. The Appalachian Regional Commission, supposedly responsible for uplifting the condition among the natives, has built highways instead, over which coal, oil, steel and chemicals move at faster speeds to the mother country. About 10,000 West Virginians leave over those roads every year, looking for work, and often coming to grief in city slums. The Tennessee Valley Authority has helped administer the kiss of death to West Virginia through its policy of buying strip-mined coal for its power plants. Since TVA is the largest consumer of coal in the world, and pays the lowest prices, this has had disastrous consequences: The producers seek the cheapest way to destroy the mountains and extract the coal, and the private utilities buy strip-mined coal too, in order to keep their costs competitive with TVA. One result is that Consolidation Coal is getting ready to open the world's largest strip mine in southern West Virginia—a mine so big it is planned to last for 100 years. Operations will begin as soon as Consol and the government finish uprooting the several thousand people who live where the mine will be.

The miners who fought for black lung compensation are up against the empire in more ways than it would appear. The disease itself is most common in the big mechanized mines where machines chewing into the coal stir up dust so thick that spotlights won't penetrate it. Mechanization has thus become ironically a bigger killer than the old pick-and-shovel mines which were thought to be the ultimate in inhumanity. Naturally big companies like Consol aren't enthusiastic about liberalizing the compensation laws, since funds come solely from employers and there are at least 20,000 West Virginia miners suffering from black lung.

The miners walked out, demonstrated, scared some of the legislators and got a bill. But its phrasing is vague, and until the state Supreme Court hears a test case—likely to be many months from now—no one will know how little it really is. In any case, compensation awards in West Virginia are low—the maximum per year total disability is less than $2,500—and the compensation board sometimes gets as much as ten years behind in settling claims. The miners may have won a skirmish (and the black lung battle appears to be headed now for the Ohio and Kentucky legislatures) but the empire still rules the colony, and until there is a major rebellion of miners, factoryworkers, students, teachers and other disenfranchised Appalachians, the colony will stay pretty much where it is, and the mother country will have nothing much to fear.

March 24–31, 1969

Ecology
Inaction

James Ridgeway

*They [conservationists who want strip miners to restore
land] are stupid idiots, socialists and commies who don't
know what they are talking about. I think it is our [coal
operators'] bounden duty to knock them down and subject
them to the ridicule they deserve.*
— JAMES D. REILLY, *vice-president,*
Consolidation Coal Co.,
in the Pittsburgh Press, *May 8, 1969*

Stripped of the current modish hysteria, the politics of ecology seem dull and complicated. They less involve radicals
and outraged liberals than quarreling groups of doctors, systems analysts, sewermen and industrialists, in the end bringing into focus the political underbelly of post-industrial America. One way to begin is to examine three major government
programs allegedly aimed at combating environmental pollution — water, air and pesticides — and in that way see how laws
for controlling pollution end by making it legitimate.

The water and air pollution control laws are written so that the burden of proving pollution exists is on the government. Federal officials must begin by demonstrating that pollution is "interstate" and then proceed through an arduous course of meetings and hearings which can last for ten or twenty years. In the end there is an agreed-on "abatement" plan stretching even further into the future, and dependent on government financing which oftentimes is not available.

Under the water pollution law, if the government believes there is interstate pollution it can call an enforcement "conference" of interested parties for the purpose of reaching agreement on an abatement plan. If the conference fails, the government can wait six months, then call a hearing. If the hearing fails, the government must wait another six months, then go to court. Since the pollution law was passed in 1956, there have been forty-six different enforcement actions; four of them have reached a hearing stage, and only one went to court. In practice what happens is that the politicians, bureaucrats and technicians get together at a conference and agree to meet at various dates in the future. Each time they meet, it is agreed that progress has been made. The conference method helps to legitimize pollution by conferring it to death.

It is only recently that pollution became such a passionate public cause. In the early 1960s, the government seldom even announced the existence of an enforcement conference to the daily papers. In those days the conferences were the scenes of in-fighting among bureaucratic sects: lawyers against doctors, systems engineers against old-fashioned sewermen; congressmen against state assemblymen. The most bitter fights took place among the doctors of the U.S. Public Health Service and a small group of lawyers, who shared control of the pollution program. The Public Health Service doctors believed their job was to channel technical information and friendly advice to the doctors in the state health services. The state health services invariably controlled the state pollution programs and, often as not, were locked up with local polluting industry. Thus, nothing got done. For example, on the Raritan Bay in New Jersey, the federal government has been involved in an enforcement conference with New Jersey for nearly ten years. While the U.S. Public Health Service had the upper hand in managing the federal program, its representatives refused to pressure their doctor friends running the New Jersey program. On one occasion a district director of the U.S. Public Health Service actually refused to send a memorandum to the New Jersey health service which showed that more than one-hundred people had come down with hepatitis after eating clams taken from polluted beds in the state; the memo urged that action be taken. The doctors in PHS argued with the lawyers, and finally in 1965 the administration of the act was taken away from the PHS and placed instead in the Interior Department, where it immediately became subservient to other sets of interests – mining, oil, etc.

In 1965 Congress amended the basic water pollution law, raising the amount of money for building sewers, and creating national water quality standards for interstate streams. Under this scheme, states were encouraged to write standards based on federal criteria. The government then could either approve them, or force the state to adopt tougher rules. If a state chose not to set standards, then the government could write them itself. At the time, these amendments were viewed as tough anti-pollution measures, but that's not the way things turned out. For one thing, while the government sets standards, the states "classify" streams by use. This tends to work in favor of special-interest groups, especially industry. If large companies don't care for pollution standards, they threaten to pull out of a state, creating the specter of diminished tax revenue and unemployment.

The water quality standard amendments were passed in 1965; the standards were supposed to be submitted by June 30, 1967. However, as 1969 draws to an end, twenty-eight states have yet to file complete sets of standards. Even where states have filed complete standards and the government has approved them, the date of implementation may be some way off in the future. A usual implementation date is 1972.

Moreover, during LBJ's reign, the then Interior Secretary Stewart Udall was caught in the embarrassing position of approving water quality standards which actually were lower than existing standards of the water in certain states. To recti-

fy this mistake, Udall sought to persuade the states to adopt
the so-called "non-degradation clause," which says they are
pledged not to lower existing water quality. That created a
fresh quarrel, and so far only fifteen states have signed non-
degration clauses. (It was Udall's misfortune to unduly alarm
people. The non-degradation clause was to save face among
the conservationists. Actually he had written loopholes
throughout. In one part, for instance, the clause says existing standards cannot be lowered unless "such change is
justifiable as a result of necessary economic and social development," a statement which could mean anything to
anybody.)

Over the years water pollution abatement programs have
made tiny steps forward whenever the federal government
paid for construction of a local sewer. This in turn depends
largely on the temper of the people in the House and Senate
public works committees who control the money. Sewer
money doesn't amount to much ($214 million this year), and
it is doled out according to a complicated ratio which is meant
to ensure that every congressman gets a little sewer for his
district. The law says the government can pay up to 55 percent of the cost of a local project, but when the Congress
appropriates $200 million and the total cost of building sew-
ers in New York state alone is $1 billion, the program ob-
viously becomes a laugh.

The members of the Public Works committees can have
considerable sway in the way pollution programs are managed: It was in deference to John Blatnik, who heads the
House pollution sub-committee, that the Interior Department
during LBJ's time suppressed a report which revealed an
enormous source of pollution was in Blatnik's district. The
Reserve Mining Co., a subsidiary of Republic Steel, is dumping 60,000 tons of ore tailings into Lake Superior every day.
But Reserve is in Blatnik's district and it created considerable
employment in an area which had been previously starving.
(After conservationists set up a cry, the government eventually called an enforcement conference.)

Industry is the biggest pro-pollution lobby. There are
others. One of the most peculiar consists of the sanitary engi-

neers, the men who man the sewers. One might think they would be solidly for more pollution control, but often they oppose pollution programs. The sewermen dislike federal bureaucrats messing about the works. They don't care much for the new systems approach with all the talk of sewage so clean you can put it back in the reservoir for tap water. They've always viewed the job as carrying the shit to the river and dumping it in. The federal systems engineers talk about fail-safe sewer plants with standby systems all set to carry the load when the big pumps jam. That's pretty far-out thinking for the sewerman. When the pumps clog in most stations, the operator looks to see if anyone is watching, then yanks the bypass switch and shoots the raw shit into the stream or lake. When he gets a spare moment, he empties the pipes and starts all over again. The sewermen sometimes lobby strongly. In Richmond, Virginia, for example, the citizenry is up in arms because the city sewermen want to turn off the main sewage disposal plant for four months while they hook up a new pipeline. During that period, the plan is to dump the raw sewage into the James River. The major proponents of the scheme include the members of the state's water pollution control board.

Since Nixon's election, things have been slower than usual at water pollution headquarters in Washington. Nixon's "Clean Water Team" consists of Carl Klein, a Chicago savings bank lawyer friend of the late Sen. Dirksen, who is assistant Secretary of the Interior; and David Dominick, a thirty-two-year-old nephew of Peter Dominick, the reactionary Colorado senator. Not long after he took office, Klein asked Edgar Speer, president of U.S. Steel, to stop by the Interior Department for one of the Mr. Clean Water awards Wally Hickel was handing out. The award subsequently proved a bit embarrassing since the government is threatening to sue U.S. Steel as one of the biggest polluters in the nation.

A couple of weeks ago the Nixon gang threw a booze party at the Washington Hilton for six-hundred executives who are interested in sewage treatment. Each executive paid $100 to get in. "Clean Water" Speer set the meeting tone: "We oppose treatment for treatment's sake," he declared, pointing out there just were not enough earnings for "ideal" pollution abatement programs. "Unless the money for pollution control is intelligently spent—not by the dictates of emotion—the citizen is paying for something he didn't get," Speer said. "Is an additional 10 percent improvement in fishing worth $100 million?" John Swearingen, chairman of Standard Oil Co. of Indiana, added, "The central question is not whether we should have cleaner water, but how clean, at what cost, and how long to do the job. These considerations are frequently ignored in popular discussions. Public enthusiasm for pollution control is matched by reluctance to pay even a modest share of the cost. This attitude will have to change."

Earlier this year, Assistant Secretary Klein told the House Appropriations Committee there was no need to appropriate more money for sewage grants. The pollution headquarters even had money left over from last year, he maintained. But when the House insisted, and voted $600 million instead of the $214 million Klein wanted, Klein said they'd just have to live with the increase. (The Senate still must act on the bill.)

Meanwhile, David Dominick has ordered his public relations men to write a book which can be published under his name. A book might improve his image as a conservationist and be useful in future political campaigns.

The government's air pollution program, which is called a "center" and is based in HEW, is a feeble imitation of the feeble water pollution program. The federal government cannot set clean air standards, but only recommends criteria for such standards to the states. They do as they like. It does periodically hold enforcement conferences. Eight have been called to date. Most involve relatively small cities, and the air pollution people stay clear of places like Los Angeles or New York, where there are big messes. The air pollution center's most celebrated case to date was its victory in federal court against a chicken rendering plant which sent bad smells from Maryland to Delaware. Major moves in air pollution, such as attacks on the automakers for conspiring to delay the development of emission control, come out of the White House. During Johnson's administration attacks on the automakers were stopped by the White House. In his last days, Johnson allowed an anti-trust suit to be brought against them. Since then, Nixon has terminated the suit. The air pollution control division remains at best a public relations maneuver. The government has no power to control air pollution, and what little regulatory machinery does exist is seldom used.

* * *

Under the Federal Insecticide, Fungicide and Rodenticide Act, the Agricultural Research Service (ARS), part of the Agriculture Department, is responsible for making sure that pesticides are both safe and effective before they are put on the market. The ARS registers all pesticides before they can be used, and if it detects a violation of the law, it can always cancel the registration, seize the goods, or ask the Justice Department to prosecute violators.

Despite these broad powers, the ARS did not prosecute one case in thirteen years, even though it cited thousands of companies, many of them repeatedly, for violations. Instead the service writes the chemical companies obsequious notes, pleading with them not to sell crummy and dangerous merchandise. In a few instances it seizes batches of tainted goods at one retail outlet, but leaves them out for sale at all the other outlets.

The law says the burden of proving safety and efficacy is on the manufacturer; but in fact, the ARS accepts the manufacturer's test data without checking into its validity. Once a product has been on the market, the ARS believes the burden of proof rests with the government, not the company.

Recent investigations by a congressional subcommittee headed by L. H. Fountain, suggest the results of this policy may be much more extraordinary then previously believed. ARS officials cheerily told Fountain that there were only 175 pesticide poisonings last year, and only half of that number involved humans. However, the Public Health Service maintains a series of poison control centers; they reported 5,000 instances of pesticide poisoning among humans, with 4,000 of these involving children under five. The PHS estimates total pesticide poisoning at about 50,000 a year. The ARS pleaded ignorance of the PHS data, and it then came out that the government has no way of sending this sort of data around to different agencies. If there were ever a sudden, severe epidemic of pesticide poisoning, the ARS, the agency responsible for taking the poison off the market, would never know about it; nor in all likelihood would anyone else. That, of course, works to the benefit of the pesticide manufacturers.

One of the ARS jobs is to make sure that proper cautionary labels are placed on pesticide packages. Here is an example of how that works out: On one side of a label for a concentrated fly and roach spray, manufactured by Hysan Products Co. of Chicago, the directions say, "Use in well-ventilated rooms or areas only. Always spray away from you. Do not stay in room that has been heavily treated. Avoid inhalation."

But on the other side of the label, the directions read, "Close all doors, windows, and transoms. Spray with a fine mist sprayer freely upward in all directions so the room is filled with vapor. If insects have not dropped to the floor in three minutes repeat the spraying, as quantity sprayed was insufficient. After ten minutes doors and windows may be opened." According to the first warning, one might have already succumbed at this point.

When a company files for registration of a new pesticide, the ARS sends the application around to other interested government agencies for their comments on possible adverse effects. The Public Health Service looks at the pesticides to see how they might affect humans. Over the years, the PHS argued that various pesticides should not be approved, and the ARS regularly ignores the warnings. There are any number of examples of what happens as a result, each one more ghastly than the other. Here is one: Some time ago the ARS approved registration of a rodent repellent paste made of thallium sulfate. The paste was distributed about the house for rats and mice to eat. A number of children ate the paste and either became dreadfully sick or died. The ARS learned of the situation in 1960 and took steps to limit the amount of thallium in the products. However, that didn't do any good, and between 1962 and 1963, 400 children ate the paste and were poisoned. Nobody knows how many died. Two more years went by, and finally the ARS took what must have seemed to it drastic action: Registrations for fifty-eight thallium products were cancelled. That supposedly means the products are off the market. However, in 1968, the same thallium products were still available in Washington, D.C. Asked to explain how this was possible, the ARS said it had no control over products already in stores or in shipment at the time of cancellation notices.

The thallium case is not an isolated instance. According to the General Accounting Office, which made a study of the ARS, 11,361 new products were referred to the Public Health Service for comment between January 1968 and March 1969. The PHS listed "objections" to 252; the ARS ignored them.

* * *

It seems pretty clear that the laws aimed at combatting pollution function to make it legitimate, providing a defensive cover for the chemical and energy industries which do most of the polluting, and at the same time encouraging the growth of competing technical staffs, whose livelihood in the simplest terms depends on continued environmental pollution. As pollution grows worse, the prevailing liberal response is to sink more money into building up the technical staffs, seeking solutions through government efficiency, and beneath that cover, proposing new laws under which the populace will be taxed to pay industries to install pollution abatement equipment. Incidentally, there is a growing market in this equipment, some of it made by subsidiaries of companies which do most of the polluting. In the future, pollution control will be a growth industry — dependent, of course, on the continued growth of pollution itself. In short, liberal ideology is creating the foundation for new consumer goods.

However, as the central government itself loses momentum, and the pollution programs become more removed from the populace, they begin losing even the appearance of legitimacy, and people turn to more direct action: picketing, lawsuits, sabotage, and eventually the seizure of land and the formation of new communities.

November 3 – 10, 1969

Slow or Sudden Death

Ralph Nader and Jerome B. Gordon

Three months ago a group of Cuban refugees escaped to the United States on a Soviet-built Antonov crop-dusting aircraft. When the plane touched down in Florida, it was immediately quarantined by federal immigration and Florida state health officials and returned to Cuba the following day. The passengers in the aircraft emerged retching and vomiting and were rushed to nearby clinics; they had been made ill by the noxious pesticide parathion that was all over the aircraft.

In 1965 twenty-eight persons in San Diego, Calif., were poisoned by the pesticide diazinon, which accidentally contaminated doughnut mix in a local bakery.

In 1967, in nearby Tijuana, Mexico, seventeen persons were fatally poisoned and 300 were reported ill when parathion was carelessly spilled on a truck which was later used to transport confectionary sugar.

But the worst disaster from pesticide contamination of food occurred in Colombia last year: 77 people were fatally poisoned, 146 were hospitalized and upward of 600 were reported ill from flour contaminated by the traces of parathion spilled on the floor bed of a truck used to transport the flour.

On September 10, the U.S. General Accounting Office issued a report on regulatory enforcement of the Federal Insecticide, Fungicide, and Rodenticide Act. The substance of the GAO review was that there was little effective compliance action and no request for prosecution by the Justice Department in thirteen years. "This was true," the GAO found, "even in instances where repeated major violations of the law were cited by the Agricultural Research Service [of the Department of Agriculture] and when shippers did not take satisfactory action to correct violations or ignored ARS notifications that prosecution was being contemplated." ARS conceded the truth of the GAO's charges.

As usual, the GAO report was hardly noticed. Little action has been taken since Rachel Carson's *Silent Spring* raised important public health issues in 1964 and the chemical-agribusiness bloc squelched them before fundamental, enduring reforms were developed.

While regulations exist in this country for registration, dosage limitations and residue tolerances, violations or misapplications can have tragic consequences reaching far into the lives of an affected people. Farmworkers in California know this to be true:

In August and September of 1963 an outbreak of pesticide poisoning among ninety-four peach harvesters was traced to the residues on the foliage of the orchard in which they were working. The cause of poisoning was the *amount* of parathion applied and not the premature entry into the orchard by the harvesting crews, according to the California Department of Public Health. (California law stipulates a waiting period between the application of a pesticide and crop harvest, so that the chemical will have deteriorated to the point where residues on the fruit are within "safe" limits.) The final cause was determined to be the presence in the spray residues of a compound evolved from parathion alteration which was considerably more toxic than parathion; but it was identified by routine analysis simply as parathion. The mishap resulted in one death and lengthy hospitalization for many others.

It is difficult to work through bureaucracies for compliance with existing safety standards – and next to impossible to campaign politically for additional safeguards. A case in point is the recent experience of Cesar Chavez and his United Farm Workers. Over the past eighteen months in California there have been six deaths among farmworkers due to accidental ingestion of pesticides mistaken for water or wine. Some of the pesticides were improperly stored in empty plastic bleach containers. The bottles were either mislabeled – or the workers, many of whom cannot readily read or write English, misunderstood the labels. This is in spite of the fact that California State Safety Orders explicitly require farm operators to properly inform farmworkers of hazards, even workers who do not understand English.

This summer, as part of their organizing operations, the United Farm Workers Organizing Committee sent legal aides into the fields to get affidavits from the grape pickers about specific instances of pesticide poisoning. The affidavits – as well as information in the application and use registers kept by the State County Agricultural Commissioner's office – would have revealed the extent of possible violations of state pesticide standards.

The information is presumably open to the public, and the Farm Workers requested access to the records through the Kern County Agricultural Commissioner. They were summarily informed they could not obtain access to such information; two hours after their appearance at the commissioner's office an injunction was issued by the Kern County Court barring them from looking at the records. A hearing is underway to determine the legality of that move on the part of the state agency.

Chavez's troubles are not limited to the effects of toxic pesticides on his workers, but also involve the pollution of the local water supply beyond the tolerance of even the most moribund suburbanites. Last summer, the State Department of Public Health condemned the use of the local water supply in Delano for the consumption of infants below the age of six months. The groundwater supply – the major source of supply for the water system in the Delano area – is loaded with nitrate residues from the applications of fertilizer to the crops in the fields surrounding the Delano area. Nitrates are normally tolerable in the digestive systems of children and adults beyond the age of one year; but to infants below one year of age — and particularly to infants during the first six months of life — the residues are highly toxic.

* * *

Prof. Barry Commoner, of Washington University in St. Louis, recently reported on the increasing incidents of nitrate poisoning uncovered by European public health officials among infants, traced to the consumption of unrefrigerated American-processed baby food.

* * *

Chavez's people now are forced to purchase bottled water for their children. On an average income of $1,232 per year for farmworkers, buying bottled water — for which local public officials provide no funds — can be an intolerable necessity.

Large-scale grass-roots efforts aimed at controlling the spread and use of pesticides have met with something less than success in California. In 1964, a petition banning the use of most pesticides in California's agriculture failed by only a few thousand signatures to reach the ballot. The Brown administration — in the wake of the 1962 peach harvester debacle — tried to avoid the problem by appointing a commission to investigate and report on recommendations for regulating the use of pesticides. The Reagan administration has done nothing to expand significant control over the registration and use of pesticides in California; and Reagan may even dismantle existing machinery for doing the job.

In California, fruits and vegetables, not cheesecake on the silver screen or the esoteric production of integrated circuits for complex electronic gear, are the leading industry. Production of table grapes is a billion-dollar industry. Over 100 million pounds of pesticides — 20 percent of the nation's total — are used in California's agri-business. Not so surprisingly the agricultural industry has the highest occupational disease rate — over 50 percent higher than the industry in second place and almost three times as high as the average rate for all industries in the state.

Pesticide poisoning is high among the most serious causes of fatal and non-fatal occupational diseases. The number of doctors' reports involving pesticides and other agricultural chemicals have doubled since 1951 and in California have ranged from 800 to 1,100 reports annually. Over the ten-year period from 1955 to 1965, about one occupational death from pesticides has been reported for each 100 reports of occupational poisoning from these chemicals. The villains in these cases are the familiar family of phosphate ester pesticides — parathion, phosdrin and thimet, demeton and tetraethyl pyrophosphate (TEPP). The wonders of chemical technology have made the unit costs of these pesticides so cheap that, for example, $5 worth of parathion is sufficient to cause the death of 7,000 people if dispensed without proper controls.

The growth and use of pesticides in this country have been enormous. More than 650 varieties have been invented over the last quarter-century. These new chemical compounds, as well as several others, have been formulated into 60,000 trade names. About 59 percent of the pesticides used are insecticides, 15 percent fungicides, another 15 percent defoliants and herbicides, 10 percent fumigants and 1 percent rodenticides. In contrast to many areas of the world, only 1 percent of all pesticides produced in the United States are used for control of diseases such as malaria. By far the greatest use of pesticides in this country is in commercial agriculture.

While farmworkers in California are exposed to considerable risk of pesticide poisoning, the most formidable record of occupational disease and injury is in the agricultural aircraft industry. Pesticides are applied by air to half of the acreage treated in California.

The complement of 1,000 agricultural pilots applies about 10 to 15 percent of the nation's pesticides, at a considerable price. One pilot is killed in an air accident for each million acres treated. In addition to having the highest fatal injury rate of any occupation in California, over half the disabling work injuries are due to pesticide poisoning. For most other industries the occupational disease injury rate is 5 percent or less of total work injuries. However, considering the amount of pesticides and other agricultural chemicals used by this group, the cost in occupational disease is considerably less than among farmworkers and ground applicators who apply the other half of these chemicals.

The frequent victims of pesticide poisoning are children. In the period from 1951 to 1965, roughly 60 percent of the accidental deaths attributable to poisoning from pesticides in California were among children. The most frequent causes for this toll are the improper safeguards—in the private home or farm—for the storage of pesticides and the contamination of clothing by adults, in the household or on the job, who apply the chemicals. Two incidents drawn from the annals of the California Department of Public Health files are representative:

An eighteen-month-old child of an agricultural aircraft pilot was found at home in a state of acute respiratory distress, semi-conscious and with "pinpoint" pupils of the eyes. She was rushed to a local hospital and treated by a physician for severe organic phosphate poisoning. Fortunately, she recovered. On the morning of her illness, her father had come home after applying a highly toxic phosphate ester pesticide. He cleaned his boots with paper towels, threw them in a nearby wastebasket and put his boots in the bathroom. The child contracted the poisoning from either the boots or the paper towels.

In the second instance, a group of families, with children, were picking berries on a farm. They were followed by a spray rig carrying a five-gallon tank of TEPP concentrate. A four-year-old girl sampled the can, which her older brother had opened. She died in twenty minutes.

Because of readily available supplies of pesticides for both commercial and private use, suicide and accidental deaths from pesticide poisoning are an increasing problem. While only 13 percent of pesticides are used in the home for pest control, 50 percent of all accidental deaths and suicides, traced to pesticide poisoning, are from non-agricultural uses of pesticides. For example, in just one of Florida's sixty-seven counties there were eight accidental and five suicidal deaths from phosphate pesticide poisoning in 1963 alone.

California is better than most states in the regulation and

use of pesticides; but the form of regulation leads to abuses by special-interest groups that have severely weakened the national pesticide regulatory program and have blocked efforts to seek increased protection of farmworkers.

The four-part regulatory structure consists of: (a) registration or licensing of pesticide products; (b) licensing of agricultural pest-control operators; (c) the registration and use by permit of injurious materials such as the highly toxic phosphate ester pesticide family; (d) sampling of crops for pesticide-residue inspection. As in the federal program and some other state programs, the responsibility for regulation of pesticides is in the hands of the Department of Agriculture and, in the case of California, the county agricultural commissioner.

* * *

With the exception of registration, testing and evaluation of specific pesticide products, the California program is effectively run by the county agricultural commissioner. For example, an agricultural pest control operator must register with the commissioner in each county in which he does business and supply a monthly report of his operations in the county. The commissioner also issues licenses for agricultural aircraft operators and administers special examinations for agricultural aircraft pilots. Most important, the commissioner issues permits for the use by farm operators of chemicals registered by the California Department of Agriculture as injurious materials. These include the toxic phosphate ester family of pesticides and fourteen other pesticides.

The State Department of Agriculture, to ensure quality control over application of pesticides, inspects and analyzes samples of fruits, produce and meats in wholesale marketing distribution facilities to check on pesticide residues on food offered for sale in the state. The U.S. Food and Drug Administration does the same thing in interstate traffic. Tolerances for pesticide residues used in California are the same as those developed by the federal Food and Drug Administration.

These tolerance levels are set for the particular crop, and practically none are developed for the foliage on which the crop is grown. The outbreak of pesticide poisoning among the ninety-four peach harvesters in California in 1963 was traced to excessive application of parathion on the foliage, *but not the crop*.

The effectiveness of this program of regulation by state and federal agricultural authorities has come under serious attack recently in a salient area—registration, evaluation and testing of pesticide products. Under the federal Insecticide, Fungicide and Rodenticide Act, the U.S. Agricultural Research Service can take action to remove products from the market, cancel the registration of products and prosecute those who ship products that violate the law.

The GAO report last September detailed that Research Service's concept of "law and order" is for the benefit of the pesticide industry. The report went on to show that of 2,751 samples of products tested and reviewed during fiscal 1966, 750 were found to be in violation of the law. Of these, 70 percent (or 520) were in "major" violation of the law. In 1967, of 4,958 samples taken, 23 percent (or 1,147) were found in violation.

Part of the reason for the situation is the old complaint of fiscal starvation and bureaucratic passivity toward vested interests. The pesticides regulation division has a staff of about 150, of whom twenty-six are field supervisors and five are supervisory inspectors. In fiscal 1968 the total budget of the agency was $3.6 million. By way of contrast, the California State Assembly appropriated and spent $20 million last year for agricultural research support for its state university and college system.

Obviously, federal and state agricultural agencies are oriented toward maximizing the productivity-increasing features of agricultural chemicals, generally, and pesticides, specifically. The fact that no research in the United States is currently conducted into the occupational health hazards of agricultural and industrial chemicals is indicative of the general lack of concern in the regulatory organization for worker interests.

A portent of the future direction of public policy in this area is the fact that the budget of the Bureau of Occupational Health of the California State Department of Public Health was cut by one-third as part of Governor Reagan's attempt to bring "efficiency" into government operations.

If a severe budget cut were not enough, the Bureau of Occupational Health was also in jeopardy of being legislated out of existence. The chief legislative analyst of the California State Assembly, Alan Post, uncovered the fact that the bureau's existence was subject to legislative approval. Recently legislation has been introduced into the Assembly to rectify the anomaly before the bureau's existence becomes an object of lobby pressure. This may seem like just another administrative oversight, but the bureau is practically the only source of information on occupational disease and health hazards among farmworkers for the United States. (California is the only state in the country where injuries among farmworkers are counted and where farmworkers are also covered by Workmen's Compensation.)

California is one of the few states to have developed safety standards for agricultural operations. The standards are administered by the Division of Industrial Safety of the State Department of Industrial Relations. Safety orders for injurious materials (as defined in Section 2461 of Title 3 of the California Administrative Code) cover four areas: first, the provision of medical services by an employer engaged in commercial operation who uses toxic pesticides; second, decontamination of equipment; third, precautions for aircraft crop dusting and spraying; and fourth, standards for equipment used in both ground and air application of pesticides and other injurious agricultural chemicals. By far the most important of these for protection of the farmworker is the standard of medical supervision over application of pesticides. Even this is weakened, since control over recommendations and reports filed with the Division of Industrial Safety covering the determination of restricted activities for employees exposed to injurious materials is under the employer.

Part of the pesticide problem comes from our failure to recognize that a problem really exists. Dr. Irma West, a leading champion of pesticide control among environmental health specialists, writing in *California Medicine*, has summarized the issues involved clearly:

"Man has manipulated his environment on so large a scale that he has inadvertently invented and produced a multitude of the most complicated new problems ever to confront the health professions. Unfortunately, we have been slow to realize that plans for health and safety should be built into technologic advances in the planning stages. By the time technical tools are in operation and their use results in undesirable and unexpected effects upon people and their environment, the best opportunity to minimize these effects efficiently and humanely is largely lost."

November 8 – 15, 1968

Part Three
The Crisis of Arms

No one could have predicted that the U.S. Army—and, indeed, the entire "defense establishment"—would be the object of revolt and attack. But from a few isolated incidents (such as the refusal of Army doctor Howard Levy to train Green Berets for Vietnam duty in 1967), the GI rebellion became an enormous factor in the anti-war movement and in the conduct of American military policy. Collaterally, opposition to the Pentagon's mighty power grew from a far-Left cause to a "respectable" liberal position.

Military Complex

Fred Gardner

Colorado Springs

The nicest thing about living in Colorado Springs is the view of the Rockies a few miles west. But one of those lovely mountains has been hollowed out to house Norad, the nerve center of the Air Force. There is another Air Force base in the heart of town, and the Air Force Academy is only five miles north. Fort Carson, the 30,000-man Army base, forms the city's southern border.

For years, Colorado Springs was a fashionable spa. At the top was old oil, ranching, mining and real estate money. After World War II the tourist trade gave way to the military trade — which adds $5 million a year to the town's payroll. The population has swelled from 35,000 in 1945 to 135,000 today. Almost all the newcomers are military, retired military, civilians directly employed by the military, or people who sell things to the military. The only industry is precision electronics; Hewlett Packard and Litton have the largest plants. Their workers are women, most of them military wives. The going rate for unskilled labor is $1.65 an hour.

Military security forces have carte blanche to tap phones, intimidate civilians and otherwise run the show. A friendly agent says that Colorado Springs is in fact a controlled experiment to see whether police state methods are acceptable to an American community. It looks like a success. The pay phones in bars where GIs and airmen gather are tapped; so are the phones of the town's few radicals. The Chamber of Commerce has created a special military affairs committee, headed by a patriotic realtor, Norman Coleman, to serve the brass.

I came to town with five co-workers—Eric and Marya Levenson, Steve Jones, Nancy Bardacke, and Jennifer Gardner—to help local resistance people set up a GI coffeehouse. We had only a few months to work and were overjoyed therefore when we found a good site after one week of searching. It was the basement of a deteriorating hotel right next door to the Greyhound terminal, only one block from the strip of bars and pawnshops where most Fort Carson men squander their leave time.

The lease was drawn by our lawyer, Norman Helwig, a McCarthy activist who had volunteered his services. It was signed on the afternoon of July 24 by D. G. Pool, manager of the hotel. That night both the hotel owner and a senior partner of Helwig's firm were contacted by Army Intelligence agents. They were told flat lies about our project and its staff—including a tale that I was a leader of SDS. The next day we were barred from the premises of our funky little café. And the lawyer for the hotel, an ambitious ex-minister named Clifton Kruse, informed us that our lease was invalid because Pool didn't legally represent the corporation that owned the hotel. Helwig dropped us like a hot potato, but still comes on like a friend. He takes it for granted that a man must bow to pressure from his boss, no matter what the circumstances.

We turned to a young establishment lawyer, Lindsay Fischer, a Harvard man and son of a former Republican legislator. He phoned Kruse and proposed that they negotiate our contract before fighting it out in court. "I don't want to talk to you, Lindsay," Kruse said, "until you've heard what the FBI and CID (the Army's Criminal Investigation Division) have to say about these people." He offered to send the agents over to Fischer's office that morning. Fischer said that wouldn't be necessary and instead spent the morning poring through his books. By noon he had concluded matter-of-factly, "Colorado law is somewhat landlord-oriented." There was no way we could get the hotel basement back, he said.

Two days later our house landlord also tried to turn us out — ostensibly because a retired colonel living across the street had complained about "hippy cars, dogs, and naked children." We went back to Lindsay Fischer's office. It turned out that his senior partner, Lee Goodbar, had been contacted in the interim and threatened with eviction and loss of clients if the firm represented us. Goodbar, a man of integrity, told the strong-arm boys that he would run his own business, thank you.

Next, we canvassed possible coffeehouse locations until it became clear that all the realtors and downtown landlords had been warned not to rent to us. The word had been spread by the FBI and by Norman Coleman, the Chamber of Commerce, man, who said that he had been shown "highly secret files" about the coffeehouse project. Our choice at this point seemed to be: Split, stay, or come back when we have the money and time to put up the kind of fight this town needs.

* * *

"Movement" seems like a mighty big word for the handful of people who are working to change Colorado Springs. The black community is on the defensive, while the El Paso County Taxpayers Committee tries to eliminate the welfare system, with its $127 monthly allotment to a family of four. The chicanos are discriminated against bitterly. (The only other case in memory of a man being unable to rent a downtown storefront involved a chicano haberdasher.) But they are trying to assimilate, not fight. They have no organization, and their self-styled leader, Art Tafoya, is cynical enough to say privately, "Let the blacks take the risks; if any benefits come we'll reap them, too." Young people, a vaguely political force in a city like San Francisco, have no impact here because all the kids with gumption have split.

Fort Carson is an explosive base. It is nothing but a holding company for short-timers back from Vietnam. Some 70 percent of the troops stationed there have returned from overseas with seven months or less remaining in the service. They are made to stand five formations a day and put through a training regimen which they find absurd. The only exercise which isn't pure make-work — riot control — is offensive to all the blacks and many of the whites. Morale is at rock bottom.

We've learned that two previous attempts to establish coffeehouses, neither under the auspices of Support Our Soldiers, had been crushed in the past year. In one instance, a white GI from Fort Carson had rented a downtown storefront, obtained a business license and health department stamp, and then was evicted on opening night after he had allowed an SDS member to join his staff. The other episode involved black GIs who tried to set up a political forum off post. They were "befriended" by a black officer who said he would try to reserve a service club for them on post. Mysteriously enough, they were all reassigned to other bases within a matter of weeks.

Six black GIs were court-martialed three months ago at Carson for lingering in the mess hall instead of joining a formation they thought they had been excused from. The real basis for the charge, according to Susan Graham Barns, their ACLU lawyer from Denver, was that one of them kept a copy of Malcom X's autobiography in his footlocker. Their commanding officer assumed that their mess hall talk was a political meeting. The six were convicted and sentenced to three months' confinement on a charge of disobedience. It is ironic that in a simultaneous case at Fort Jackson, S.C., eight GIs who *were* trying to hold a political meeting beat the charge. For some time now the Army has been much harsher in unpublicized trials. Army Secretary Stanley Resor intervened in the Fort Jackson proceedings as soon as *The New York Times* picked up the story. The Fort Carson trial, on the other hand, attracted no national attention.

The situation here seems to call for more than just a coffeehouse for GIs who want a respite from the Army. When the nationwide project was begun in 1967, we saw our task as creating non-military hangouts where men could gather and get a sense of their common problems and common strengths. It was a prerequisite to organizing. That job could only be undertaken by GIs themselves. But now they've done it. The GI movement exists and it has new problems and needs. One of these is how — whether — to relate to the civilian movement.

We had figured that the Colorado Springs coffeehouse could in sort of parable form tackle this problem. We had planned it as an out-front Movement center in which various groups of fucked-over people — soldiers, women, kids, blacks, chicanos, peacers — could partake of one another's experience. Perhaps a newspaper would come out of the place: Not just a GI paper, but a hip/radical paper that contained a few pages of and by GIs. In place of a radical political party, a paper can serve crucial communications functions. It can pull isolated people into the national Movement and it can define events in a radical way. The second day we were in town a cop shot and killed a fifteen-year-old kid in a suspicion-of-robbery situation. There was a little story about it in both local papers, no demonstration or formal demand that the cop be fired. In fact, there was no force in this city of 135,000 that defined the killing as a political event.

People driving back from the United Front Against Fascism Conference in Berkeley have been parking their old hippy vans in our driveway and giving us the revolutionary rap. It sounds swell.

August 11 – 18, 1969

Crackdown on GIs

Andrew Kopkind and Fred Gardner

Columbia, South Carolina

There's nothing that people in these parts like better than a famous failure. The local television station's annual "man of the year" citation was given last week to Judge Clement Haynsworth, in recognition of his losing the Supreme Court appointment. Last year, the award went to Gen. William Westmoreland, for losing the war in Vietnam. The elevation of local losers to international heroes is a peculiar feature of oppressed peoples, and it's no wonder that South Carolina follows that rule. More even than most white Southerners, South Carolinians see themselves in some conquered province, occupied—or at least besieged—by the armies of the North.

The source of evil in Columbia these days is not, as some might expect, the 23,000-man Union encampment at Fort Jackson, the vast basic-training post that adjoins or, in a sense, engulfs the South Carolina capital city. The prevailing atmosphere at the base is Southern, not federal, and in any case the Army is the major industry in town. But what really offends public morality and integrity is a small coffeehouse called the UFO, directly across Main Street from the City Hall, in a seedy block of pinball parlors, bars and would-be brothels where the GIs from Fort Jackson hang out in their off hours.

The UFO was the first of a half-dozen coffeehouses which have been set up in the past two years by anti-war movement people as a focus for organizing the consciousnesses — and occasionally the activities — of GIs. Most of the work has been played in the lowest of keys: The coffeehouses serve more as collecting points than indoctrination centers. Dissent within the lower ranks of the service is so widespread that it takes little more than a conversation pit to bring GIs to an anti-war or anti-authority position. But the pro-war, pro-authority forces find it hard to believe that opposition can develop of its own accord, and they have naturally focused on the coffeehouse movement. At Fort Lewis, Wash., the Army is trying to declare the local coffeehouse "off limits" (see Fred Gardner's report below). Various officials and un-officials have harassed all the others, at one time or another. But the heaviest repression of a coffeehouse to date is in Columbia: One day two weeks ago, city police rounded up the staff, arrested them on several charges of "creating a public nuisance," and locked them up in the local pokey. Bail for the four (one was not apprehended) totaled $28,500; they face sentences, if convicted, of up to ten years. Then, two days later, the UFO was closed and padlocked by a municipal judge's restraining order.

The old patriots in the White Power elites of Columbia have a theory about the troubles that have lately beset their town. To their way of thinking, the problem began when Dr. Howard Levy came to Fort Jackson, called by the government to serve his country as head of the dermatology clinic at the U.S. Army hospital at the base. Levy incorporated three original and indissoluble sins: he was a Jew, a liberal, and a New Yorker. From such corruption even more than from any activities he engaged in flowed the surprising growth of a student movement at the University of South Carolina, the GI "pray-in" at an Army chapel, the trial of the anti-war "Fort

Jackson Eight," the development of a hip/radical community in Columbia, and perhaps certain ineluctable meteorological phenomena, such as unseasonable cold waves and thunderstorms in December.

As it happens, the theory is in many ways correct. Levy may not have brought on the bad weather, but he did a bang-up job of organizing local kids and GIs, and a lot of the action that has come to Columbia in the last three years derives from the work he did or the energies that he spawned.

Howard Levy tooled into town one day in 1965, and things haven't been the same since. Hardly aware of his historic role but possessed simply of a healthy distaste for the Army, Levy managed to pique the brass at a number of vulnerable points. He refused to join the officers club, showed disrespect for his uniform, and failed to master a proper salute. Soon simple protest passed into politics. Levy began working in a voting rights project in Newberry County and started a civil rights newspaper out of Columbia. About that time, the Army's Counter-Intelligence Corps decided that Levy was a communist and reported him to his superiors. The end came, of course, when Levy refused to instruct Vietnam-bound Green Berets in the practice of minor medical techniques which they were to use to win the hearts and minds of Asian peasants. The local brass brought Levy to trial, and in June 1968, to the accompaniment of world-wide media coverage, he was convicted of various military crimes and sentenced to three years at hard labor.

But that was hardly the last that Columbia heard of Dr. Levy. From his cell in the prison ward of the hospital at Fort Jackson he directed the development of the civilian and GI anti-war movements, and by the time he was transferred to Leavenworth, in December 1967, a permanent base of protest had been built. Those who had met Levy were moved by the ferocity of his own struggle, and the many more who had never seen him were excited by his example. In the month Levy left, Fred Gardner and a handful of local and out-of-state activists got the UFO going.

* * *

In those days, there was little interest in GIs as a "base" in

the radical movements. No one had tried to organize GI protest; the Movement stopped at the point of induction. Those
who went into uniform went over to the other side. Even if
there were dissidents in the Army, how could they express
their dissent within the confines of a totalitarian institution,
where even the blessed Bill of Rights did not apply?

That analysis was good as far as it went, which was not
very far. For before long there were the beginnings of a GI
movement which confounded the middle-class radical kids
who were devoting all their time and theories to draft resistance. What happened was that the conflicts urging civilians
on to protest appeared logically, if a bit tardily, within the military establishment. On the simplest "cultural" level, young
Army draftees wanted to smoke dope, listen to rock records
and trip in the park just as much as anyone else of their generation. The fact that they were inducted before they could
organize resistance made their desire to escape even stronger.
And on a deeper "political" level, the contradictions of racism and authoritarianism were even more pressing in the
tightly structured military institution. Civilian blacks could
grow afros, wear dashikis or surround themselves with black
culture, but in the Army it was not so easy. Similarly, civilian
white kids could freak out and live in one or another stage of
hippiedom — in communes, on campus, or even at home — with
only a glance over the shoulder at the infrequent narc. Dress
codes and hair-length rules are falling by the dozens at high
schools around the country; and it's easy to drop out of college or a job. But wear long hair in the Army or try to sleep
late during basic training, and the Man cracks down at once.

The revolt which began in the sixties may have had class or
racial attributes, but it was overall a generational phenomenon, and its appearance in the Army (and, not illogically, in the
super-uptight Marines) should have been expected. When it
came, there was the predictable flurry of organizational activity, media interest, establishment bafflement — and repression.

The realist organizing within the Army had been done by
Old Left groups (on the wrong analysis, but it doesn't matter).
While New Left kids were resisting the draft, some Trotsky-
ists and communists were deliberately joining up to organize

on the inside. The earliest revolts reflected their work. But the coffeehouses represented the first significant attempt of the New Left—with its independent ideologies and its emphasis on the generational culture—to break into the world of the GIs.

The coffeehouse project was so obviously a good idea that older Movement types began thinking of ways to expand it quickly. Projects at Fort Hood, Tex., and Fort Leonard Wood, Mo., followed the successful Fort Jackson model, and a larger organizational umbrella unfolded around them, operated by the (old) Mobilization to End the War in Vietnam. A "Summer Of Support" was planned for 1968, and work began to recruit and train hundreds of kids—and raise money—for a string of coffeehouses in Army towns throughout the United States. But the election year was more immediately important to the Mobe, and by late spring its energies—as well as those of the best radical cadre—were draining off the coffeehouses and into the Democratic Convention demonstrations.

The Missouri coffeehouse folded in the rush to and from Chicago, and the national umbrella folded, too. Summer Of Support became Support Our Soldiers; and more careful, if leisurely, organization of the coffeehouses began in the fall of the year. Since then, projects have been set up at Fort Lewis, Wash.; Fort Dix, N.J.; Fort Knox, Ky.; and Fort Carson, Colo. There is a SOS "presence" at Camp Pendleton, the Marine Corps base in Southern California, and a coffeehouse is due to open this month at Fort Ord, near Monterey, Calif. Another is projected for a big base in the South—the first at a non-basic-training Army post.

Initially, the coffeehouses were set up near the big basic-training forts because the draftees there—in the most dehumanizing and humiliating phase of their military service—were considered to be most in need of the support the movements of their generation could provide, both culturally and politically. The coffeehouses were to be alternatives to the exploitative and tawdry pinball culture that traditionally has served GIs in Army towns, and they were to offer some avenues for expressing the political gripes the GIs had against the Army system. But there were disadvantages in restricting the projects to basic-training posts. For one thing, GIs in training have little time for extracurricular activities. More important, post populations at places like Jackson, Dix or Ord are highly transient; thousands of new GIs come in for two or four months and then are shipped out – or over.

* * *

The UFO at Fort Jackson (the name was a pun on the military establishment's own USO) prospered and suffered according to the vagaries of the GI movement, the energies of the staff, and the oppressive atmosphere of Columbia. The GI "pray-in" at Fort Jackson and the organizing work of a black GI named Joe Miles – which led to the "Fort Jackson Eight" anti-war petition and their court-martial – gave focuses to UFO activities. Civilian students and local freaks added to the coffeehouse clientele in various proportions, and to one or another effect. In one way, the GIs appreciated a chance to get together with their generational brothers and sisters; but there were tensions, too, and the staff was always worried about dope dealing and other illegalities that might happen around the coffeehouse and give the Army or local authorities an excuse for closing the shop. Everyone knew (and now Columbia officials admit) that there were narcs, Army CIC agents and sundry pigs and informers at the UFO all the time, but the staff tried to stay as clean as possible. On one occasion, staff members asked the police to help them keep dealers out of the coffeehouse. The police refused.

Except for some minor incidents and threats, the UFO managed to avoid the repressive measures that were coming down on other coffeehouses. At the Oleo Strut, at Fort Hood, for example, one staff member was busted on a spurious marijuana charge and held on $50,000 bail (the charges were ultimately dropped). At the Shelter Half, at Fort Lewis, two staff members were arrested for "contributing to the delinquency of a minor," the project house garage was fire-bombed and its automobile destroyed, and the base commander began the process of declaring the coffeehouse off-limits. The FTA, at Fort Knox, was charged with creating a "public nuisance," staff members have been held in contempt of a grand jury, and the project's garage has twice been bombed. In some towns, coffeehouse organizers have been unable to lease space for their projects.

Army action against individual GIs who are connected with the coffeehouses has been even heavier. Stockades are full of soldiers who have been court-martialed for distributing "unauthorized literature" — usually the post underground newspaper, such as Fort Jackson's *Short Times* — or busted in one protest demonstration or another. The GI editor of the Fort Hood underground paper was arrested for possession of microscopic traces of marijuana "discovered" in an analysis of the lint in his pants pocket (and never produced in court); he was sentenced to eight years at hard labor, and served two of them, without the right of bail, until the conviction was overturned.

Authorities at Fort Jackson were apparently of two minds about the UFO. The trials of Howard Levy and the "Eight" had obviously boomeranged. The cooler heads at the Pentagon strongly advised against precipitous repression. It was more sensible, they thought, to keep the UFO wired with agents and informers and to keep a tight rein on GIs who frequented it, than to blow up and risk more bad publicity.

In reality, there was not much for the Army to worry about this winter at the UFO. The staff — mostly people "new" to the Movement and of a more passive political bent than the activist staffers at Fort Dix or Fort Lewis — had done little serious organizing work with GIs, and the coffeehouse was at a low point when the Columbia cops rounded them up. The reasons for busts remain obscure. One local establishment type told me that federal authorities in Columbia had been trying to "get something" on the coffeehouse for some time, but had failed, and the local authorities acted themselves. There is some suggestion that the "evidence" of wrongdoing at the UFO was provided by a disturbed teenage doper who lived with staff members for a short time last year, stole a lot of their belongings, and then "informed" on the project to the special South Carolina state police called SLED, a kind of official vigilante squad controlled by the governor. The teenager later confessed to UFO staffers that he had invented elaborate fantasies about "arms caches" and dope rings to impress the SLED agents.

What is not known at all is the connection between the Fort Jackson command and the city UFO busters. But one Columbian suggested the likely link: "The Army didn't particularly like the place, but they didn't want to do a job on it themselves. They left it to our people." Given the national ambience of repression against insurgency of all kinds, the local solicitor and his men knew they had green lights all the way.

* * *

Four staffers were arrested; a fifth who had been indicted slipped through the police's fingers and was thought to be organizing an extra-territorial political protest against the repression of the UFO. Two of those jailed, including a woman four and a half months pregnant, were freed on bond several days after their arrest; the others, including the pregnant woman's husband, were trying to raise bail money last week. Motions to reduce the exceedingly high bail ($7,500 on the men, $6,000 on the woman: one cheer for Southern male chauvinism) were, of course, denied. The ACLU has tentatively agreed to take the case and will try to remove the restraining order — and the padlock — on the UFO.

Now the political response has started. The community of GIs, local students, freaks and the few lonely liberals of Columbia have rushed in to save the UFO with a confusion of political tactics but a clarity of commitment. On the Sunday after the busts there was a rally in a park (the university had agreed to let one of its lecture halls be used but demanded that speakers be "approved" and that only ID-card-holding students and teachers could attend; the rule was enforced, and the rally organizers moved out of doors). Howard Levy flew in to make a short speech of encouragement, and no doubt the city fathers saw the whole conspiracy very clearly. But Levy's only a spiritual ancestor now. There's a Movement in Columbia, and after the rally it marched through town, past the Capitol, down Main Street to the padlocked, pig-protected UFO. There were four or five hundred marchers—an astounding number in this confining city—and a quarter of them were active-duty GIs, risking whatever horrors the brass has in store for them back on the base. There were CIC agents and MPs on every corner taking pictures. But the GIs held up their green service identification cards in defiance—and to wave the scores of GIs on the sidewalks into the line of march. A lot of the bystanders held up a "v" or a clenched fist, and some ran into the parade. The other marchers hugged them like brothers.

It's difficult for the UFO "community" and the remaining staff to see their way out of the traps that Columbia has put them in, and it's even more depressing when they see the problems that the other coffeehouses are facing. But seen another way, the forces set against UFO may have saved it— or even moved it ahead—at the moment it was running down. If there were no movements behind the hundreds of radical projects and parties now blooming in America, repressive attacks by the government or the institutions of the Right would finsh them off, one by one. But when radicalism expresses real contradictions and while movements can still believe in themselves enough to fight, repression is not so simple. It is not 1950 after all, despite a few familiar faces.

DOWN AMONG THE SHELTERING HALF

Tacoma, Washington

The Army's indoctrination of a soldier, particularly a trainee, doesn't end when he goes into town on pass. The typical base town, with its sordid environment of bars and clip joints, does as much to transform a boy into a killer as the classrooms back at the fort. The generals understand this and traditionally have gone easy in exercising their power to place an establishment off limits. They have let the dollar-a-shot bars stay open until men start getting rolled there; the syndicate game continues until a man turns up dead near their trailer; the whorehouses remain on limits until syphilis becomes epidemic. But on December 11, 1969, the military took preliminary steps to place the Shelter Half—a Tacoma coffeehouse catering to Fort Lewis GIs—off limits because of its employees' politics. A letter from the Armed Forces Disciplinary Control Board ordered the "proprietor" of the Shelter Half to appear at a hearing on January 22 to "show cause why it should not be placed off limits" as "a source of dissident counseling and literature and other activities inimical to good morale, order and discipline within the Armed Services."

Friends inside the Army told the Shelter Half staff that it was Gen. Stanley R. Larsen who had initiated the move against them. Larsen's jurisdiction as Sixth Army commander includes the Presidio of San Francisco as well as Fort Lewis; he is the hard-liner who pushed ahead with the mutiny trials last year despite opposition from the Secretary of the Army. A panel of Fort Lewis officers subsequently ratified Larsen's recommendation by a vote of six to one. The one dissenter, a medical officer, has already been transferred from his hospital job to a new one, riding the Army's poison-gas train on its run from Maine to Fort Detrick, Md.

Staff members at the Shelter Half feel that the off-limits order reflects the strength of the enlisted men's movement at Fort Lewis. They make no attempt to deny their role in sustaining that movement. Whereas staff members in an earlier phase of the GI coffeehouse project saw themselves as passive (merely providing a hangout at which soldiers could talk politics if they felt like it), the current tendency if for staff people to function as organizers. The Shelter Half staff—three women with Movement backgrounds, four recent vets and a fifth man who is an experienced organizer—have taken down last year's Fillmore posters and replaced them with Cuban graphics and portraits of the Cleaver family. They no longer absent themselves when the American Servicemen's Union holds its weekly meeting at the coffeehouse; and two staff members play active roles in the Union, having been discharged from Fort Lewis only recently.

The ASU chapter is large and imaginative. Last October it held a spirited 35-man meeting at a service club on post. Its members have exposed the Sixth Army's policy of flying conscientious objectors to Vietnam at gunpoint; they have vocally opposed military purchases of California grapes; and they regularly circulate 5,000 copies of *Fed-Up*, one of the most spritely and forceful GI underground papers. The brass evidently think that an attack on the coffeehouse, the Union's occasional home base, will destroy the Union. This is the kind of misjudgment that U.S. commanders have been making in Vietnam for years. It is no coincidence that Gen. Larsen, when he was head of all Army forces in Vietnam in 1966, insisted that hot pursuit into Cambodia was the final solution to the problem of NLF guerrillas.

According to Michael Kennedy and James Vonasch, attorneys for the coffeehouse, the original notice ordering the "proprietor" to appear at an off-limits hearing was illegal in its vagueness. Kennedy sent a three-page letter to the Armed Forces Disciplinary Control Board demanding a bill of particulars: What, precisely, was illegal about the activities taking place at the Shelter Half? The board did not reply with any specific allegations — perhaps because they had none to make. The law in this area is itself very vague. In the spring of 1969, Gen. Westmoreland asked the Army's General Counsel to provide commanders with a handy checklist of repressive measures they could use against dissenters. But several young lawyers on the General Counsel's staff seized the opportunity to write a relatively liberal guideline, reminding commanders that they had to accept certain constitutional constraints. One section was devoted specifically to coffeehouses, and advised that they could only be placed off limits for perpetrating "illegal acts." (The well-meaning lawyers wrote their document with Gen. Larsen and the Presidio mutiny case in mind.) Like most attempts at reform within the Army, the General Counsel's affirmation of GI rights was killed. Mendel Rivers castigated it, then the Defense Department superseded it with its own "directive on dissent." The newer directive frees commanders from any obligation to find illegal acts; it establishes "acts with a significant adverse effect on members' health, morale or welfare" as sufficient grounds for an off-limits order.

While Kennedy and Vonasch were preparing the legal defense, the Shelter Half staff and their soldier friends organized a political counteroffensive. The GIs began writing and collecting affidavits to the effect that the Army and the war — not the coffeehouse — were bad for morale. The staff scheduled two major rallies — one for the University of Washington the night before the hearing and one to take place in the street when the Disciplinary Control Board convened. Arrangements were made to fly in a few expert witnesses on the broad question of morale — among them Dr. Peter Bourne, a former Army psychiatrist who has published a medical text analyzing the way in which military training undermines a man's identity.

Then, three days before the hearing, the Army sent a letter to Kennedy — and provided tapes to the local radio stations — announcing that the hearing had been postponed at the Shelter Half's request. No new date was set. Kennedy says the postponement is a farfetched interpretation of his letter and thinks it may be a euphemistic way of backing down. "When their lawyers in Washington realized what a shoddy case the Sixth Army had," he speculates, "they probably told them to call it off. I don't think they're going to let Larsen embarrass them again."

The Shelter Half decided to go ahead with its rally at the university — to test their community support and to rehearse the defense in case the board sets a new date for the hearing. A jury of GIs and a crowd of more than 1,200 people (including many vets back in school on the GI bill) came to hear some twenty servicemen give their accounts of Army life to a "people's prosecutor," Terry Cannon of the Oakland Seven. All the testimony was terse, personal and compelling. The first witness, Denny Leonard, said he hadn't taken his identity as an American Indian seriously until he saw a basic training film showing the cavalry wiping out his people. He stood up to express his misgivings, and his commanding officer accused him of disrupting the class. Then and there he decided not to fight in Vietnam. He wound up in the Presidio stockade, where he was beaten.

Next came Roger Broomfield, who had been a guard at that stockade. He described the pressures on the guards, the reward-and-punishment system that encourages brutality. A black airman discussed racism in the Army. An information specialist showed the photos that his commanders had censored — not just atrocity shots, but pictures of GIs in positions of fatigue and despair. Jim Turk described last year's rebellion at the Fort Dix stockade. One after another the soldiers and vets said that the only way back to honor was through shame, and through resistance. Bruce McClean told of the Army's attempt to shanghai him at gunpoint to Vietnam. "They took me to the airport under guard. I told them I had to take a shit and went into the latrine. The guard stayed outside and I jumped through a window and got away."

"What's your status now?" Cannon asked.

"I'm AWOL from Fort Lewis," McClean explained. A cordon of eight soldiers materialized around him and led him out of the auditorium while Cannon warned the crowd not to follow.

Several of the speakers had been wounded in action. Mike Day, shot near the Laotian border, recalled, "I saw this North Vietnamese soldier off in the distance. I had time to shoot him, but I was going through an extreme change. My sergeant had said, 'In a fire-fight, it's you or him.' I figured it had to be me, since I was the one who was in the wrong place."

"Do you think of that Vietnamese soldier?" Cannon asked.

"Yeah," Day said. "I think about him and his family back in Vietnam, and I just hope they're OK."

Day blamed the brass for forcing him to fight a war that he considered unjust. Blaming the brass was becoming a litany until Bruce Whitver broke it. Whitver has nine scars from Hamburger Hill. "I don't want to excuse the brass," he said, "but I did a lot of maintenance on my helicopter and I was always staring at these names: Bell and Sikorsky and Remington."

The passion of the speeches and the impact on the crowd convinced some observers that the time is ripe for setting up a speakers' program for GIs and vets. The Army spends millions of dollars foisting publicists and recruiters on the youth of this country. The Movement should challenge them. There are so many men back from Vietnam now, yearning for a chance to dissociate themselves from the war machine, that we could confront the Army flacks whenever and wherever they ply their trade. And if a speakers' network were established, it would be the basis for a vets' anti-war organization that had roots in real work.

In many ways, the GIs' "Trial of the Army" at the University of Washington suggests that certain functions of the GI coffeehouses can be continued even if the coffeehouses themselves are wiped out. It is difficult to tell whether the postponed hearing represents a victory for the Shelter Half or a shrewd move by the Army to deflate the defense. The brass may simply leave the dirty work to politicians and cops in Tacoma, the way they have left it to local authorities near Fort Jackson and Fort Knox. Our consolation should be that no institution is worth more than the sum of the jobs it performs, and the jobs the GI coffeehouses perform can be taken over by groups of civilians who have the guts to work in Army towns and a little sense of street theater. The only aspect of our work that will die with the coffeehouses is the do-gooder aspect — providing respite for men strung out by Army life. And staffers seem willing to dispense with that.

There is another consolation. By striking at the coffeehouses (and GI papers), the Army is making its customary poor choice of targets. GI dissent manifests itself across a whole spectrum; the coffeehouses and papers are only the visible center; the invisible bands are sabotage at one end, a quiet but paralyzing disaffection at the other. These are the forms of dissent which materially hurt the Army's combat efficiency. The crackdown against the coffeehouses will not eliminate them.

Ultimately, the brass will find themselves unable to "sanitize" the Army. Just as the bombing of North Vietnam led to a flood of men and women marching south, so the attempt to cut off liaison between Movement people and GIs in base towns should lead to mass enlistment on the part of Movement kids, street people, anti-war medical and law students. Others have learned that when the bombs start falling you dig tunnels.

February 2 – 9, 1970

Bury the Dead

Fred Gardner

On December 5, Rod, Ricky and Dwyane Stevens, Jr., got an order from a court in Redding, Calif., barring a military funeral for their brother Dennis, twenty-one, killed in action around Chu Lai. Dennis's legal guardians, an aunt and uncle named James and Joyce Stevens, insisted that he be buried "with dignity and with high military honors." A hearing to settle the matter took place three days later.

Redding is a city of some 15,000 near the top of California's great Central Valley. Sprawling farms to the south produce rice, olives, prunes and almonds. Lumber and sheep-raising are major sources of income. The mountains and streams bring in tourists. Redding is the seat of Shasta County, and it was outside the courthouse that the two feuding sides of the Stevens family gathered December 8.

They looked like the silent majority embodied: powerful men with leathery cheeks and broad hands, mortar under the nails, dressed in windbreakers and gabardine and Ban-Lon; grim women in bouffant hairdos; teenagers with crewcuts.

139

The teenager wearing round-rimmed granny glasses turned out to be Dwyane Stevens, Jr. He told me that this whole crowd sided with him and his brothers against the Army. Uncle Jim — "I don't even think of him as my uncle now" — was standing some 40 feet apart, with his wife and stepson and some military personnel.

Dwyane laid out the complicated family history. The older generation of Stevenses — Dwyane, Sr., Bud and Jim — had come to Redding from Iowa some thirty years ago. Dwyane, Sr., married and had four children. Then, in 1952, his wife disappeared, never to return. When he died a few years later, his three oldest boys, Rod, Dennis, and Ricky, went to live with his brother Bud, his wife Ioia and their five children. Dwyane, Jr., the baby, was adopted by a union brother of Bud's. All four boys grew up in Redding — healthy, athletic, good in school.

When Dennis was fifteen, he spent a summer down in Vallejo with Dwyane, Sr.'s other brother, Jim. Jim's wife, Joyce, had four kids by a previous marriage and she found Dennis a good companion for them. She invited him to spend the school year and promised him a motorcycle. She also requested, and got, the $20 a week from Dwyane, Sr.'s pension which Bud conscientiously had been putting into a bank account for Dennis. Lest there be any squabble about this, Joyce and Jim had a court make them the boy's legal guardians. Dennis played varsity football at Hogan High School in Vallejo for two years. Then he moved back to Redding. He later complained that during his stay in Vallejo, Joyce Stevens had dipped into his small legacy to buy a washer and drier.

Dennis was drafted in the summer of 1968, spent six months at Fort Lewis, Wash., training for the artillery, then shipped out for Vietnam in August 1969. He was killed on November 14. The Army owes somebody $10,000 life insurance.

"Joyce is a bit of a flag-waver," Bud Stevens said that morning outside the courthouse. "But I don't think that's her real reason for insisting on a military funeral. I hate to say this about anybody, but I think maybe money's behind it. She might think the Army will make her the beneficiary just 'cause she supports the war." He shook his head and chomped his cigar butt.

* * *

Joyce Stevens, a stocky woman with close-cropped black hair and a tense manner, seemed upset that Dennis's high school football coach was not on hand. She had wanted him to testify that the boy loved drill-and-ceremony. "The boy is being dishonored," she said. "I raised him and nursed him when he was sick. We are his legal guardians, we are his next-of-kin, and it is so noted on the Army records." Her husband, a big, blue-eyed man who resembles Bud, stared hard at the ground. None of his relatives would speak to him.

She introduced her son, William Koontz, as "Dennis's brother, who has a top-secret clearance from the Navy."

I said I thought Dennis only had three brothers.

"Dennis was my foster brother," the top-secret man said.

"They were *like* blood brothers," Joyce insisted, "and my husband, of course, was a blood brother of the boy's father."

The military men hovering around were the Vallejo Ste-venses' lawyer, a Maj. Workman, and their key witness, Sgt. Richard Moulton. It was Moulton, a tall, fat man with "es-cort duty" inscribed on his nameplate, who had accompanied Dennis's body to a nearby Memorial Chapel. His orders list-ed James and Joyce Stevens as next-of-kin. Escort duty is voluntary in the Army. You have to be very humane or very malign to want the job of telling people their sons are dead. And the Army doesn't attract many career humanists. "It's funny," Sergeant Moulton reflected, "but I had a very similar case just two weeks ago in Columbus, Ohio. The boy had been recommended for a private showing, but that was some-body's error of judgment. He had had a lot of waxwork, and the parents just couldn't recognize. They insisted it wasn't their son. Said they couldn't locate a certain scar. In the end it turned out all right, though."

"What do you mean?"

"Well, they took my word it was him."

Dennis Stevens described his increasing revulsion over the war in letters to his family and friends in Redding. Almost all the thirty people gathered outside the courtroom had a letter from him in hand or back home. The letters said that Dennis's battery had been decimated—23 men left out of 130—and that he had been reassigned to an infantry unit by a captain who hated him. "Now you're gonna get it, Stevens," the captain had promised.

"If you ask me, the Army killed him," says Glen Jeffries, the retired plasterer who brought up Dwyane. "He had no infantry training and they put him in the infantry."

Ricky Stevens, home on emergency leave from Fort Dix, had a letter saying, "The captain told me he was going to send me into the field with 'A' Company—that's the infantry. Rick, if you can get the fuck out of the fucking Army, do it!"

Dwyane, Jr., says simply, "I won't go. That's that. Don't ask me 'What if . . . ?' I'm telling you I won't go." He is a student at Shasta Community College, where "just about everybody's against the war. They support us in what we're doing about the funeral." What about the vets? "Especially the vets. Vets have been coming up to me after class to say we're doing right fighting the Army."

The hearing itself took only ten minutes. Rod, the oldest at twenty-two, testified that he was next-of-kin and wanted to make the funeral arrangements. Ricky and Dwyane took the stand in his support. Then Joyce Stevens showed her certificate of guardianship to the judge. Her tone was Hollywood grief; her language, strictly military. She whimpered: "According to Army regulations he never changed his status with respect to these papers, as would have been his prerogative." Maj. Workman said that even though Dennis had turned twenty-one in Vietnam, the Army recognized the legal guardianship of James and Joyce Stevens. "Doesn't the Army recognize the legal impact of adulthood?" the judge asked. "No," the major said.

The judge scowled and ruled in favor of the brothers.

Ioia Stevens was sobbing in a daughter's arms. "It don't bring anybody back to life, does it?" she asked.

Joyce Stevens went into consultation with Maj. Workman about when the life insurance payment would come down.

"Do you know that the policy was made out to you?" I asked.

"The paperwork is in the hands of the Sixth Army," she replied. "Processing takes four weeks." Maj. Workman nodded. Then he put on a smile and approached Rod Stevens in the hall outside the courtroom. "I'm here to be of assistance to you," he said. Rod glared at him. Dwyane said, "First you kill him, then you want to help. You lifers make me sick."

Jim Stevens was trying to get a hello out of some of his relatives, but to no avail. Finally Bud walked up to him and said quietly, "You shouldn't have pushed it this far, Jim. The boys have a right to bury their brother the way he would have wanted."

An hour later a CBS-TV crew showed up at Rod Stevens' house, where the brothers were drinking beer and listening to Santana.

"Which did he object to, exactly, the military or this particular war?" the interviewer wanted to know.

"Well, he hated the military," Rod said, "and he hated this war. He hated them both."

"There seems to be particular feeling against *this war*," the CBS man hinted.

"He hated this war and he hated the Army."

"Why didn't he resist the draft?"

"How could he know before he went in what the Army was like and what the war was all about?"

"Why do you think he disliked the Army?"

"He *hated* the Army," Rod said. "He wrote my brother Rick he should get the fuck out."

The interviewer blushed, stammered and cut off the conversation. He asked if they had a photograph of Dennis around. Rod brought out a Polaroid shot of a broad-shouldered, handsome young man in fatigues. In the background was thick jungle foliage. The soldier had a flower in one hand and was giving the peace sign with the other.

December 22–29, 1969

Army Games

Fred Gardner

Lindy Blake is a very tall, sandy-haired Southern Californian who likes to sing Dylan songs and write poetry. His father works in an L.A. defense plant. When he was drafted a year ago, Lindy decided to go along with soldiering as far as he could—"but not to kill another human being." He was ordered to Vietnam after finishing Army bakers' school. "We need riflemen more than bakers," a sergeant told him.

Blake put in a conscientious objector's application before he was due to ship out from Oakland; it was refused by a Sgt. Sota, in Personnel, who told him he had no religious basis for filing for C-O status. He went AWOL; and the next stop was the Presidio stockade.

Blake was a member of the stockade work detail on which Richard Bunch, a fellow prisoner, was shot and killed by a stockade guard last October 11. This is how he remembers it:

"We were to go to the supply company for the hospital and put together wall lockers. The boxes of parts for the lockers were on the sidewalk in front of the supply room, across the street from a barracks where we went to get a drink of water.

144

There I noticed Bunch was bothering the guard, asking him questions such as, 'Would you shoot me if I ran?' As we went back out into the street to cross it I heard Bunch say something like 'Aim for my head,' or 'You'd better shoot to kill.' I wasn't paying too close attention. I said something to Bunch like 'Don't bug him, he's got a gun.' Bunch and the guard were in the middle of the street, two other members of the detail, Colip and Reims, were in the supply room, and I was on the sidewalk with my back to Bunch and the guard. I heard footsteps and the click of the shotgun being cocked, and I turned to see the guard aim and fire, hitting Bunch in the small of the back. There was no command of 'halt' given by the guard, and Bunch was 25 to 30 feet from the guard when he was shot. There was one shot fired. After shooting Bunch, the guard whirled, pointed his gun at me and yelled, 'Hit the ground, hit the ground or I'll shoot you too.' Then he seemed to have flipped and said, 'I hit him right where I aimed, in the lower back,' and then, 'Why did I do that? I didn't want to kill anybody, I should have let him go, I didn't want to kill anybody.' "

Lindy Blake escaped from the prison ward of the hospital. "We called it 'the dungeon,' " he says. "It used to be for the insane. There were old chains on the wall, and things to hold your arms in place, and a lot of incoherent writings."

Blake and Randy Rowland were sent to the hospital in late February with hepatitis. "A friend smuggled a hacksaw blade in to us," Blake says. "Randy couldn't make up his mind whether or not to escape. For a few days I changed my mind about escaping and stopped work. I was so scared to do it alone. Then I realized I was gonna die if I stayed. I was gonna be a martyr. But that wasn't my thing, martyrism. My conscience told me my thing was life.

"I sawed all night long for almost two weeks. We had to run the shower all the time and sing so the guards wouldn't hear us. We sang every song we knew, and added a lot of verses to them, too. We made up a lot of groovy verses to 'Swing Low, Sweet Chariot.' Since we couldn't carry a tune, the tune would change; then we felt entitled to change the words.

"Escaping is not like the movies, man. There was a whole

gridwork of bars. I scraped all the skin of my thumb. At first I just had a blade. Then when I got a whole hacksaw — it was thrown in through the window — wow! The afternoon I finished the last bar, sort of to celebrate, I had a long conversation with this really stupid guard. I said, 'I don't know why they have all these tight security measures around here. Everybody knows it's impossible to escape.' He said, 'Yeah, it sure is, man.'

"That night I bent the bars back and wriggled through. It was really tight. I had to take off all my clothes, and even so I cut the hell out of my hips. Not like the movies at all.

"My friend was waiting and she had a car nearby. I went to an apartment in the Haight, saw some beloved friends, and that night I just couldn't resist dancing in the streets. I danced around the Panhandle, man."

* * *

Lindy Blake is now in Canada, along with two of his fellow fugitives from the Presidio stockade. Blake left the United States in March; the other two — Walter Pawlowski and Keith Mather — escaped from the stockade on Christmas Eve and made their way to the North Country Fair some weeks later. Twenty-four others have been, or are about to be, on trial at West Coast posts, for demonstrating in the aftermath of Bunch's death. What they did was sit down in a circle on the Presidio grounds and sing "We Shall Overcome." The prisoners called it a sit-down. The Army called it mutiny.

In a sense, the Army was right. The kind of spontaneous action the prisoners undertook that day was moderate in its form, but contained a revolutionary element which the military authorities must find threatening. The twenty-seven were not bright young collegiate radicals performing a political tactic around an opportune issue. They were thoroughly apolitical, small-town, working-class youths who had never conceived of themselves as organizers or agitators. Their median educational level was ninth grade; only four came from families either willing or able to get them civilian counsel. It was the Army that made them rebel.

The Presidio mutiny of Monday, October 14, marks a turning point in the movement of GIs against the war and against military authoritarianism. Until that point, the publicized cases all involved individual acts of witness by well-educated or highly political people: Dr. Howard Levy, Capt. Dale Noyd, Lt. Susan Schnall, Airman Michael Locks, Pvt. Ronald Lockman; or Andy Stapp at Fort Sill, Howard Petrick at Fort Hood, or Henry Howe, Jr., at Fort Bliss. The only collective political action had been done by blacks—the uprising (close to a race riot) in the Long Binh jail and the refusal of forty-three black soldiers at Fort Hood, Tex., to accept duty in Chicago at the time of the Democratic Convention.

The Presidio twenty-seven was an all-white group, "typical of the GI sub-culture that fills every stockade," as a lawyer for them once put it. All were imprisoned for AWOL offenses. If there is a *lumpen* class in the Army, they were it.

The Sixth Army regards Pawlowski and Mather as the leaders of the sit-down. It is a logical conclusion for the Army to draw, since it was Pawlowski who stood up to read the group's grievances and Mather who demanded civilian counsel for everyone. Pawlowski, a tall, articulate New Yorker, and Mather, a powerfully built Californian, escaped long before the trials began, so in their absence the prosecution has tried to identify other leaders for special punishment by such subtle criteria as who changed the song the mutineers sang from "We Shall Overcome" to "This Land Is Your Land." Of the twenty-seven, eight were sentenced to various terms in prison, from nine months to sixteen years; two have had their trials deferred for medical reasons; fourteen are on trial now with civilian defense counsel; and three escaped.

Those three escaped "mutineers"—though they're hurting for money—declined to sell their stories to the straight press until they could break it through the Movement. I have been in touch with them over several months. The last time we talked we were joined by Frenchy Kight, the prisoner who bunked under Richard Bunch and retrieved his pathetic suicidal notes. Kight did not join the demonstration because he had five charges hanging over him from a more violent protest staged immediately after Bunch was shot.

The four escapees are able to shed light on the "mutiny"—how it was planned, who took part and why—more thoroughly than the prisoners now standing trial.

"When Bunch was killed that Friday morning," Pawlowski

recalls, "the first word we got back at the stockade was that Walker [another prisoner] had been shot. He was very well liked, and a lot of us knew he was going to try an escape. Bunch? It was hard to imagine him trying to cut out."

As word filtered in, everybody in the stockade's main building gathered in cellblock 4. "It was the best place to hold a meeting," according to Kight, "because we had jimmied the lock. The guards couldn't get in but we could get out. At that time it was called the Resisters' Cell, or the Instigators' Cell, because Woodring [the sergeant who effectively ran the stockade] had put five guys in there whom he especially hated."

"Everybody was talking revenge," Kight says. "The feeling was we ought to take over the whole compound and lock the sergeants in the cellblocks. We could have done it, too."

As more and more men headed upstairs to the Instigators' Cell, the meeting spilled across the catwalk to cellblock 3. There, says Pawlowski, "People stared for awhile at Bunch's bunk, then began breaking the iron rungs off the bunks to use as weapons. We broke windows, overturned bunks, threw things, a couple of people tried to get a good fire going. . . . Sgt. Morales came up, but he was afraid to try and break it up. He went and got Woodring and five or six more guards. Woodring stood by the door and yelled, 'I want you men to stop this right now.' Harrington, who was closest to the door, said, 'How come you killed Bunch?' Woodring took him and threw him down the stairs. They put him in the box (one of four tiny segregation cells) with a dislocated shoulder.

"I went up to Woodring next. He was ordering everybody to move back, stand by the bunks. He shoved me and said, 'Get back.' I pushed his hands off and said, 'Don't you touch me!' He grabbed me and pushed me down the stairs. I sort of caught my balance on the landing, but Sgt. Yamauchi pushed me the rest of the way."

Woodring then ordered the men to start cleaning up the debris. Joe Stephens, a black man from Oakland who knew and admired Huey Newton, turned to his fellow prisoners and said: "You were right to tear this place up. You got a right to protest about a dude being shot. If you clean it all up now, you're going back on yourselves." Stephens was imme-

diately sent to the box for this remark. His detention there for
the next few days deprived the ten black prisoners of their
most dynamic leader—and the only one who was on good
terms with the whites.

Since there weren't enough boxes to lock up all the men
involved in this outbreak, Woodring made a shrewd move to
take the others out of action. He listed the violations they had
committed—Kight, for instance, was told he had incited to
riot, participated in a riot, destroyed government property,
disobeyed a lawful order and showed disrespect to an NCO—
but promised not to press charges if the men would cool it.
This kept a number of activists—including Jack Ortez, a leader of the Chicano prisoners—from taking part in the subsequent protest.

The official announcement of Bunch's death was made by
the stockade commander, Capt. Robert Lamont, at a Friday
afternoon formation. Lamont said a preliminary investigation
showed that Bunch was trying to escape, and the shooting,
therefore, was justified. He also announced that the stockade
chaplain would hold a memorial service the next day.

"Very few people went to this," Pawlowski says, "because
we knew it was complete hypocrisy. At that very formation
Woodring and Yamauchi had gone around ripping off our
armbands—some of us had dyed them black with shoe polish
as a way of mourning. And Woodring made a joke about
Bunch's death. He said, 'Well, one guy made it, one got
zapped. That means you all have a 50-50 chance. There's the
gate.' Cohen, a guard, said he wished he'd shot Bunch so he
could get transferred to Fort Dix. We heard that the guard
had already been court-martialed and fined a dollar for the
shell—so any other prosecution would be double jeopardy—
and transferred to a post of his choice. And, of course, we
knew from Lindy and others on the detail that the killing
wasn't justified, that the guard hadn't called 'Halt.' We also
knew from the way Bunch always acted, talking to himself,
that he belonged in a hospital to begin with. In fact, that
morning he begged Raines [the employment NCO] not to
send him out on a shotgun detail. I guess he felt this suicide
impulse and was afraid, you know."

Mather adds, "Another reason we had to do something was that there were others in the stockade who seemed as bad off as Bunch. There was a kid named Ferris who used to lie on his bunk all the time, brushing cobwebs from in front of his eyes. He said he was brushing the cobwebs away so he could see. The FBI brought him to the stockade with a note from his doctor saying he had to have his thorazine. Woodring refused to give it to him because the prescription on the bottle was from a civilian, it wasn't an Army prescription. There were a lot of sick people: Fields, Lee, Reidel all slashed themselves to ribbons. Heaston, too. Osczepinski kept talking about cutting out his eyes with a razor blade."

On Sunday, October 13, Terry Hallinan, a young, forceful civil liberties lawyer, came to the stockade to visit a client, Randy Rowland, a C-O who had gone AWOL from Fort Lewis, Wash., and had turned himself over to military police after the October 12 GIs and Veterans March for Peace in San Francisco. A long line of prisoners formed to see Hallinan — and from this episode stemmed the Army's charge that he was the outside agitator who in fact initiated the mutiny.

"What happened," Pawlowski recalls, "is that Hallinan said a group of lawyers in the Bay Area were willing to handle GIs' cases. This news had a magic effect — but it had absolutely nothing to do with the sit-down, which we had been discussing for days. You see, there'd been a vicious circle that kept you from getting a lawyer. In the stockade you couldn't write to anyone but family [according to Army rules], yet a lawyer couldn't come unless he had a letter from you, requesting him. That night I went around asking people if they wanted a civilian lawyer. Everyone said yes. You felt — everybody did — that a civilian lawyer was the key to getting out, a miracle worker.

"Because everybody wanted a lawyer, because almost a hundred guys had signed a letter Rupert was sending to his congressman, because the blacks were talking very tough, we thought just about everybody was going to take part in whatever we decided on. We held a sort of meeting in cellblock 3 that Sunday night. It wasn't a real meeting with a chairman or anything, just a bunch of people sitting around on the bunks, on the floor, leaning against the wall, trying to figure out what to do. We weren't allowed to see the regulations on stockades, but we had a contraband copy, and X [a prisoner yet to be sentenced] went through it, marking off the ways in which the Presidio stockade broke the Army's own rules. Everybody would get up and tell about the things that had happened to them. Finally I started writing some down. That's how I got to be spokesman," Pawlowski says.

"I wrote down the grievances and an example after every one. First, of course, we wanted an investigation of the Bunch killing and a psychological test for the guards. Man, they had some sick guards there. Raines took tranquilizers all the time. He was so high-strung, he used to scream instead of talk. Damaged his throat. He was transferred to stockade duty straight from Vietnam, no rest. Woodring drank a lot and he was a mean drunk. I smelled alcohol on his breath that day he pushed me down the stairs. Cohen told us he dreamed he was an SS trooper. The psychiatrist gave him a compassionate leave. Whether or not he really dreamed that, he did break one guy's back.

"We wanted an end to shotgun work details. We wanted the stockade brought up to the Army's own regulations. We wanted adequate time and facilities for visits. We wanted an end to discrimination—two guards, Myer and Luchi, really hated the blacks. And of course we wanted our constitutional rights."

How come the blacks didn't join?

"There were a couple of reasons," Mather thinks. "First, we had decided to be non-violent and they weren't exactly into non-violence. Second, they figured if they were in the group, when the MPs came it wouldn't be just a peaceful arrest, it would be gas or billyclubs or something. They also figured they'd get punished worse."

Blake adds, "I know some of them wanted to, but they had decided that whatever they did, they'd do it all together. Maybe a few were just chickenshit. Some white guys were certainly chickenshit." He turns to punch Kight on the arm. Kight's arm says, "Born to raise hell." He's a biker, very tough and very together. He asks about the fighting in Berkeley. "Is this *it*, man? There are ten thousand of us up here. Is it time for us to righteously return?"

"Even so," Mather concludes about the blacks, "they left it tentative till the last minute. If most of the white prisoners were going out, they would have, too."

As the list of complaints was being compiled Sunday night before the "mutiny," the exact form of the demonstration was still undecided. A few men still wanted to take the prisoners' compound. (Several black veterans of the Long Binh jail uprising had come through the Presidio stockade, and their story was retold as a possible plan of action.) At the other extreme was Pawlowski, who thought everybody should take off their clothes and refuse to cooperate with stockade officials until the grievances were acted on. The idea of sitting in a circle and singing "We Shall Overcome" had been obvious all weekend. "That's the classical way you have a demonstration." Mather observes. "We all had seen it on TV. No one had to suggest it."

When the course of action was finally settled—long after many of the participants had drifted back to their own cellblocks—Mather snuck across the compound to Building 1212, the low-security barracks, to relay the news. "It's ironic," he says, "that the guys in 1212 decided not to take part because Dounis and Jones argued against it. They were peacers—resisters—and highly respected. They thought it just wasn't worth the risk; and since they were political, lots of people took their word. Of course, I was in for the same thing." (Mather, George Dounis and Chuck Jones were among the "Nine for Peace"—nine members of the Armed Forces who chained themselves inside a Haight Street church in June 1968 to protest the war.)

Not the smallest irony of the case is that two of the most highly political prisoners had argued against the action; but in the way it is happening from Telegraph Avenue to Mifflin Street, the "street people" took the initiative against the restraining advice of the old Movement hands.

"Yes," Lindy Blake says, "we *were* street people. That was our identity in the stockade. Some of us in the twenty-

seven had even known each other when we were AWOL in
the Haight."

The prisoners' plan was for people to answer "Here" all
together as a group as soon as the first of the names was
called at work formation. Then everyone would move out and
sit in a circle. Many of the prisoners had stayed up all night,
and tension hung thick at breakfast; there was a vicious fight
in which one man's jaw was broken. Mather and Pawlowski
had reason to hope, until the last minute, that about one-
hundred men — 80 percent of the population — would join the
demonstration. "But only eight or nine people yelled 'Here,' "
Mather remembers in anguish. "It was terrible: 'Here' . . .
'Here.' . . . I moved out, and then I looked behind me and
there were about twenty men starting to move. Wow! I felt
better. . . . But I still feel that the first bad moment, when
everybody wavered, convinced the majority not to take part."

"When we sat down," says Pawlowski, "it was really a
beautiful instant. People were finally resisting, were finally
getting together and accomplishing something. For me it was
a moment of liberation. We'd been so impotent, so uptight.
Now we weren't just going along with everything, we were
resisting. It was a wonderful feeling, singing. Woodring was
shouting, 'Get back in line, get back in line.' But we were
louder."

Did they expect to be charged with mutiny?

"No," says Mather. "We figured the stockade was such a
scandal they'd want to hush it up. 'Go back to your barracks,
things'll be improved. . . .' "

Kight adds, "Hell, if I knew it was going to be such a big
thing I would have joined — even with all that time hanging
over me. Yeah, I definitely would have gone out there if I
knew it was going to be a *mutiny*."

June 9–16, 1969

The Future
of Desertion
Fred Gardner

Three American deserters were informally and illegally de-
ported from Canada in mid-January. "They were simply kidnapped by the RCMP (Royal Canadian Mounted Police),"
according to Don Rosenbloom, a young Vancouver lawyer
who pressed for an investigation of the episode. "It emerged
at the hearing that the RCMP have a 'gentleman's agreement'
with your FBI to hunt these kids down. It's contrary to official Canadian policy, of course. Yet the people at the Committee [to Aid American War Objectors] tell me it happens all
the time."

John Kreeger, Billy Leonard and Earl Hockett, Californi-
ans on active duty in the U.S. Army, came to Vancouver on
their Christmas leaves, intending to stay. They heard that
jobs for the unskilled could be found only in the East (such is
the nature of hard times: in Montreal you hear that they need
loggers and quarrymen in the West) and began hitching that
way. After one ride, in a town called Bridal Falls, they were
detained by police and escorted to the Huntingdon-Sumas

border station. A Canadian immigration official named K. A. Smith called the U.S. Shore Patrol to come get them. Kreeger tried to convince the Shore Patrol cop that he was Canadian, by improvising a song he claimed was the national anthem: "O, Canada, I love thee, it's so free, you don't have to go in no Ar-my. . . ." It didn't work. Throughout the ride to the Mt. Vernon, Wash., police station he and his buddies swayed from side to side, hoping to tip the van. "It had a narrow wheel base," he reminisces. And then, when the Shore Patrolman parked and went into the station to announce his catch, they busted out. The others were caught, but Kreeger made it back to Canada. In March, under pressure from some of Rosenbloom's friends in the Canadian New Democratic Party, the Manpower and Immigration Department called a judicial inquiry into the affair. The story drew wide attention. I heard a group of deserters discussing it in Vancouver, bemused at the random way in which the press seizes on issues. "We get vamped on all the time," said an ex-Marine nicknamed Ozzie, "but usually we're invisible." An ex-sailor then ran down the story of Seaman James D. Autry, imprisoned at the First Naval District Headquarters Correctional System in Boston. He had been kidnapped by Canadian immigration authorities in October 1969, but the case was not publicized.

* * *

The more political Americans in Canada have been considering the whole question of *visibility* recently. At present, the Americans are physically spread out—and in many cases, strung out. Speed freaks from the States have joined the drunks on the sidewalks of Gastown, Vancouver's Bowery. Americans have moved into the old immigrant sections of Montreal and Toronto, and one sees an occasional head shop among the Greek restaurants and Portuguese bakeries and Ukranian tapestry displays. But the vast majority have gone off in search of work and have not kept in touch with the various committees that help deserters. This is not surprising, since the committees are geared almost exclusively to helping newcomers get settled. The largest operation, run by the Toronto Anti-Draft Programme (TADP), provides job tips, housing information and advice on how to obtain landed-im-

migrant status. The Vancouver Committee to Aid War
Objectors and the Montreal Council to Aid War Resisters are
service-oriented analogs of the TADP. They distribute the
Toronto group's excellent "Manual for Draft Age Immigrants
to Canada" and collect practical lore which is of use to applicants for landed status. The Vancouver Committee, for example, had pegged K. A. Smith as a particularly vicious character long before his involvement in the kidnapping of Kreeger et al., and used to advise people not to cross the border at
Huntingdon during his shift.

Working parallel to the counseling groups is the American
Deserters Committee, which has offices in Montreal and
cadre in Toronto, Vancouver and elsewhere. The ADC as-
pires to be the political forum through which Americans in
Canada can define their own needs and goals. Its staff members do not put down the other committees as do-gooders;
they understand the worth of getting people housing, jobs and
help with immigration procedure; they, too, run a hostel and
provide a nitty-gritty orientation talk for newcomers. But the
ADC people want—for themselves and their constituents—to
retain their political identity as Americans. The objective of
their counseling is not a smooth adjustment to Canada, but
continued opposition to the war and confrontation with the
mother country. They do not see Canada as a haven but as a
waystation on the long march, a potential Yenan.

It is the ADC people in particular who now question the
value of remaining inconspicuous. They realize that you can't
organize anybody if you can't reach them (in the most literal
sense). But they're in a terrible bind. "We haven't kept records," explained Dave Beauchene at the ADC's small storefront office in Montreal, "because we don't want to make the
FBI's job easier. They could close out their files on hundreds
of men if they knew who was here. Why should we do them
that favor? Let 'em keep searching. . . ." Beauchene's group
had a brush with infiltrators this winter, exposed and expelled
them. The provocateurs, true to the book, formed a rival
group, but it soon folded under the weight of its own absurdi-
ty. "Anyway," Beauchene concludes, "we can figure out
roughly how many deserters and resisters are up here. It var-

ies with the weather, but say we handle six a day; Toronto, twelve; Vancouver, eight. . . . We figure that for every man who gets in touch with us, one doesn't. . . ." Beauchene's guess is that there are 60,000 draft-age Americans in Canada, with resisters outnumbering deserters by ten to one. Other ADC people reach the same conclusion. "To find out how many draft resisters are in Toronto," Dennis Jolly advised, "count the handlebar moustaches in Toronto."

Canadian immigration and U.S. Selective Service sources would put the total around 12,000. And the Army contends that there are only several hundred deserters in Canada. But whatever the sum, it is ironic that the deserters and draft resisters remain inconspicuous because nothing could serve the U.S. government's purposes better. Richard Nixon certainly doesn't want the moral pressure of 50,000 — or even 10,000 — young exiles weighing on the national conscience.

* * *

It is not only fear of infiltration that prevents the deserters and resisters from proclaiming themselves, getting a sense of their true numbers, and announcing their strategic goals. There is also the fear that Canadian immigration policy would change the minute the United States feels a threat from the north. The decision to grant landed-immigrant status to deserters, announced by Prime Minister Trudeau's Minister of Manpower and Immigration in May 1969, was a political coup for the prime minister. Trudeau stands for the quickest and fullest integration of the Canadian and U.S. economies. By seizing on the dramatic but fiscally insignificant issue of desertion as a way of showing off his independence, he covered his political weak flank. Trudeau has not wedded himself to the liberal immigration policy by subsequent statements, nor has he offered Americans the preferable status of humane asylum. Thus the fear lingers that if push came to shove with the State Department, the mod young prime minister would withdraw landed-immigrant status as opportunistically as he granted it. This same anxiety, incidentally, prevents the American exiles from forming any alliances with the New Democratic Party in the West or the separatists in Quebec — alliances which would be logical around such issues as U.S. corporate penetration of Canada, Canada's economic complicity in the Vietnamese war, and Canadian imperialism, which is particularly blatant in the West Indies.

Yet another factor militating against organization is the individual experience of the deserter and the draft resister. Men who have been on the lam develop deep-grained habits of inconspicuousness. When your survival has depended on successful hiding, you don't proclaim yourself just because the ADC says you're 60,000 strong. Ex-soldiers, moreover, have an explicable fear of being used, manipulated by bureaucracy or set up for danger in someone else's crusade; so they don't relate easily to an organization like the ADC, even though the vast majority approve its purposes. "Soldiers are the most over-organized people in the world," a fellow named Tip warned an organizer shortly before he deserted from Fort Carson last fall. I didn't see him hanging around any ADC offices, solid anti-imperialist though he is.

How can we now end the physical fragmentation and the legacy of fear that has kept deserters from getting a sense of their potential strength? One way would be to develop institutions that bring people together in a low-risk situation. My mind runs not to coffeehouses, but a summer camp, an efficient farm, a Judy Collins concert, a free university or speakers program featuring Movement academics up from the States: Each of these undertakings would give people a glimpse of one another, a sense of their true numbers and a hint that problems they have been trying to solve individually might best be solved collectively. A number of the Americans in Canada are keen to proceed with such projects. The ADC has called a conference for the start of June, at which an estimated one hundred deserters and resisters will draft some kind of manifesto around their needs and goals. Representatives of stateside Movement organizations have been invited. Their support is wanted, but the exiles are not optimistic that it will be forthcoming. For years now the committees have operated hand-to-mouth, virtually abandoned by the American Left. The ADC press releases have not been picked up by the underground press. There have been no speeches or concerts or love-ins organized on their behalf, and almost no money channeled toward the ADC. (Clergy and Laymen

Concerned About Vietnam raised some recently, but they disbursed it through an apolitical Canadian church group.) In fact, there has been considerable criticism of those who go to Canada—by Resistance spokesmen such as Joan Baez and by organizers within the GI movement. I have even heard coffeehouse staff members speak bitterly about deserters, angry that they had not stuck around to circulate the petition (or whatever the current on-base organizing effort may have been).

* * *

GI organizers should re-examine the question of desertion, if for no other reason than that the GI movement itself is at a tactical impasse. This is how that impasse developed:

In the fall of 1967, when Howard Levy was in the unused officers' wing of the Fort Jackson Army Hospital confinement facility (prior to his transfer to Leavenworth), the GIs who used to visit him, and thousands of others across the country, wished there were something they could do, *short of jail or exile*, to express their own anti-war sentiments. As one of them put it then, "It's not just that I don't have Levy's guts; it's that you can't build a whole movement of martyrs. I don't mind being a martyr, but I'd rather be an unknown guy within a movement." The Fort Jackson GIs finally did hit upon a tactic enabling them to involve thirty-five men: the anti-war meditation at the post chapel. All the anti-war gestures devised that year—newspapers, union meetings, rap sessions at service clubs, political meetings in the barracks, off-post marches, anti-war rallies at coffeehouses or in parks—were aimed similarly, at creating the mass movement that jail or exile could not achieve. These tactics, properly described as dissent, were not employed by men who thought that a march or a petition was the be-all and the end-all of resistance. The anti-war GIs hoped that the relatively safe actions would involve growing numbers of men, and that when hundreds and then thousands found themselves in opposition to the war, the vision of their own collective strength would enable them to plan and carry out heavier acts of resistance, acts that would tangibly undermine the war effort: mass refusal to train or fight in Vietnam.

The brass understood this threat and decided to crush dissent before the hundreds had turned into thousands. In the spring of 1969, the Department of the Army drafted "guidelines on dissent," providing commanders with legal ways they could punish protesters. These guidelines were revised by the Defense Department — at the urging of Mendel Rivers and the Pentagon's manpower chief, Roger Kelly — so as to de-emphasize the constitutional restraints on commanders and add to their repressive options. As a result of the DoD directive, soldiers can no longer distribute their anti-war papers on post. Having two copies of a paper in your possession is proof of intent-to-distribute. A soldier named Wade Carson is now serving six months in the Fort Lewis, Wash., stockade for precisely this crime.

In addition to the repressive legislation, the brass can use an extra-legal trump card called "punitive reassignment." Without going through the trouble of a court-martial — which also entails a public record — a commander can phone the Pentagon and put a man on "hot levee" for another duty station. Depending on how vindictive the officer involved, the assignment can be to Germany, or a stateside post, or to Vietnam. At Fort Jackson this spring, a bright, honest soldier named Bill Mackey, assigned by Military Intelligence to infiltrate the GI movement, instead joined the staff of *Short Times* and told how he had been used and coerced. He was immediately reassigned to Vietnam and is due to ship from Oakland on May 23.

Suffice it to say that union organizers, coffeehouse patrons and other anti-war GIs face this same kind of treatment day-in, day-out. The brass is waging total war on GI dissenters but, in the manner to which they've grown accustomed in Asia, it is a hidden and deceitful war. The GI movement, finding its institutions under attack, has been trying in the past year to defend itself; unfortunately, the fight has been conducted on the enemy's battlefield: the courts. This rearguard fight looks like a loser. Of course we should not fold up whenever attacked; that would be a fatal display of impotence. And there are times when the movement must demonstrate its professional competence — by building a splendid coffeehouse or publishing a superior paper. But the institutions of dissent have no value beyond the sum of their functions, and if we can't have a coffeehouse we can still have a bookstore, a staff house open to GIs, a free university, a be-in at the park. If men are being busted for distributing lithographed, easily recognizable papers, it might be best to go back to mimeographed broadsheets (which are often punchier). The irrefragable fact is that the forms of dissent developed in the past two years are no longer safer than the acts of witness that touched off the GI movement. Nor is dissent any safer than desertion. We must question, therefore, whether dissent is the likeliest way to build an anti-imperialist movement among soldiers.

Judging from the history of how armies fail, it appears that disintegration, not dissent, may characterize the final crisis. There has never been an army that fell apart through the exercise of civil liberties; but there have been some big ones cracked by mass desertion. As a tactic, desertion has the underrated virtue of simplicity. It is the archetypal anti-war act.

Why have people in our movement written it off as an apolitical gesture? Granted, not everyone who refuses orders for Vietnam does so because he opposes the illegal, immoral war. The majority of men I've spoken to in Canada—out of perhaps 200 in the past two years—do not give the wrongness of the war as their main reason for splitting. But somewhere in their list of reasons comes a phrase such as "and what's this war all about, anyway?" Soldiers who desert have acted politically whether or not they say so out front. Any glib son-of-a-bitch can express a noble motive; but few people act so directly against the war as the soldier who refuses to take part. It is snotty of American radicals to put them down as escapists. Escape from oppression is a political act; not the highest form of struggle, obviously, but political just the same. The GI movement, like the women's movement, is rooted in real oppression and operates on principles of self-interest. Maintaining an empire might be fine for most other Americans, but it's not worth it to the soldiers who pay with body, mind and soul. That's what the GI movement is all about. To criticize deserters because they merely want to stay alive is inhumane; to dismiss them as apolitical is not only wrong, but has the elements of a self-fulfilling prophecy.

The way out of a tactical impasse is to develop new tactics, never yielding the initiative. We should not think of desertion, mechanically, as an alternative to on-base organizing; that's like saying the forehand is alternative to the backhand, and therefore a tennis player should only rely on one. The fact is, desertion and dissent are two aspects of the same movement and re-inforce one another. It's no coincidence that the desertion rate shot up in the spring of 1968, just at the time that on-base organizing became widespread (and in the wake of the Tet offensive).

At present, men are reluctant to engage in on-base organizing because they don't want to wind up in jail, Vietnam, or an exile that would effectively end their political lives. That's why the success of the GI movement hinges on whether or not the deserter community can begin to thrive. If the ADC had the resources to run a stable and efficient office; if they had a large collective farm just north of the border where newcomers could go to get their heads and bodies together; if they could put on a Judy Collins or Arlo Guthrie concert every month; or sponsor Carl Oglesby or Angela Davis or Roxanne Dunbar speaking on the state of affairs here in the United States—not only the desertion rate but GI dissent would pick up. The physical and moral presence of thousands of American exiles would be felt within this country. Their parents could be organized as a counterpoise to those Air Force wives Mr. Ross Perot flies around. Every college could be turned into an underground railway station, giving campus politics a heavier anti-imperialist content and a grounding in reality.

One could speculate endlessly about what the deserters might achieve once they get organized. A minimum goal would be to make the brass rue the day they decided to outlaw dissent.

May 4–11, 1970

Part Four
The Crisis
of Empire

The American system of political and social organization—the "empire"—defines and controls people's lives both within and outside the walls of the nation. "Imperialism" became a slogan of opposition as people on the outside and inside—Vietnamese and American blacks, laborers and students—began to fight for their own definitions and their own controls.

World Cop

Joe Stork

Exposés of U.S.-aided torture and terror in Saigon's prisons have created a predictably brief flurry of liberal breast-beating and editorializing; but the exposure is not likely to challenge the U.S. policies and programs that have openly supported and financed police repression in Vietnam for the last fifteen years. One result of the belief that most wars in the world today are "police actions" is AID's Office of Public Safety, dedicated to international police-military cooperation and the development of national police forces as the "first line of defense" against existing or potential insurgencies. Con Son Prison is part of its program for "prisoner rehabilitation"; Public Safety is a Third World – wide program to foster "an atmosphere of confidence in law and order" – as its own propaganda proclaims.

Americans who were in Saigon in the late fifties under the Michigan State – CIA police advisory mission noted at the

(Research for this chapter was also provided by Mariette Wickes.)

time that opposition politicians were frequently carted off to Con Son. The U.S. government's own figures state that at least 70 percent of the prisoner population throughout Vietnam is political, and another 9 percent is "military" — that is, POWs. It has been said for years that, to know the status of the non-communist political opposition, Con Son was the place to go.

Both Congress and the U.S. press corps in Saigon have ignored persistent attempts over the past year by tortured student leaders and others to bring public attention to the systematic political repression and terrorism that mark the staying power of Thieu, Ky and U.S. forces. Instead, they took the word of Saigon's U.S. Public Safety Advisor Frank Walton, who declared Con Son to be "a correctional Institution worthy of higher ratings than some prisons in the United States" with "enlightened and modern administration."

Walton, former Los Angeles deputy chief of police, with a reputation for being hard on minorities, is one of 225 Public Safety Advisors with the Agency for International Development in Vietnam. AID says that "all have been carefully screened and trained to undertake a job that requires considerable courage, stability, resourcefulness and initiative in order to rapidly adjust to the daily strain . . . inherent in this unique operating environment." Walton's resourcefulness was most strained by his unsuccessful attempts to persuade two visiting congressmen to visit the prison curio shop rather than the "tiger cages" that were clearly the most unique part of his environment.

One of those congressmen, Rep. Augustus Hawkins, has demanded to know what in Walton's record recommended him for the job of advising the Saigon National Police. He should have the opportunity to meet the other 224 of Walton's Public Safety colleagues. Persons who have spent years in Vietnam in the provinces say that Public Safety Advisors are racist and that Walton is typical of the group. The advisors generally manage to alienate even their Vietnamese police "counterparts." A large number come from Los Angeles, Oakland and several Southern U.S. cities. They are usually retired or close to it, and they view AID as a chance to get away from home, pick up some money, enjoy the amenities of PX life, and do their part in the war against international communism.

* * *

Public Safety is the AID program most fully incorporated into the military part of the pacification program under the reorganization of 1967, and it is also the program that initiated the direct and full-scale involvement of the United States in Vietnam as far back as 1955. Both before the major troop buildup in 1965 and now under Nixon's Vietnamization game, Public Safety is regarded as a key program in defeating the NLF. In 1969, nearly $20 million was budgeted for Public Safety by AID; in addition there were sizable contributions from the Pentagon and CIA.

The original involvement of the United States after the Geneva Accords was the Michigan State University group brought in at the behest of John Foster Dulles and facilitated by AID's John Hannah, then president of MSU, to train, equip and otherwise modernize Pres. Ngo Dinh Diem's police forces. The largest section in the group was instructed to deal with Diem's Special Branch, the equivalent of the FBI, and these Americans were CIA operatives. The program continued under these auspices until 1959, by which time its proportions were so large that the MSU cover no longer fooled anyone, and it didn't much matter any more what people thought. The Public Safety program was taken over by AID's predecessor, the International Cooperation Administration. It developed as the main support for the regular National Police and also served to legitimate large shipments of arms and telecommunications equipment. The CIA operations with the special police and reconnaissance units continued, but directly out of the embassy, avoiding even the nominal supervision of AID.

The main responsibilities of the Public Safety Division have been in the areas of "resources control," "population control" and "national identification." "Resources control" means the interdiction of NLF supplies: arms, food or medicine. The Public Safety Advisors are assigned to work with Vietnamese counterparts on the national, regional, provincial and local levels, and on all levels close coordination is necessary with both ARVN and the U.S. military. (As part of the most crucial "non-military" program in Vietnam, the advisors also serve to monitor local activities and channel pertinent information from other AID "team members" on health, education and similar projects to the military fixed and mobile checkpoints. And a special Water Police capability has been developed.)

In a people's war, the main resource to be controlled is people, and AID says that the number arrested for moving illegally has steadily mounted. This includes those "moving illegally" back to their homes after being forcibly removed to "strategic hamlets" or their equivalents. In the Vietnamization scheme, population control is important. The strategy of free-fire zones and saturation bombing of the countryside forces people by the millions into the cities, where, it is presumed, they can be more easily controlled and kept separated from the revolutionary forces. (The population control program is to see that they move where they are told and stay put.)

"An integral part of the population and resources control program," says a Public Safety brochure, "is identification of the populace." Since 1957, Saigon has promulgated a series of laws, at the Americans' request, requiring all persons to carry IDs. "Through the passage of time and the exigencies of the struggle," some AID bureaucrat writes wistfully, cards have been progressively mutilated, defaced, or otherwise "compromised." The latest card project was begun in 1967 and, besides lowering the registration age to fifteen, requires photographs, fingerprints, biographic data, "plus greatly improved tamper resistance." Such information is the basis for the intelligence and political data by which the Special Police isolates NLF cadres or, as AID puts it, "separates the bad guys from the good." The five classifications for citizens of South Vietnam are: (1) "element of good will"; (2) "fence-sitting: escapists"; (3) "known to have had relations with the VC"; (4) "dissatisfied citizen"; (5) "hoodlum or crook." AID cites "the past and continuing VC efforts to frustrate registration efforts by ambushing registration teams and conducting anti-registration propaganda campaigns."

Besides providing a multi-million-dollar contract for Systems Development Corporation of Santa Monica, Calif., the population control program frequently provides the night-to-night entertainment for the Public Safety Advisor assigned to the hamlet level. Every so often he relieves his boredom by rousing a counterpart to two and conducting house-to-house no-knock searches for contraband and contra-people; he can always find a few visiting relatives without ID cards or proper authorization to travel.

Much of the emphasis in the Public Safety program has been on organizing and managing national telecommunications and identification and control systems. While it doesn't aid much in the struggle with the NLF, the increased intelligence and outright control prevent the emergence of any independent non-Communist political opposition. As far as the prisons are concerned, AID admits that "the [Saigon] GVN interest in prisoner rehabilitation could be described as minimal." Nearly a million dollars of Public Safety assistance was granted for this purpose in 1968, but most of the funds were used to construct new, soundproof interrogation centers in each province. In more than a few instances, the Public Safety Advisor's telephone has been "borrowed" for use in electrode interrogation, where the live wires are applied to the testicles.

The Public Safety Advisor plays a limited direct role in the counter-insurgency and "neutralization" aspects of the police and para-military work. He serves more as a supporting fixture than a crucial component. The heavier stuff has been handled, until recently, through the CIA operative on the provincial level who holds the office of Special Assistant to the Ambassador (OSA). Besides channeling intelligence gathered by the Special Police to the embassy and military headquarters, the OSA man directly advises the Special Branch and chooses targets and actions, based on that intelligence, for the Provisional Reconnaissance Units. These PRUs are elite, highly paid, and have provided the manpower for the notorious "Phoenix" terror campaign, designed to "neutralize" the NLF infrastructure. Each PRU has his own American — as intelligence analyst and tactical advisor.

Operating between the Special Branch and the PRUs on the one hand, and the routine support operations of the National Police on the other, are the Field Forces, who engage in light combat operations, perimeter security and crowd control. The Field Forces were formed around the nucleus of Diem's crack Combat Police (equipped and trained by Michigan State), and are funded directly by AID and the Department of Defense. The "advisory" positions are filled by contract and loans from the military. Former and present Green Berets are often employed in that capacity. The role of the Field Forces has been developed by Nixon's favorite foreigner, British anti-guerrilla expert Robert Thompson, with the help of Australians and Malaysians as well as Americans. The Field Forces are described in one AID memo as the "primary action arm of the police intelligence system." They are supposed to maintain security in those areas under nominal government control after military pacification, but in the past their most frequent employment has been in crowd and riot control in the cities, notably Saigon and Hué. It was the Field Forces who were airlifted by the United States to Hué to put down the popular student and Buddhist rebellion there in 1966, thereby saving the regime of Premier Ky. They were also the ones who invaded and wrecked Saigon pagodas during different periods of open Buddhist opposition.

Under the Vietnamization scenario, the Saigon army has had to go out into the countryside, and the defensive security role is being handled increasingly by the Field Forces. Crowd control and riot situations fall to the National Police, who have shown their adeptness on several occasions recently by beating back a parade of crippled war veterans and by trapping and gassing a peace demonstration that included a delegation of Americans. The increasing efficiency and capacity for brutality that the National Police have displayed can be largely accredited to the money, equipment, arms and advisors provided by the imperial Office of Public Safety.

* * *

Public Safety operations in Vietnam have been largely obscured from publicity by the more blatant military operations. Throughout the rest of the Third World, and notably in Latin

America, the Office of Public Safety plays a similarly low-profile but proportionally much more crucial role in promoting the effective counter-insurgent role of national police forces in defending U.S. and local elite interests. Through the activities of the OPS, the notion of the United States as world policeman is transformed from a metaphor to a reality.

OPS traces itself back to the first Indochina programs in 1955, but the United States has engaged in a police-support role at least since the end of World War II, particularly in Germany, Japan, and the Truman Doctrine countries, Turkey and Iran. From rather humble, supplemental beginnings, the Office of Public Safety has attained a special status within the AID administration, with considerable autonomy and powers of review over the other AID programs as they relate to political developments.

Public Safety's unique status and privilege is rooted in the shift under the Kennedy brothers to developing an invincible counter-insurgency capability for coping with wars of national liberation. Institutions and programs from the Green Berets to the Peace Corps were initiated under the premise that the struggle against international communism would be lost or won in the arena of the Third World. After communism lost, "internal stability" became a typical watchword of the New Frontier. At the foreign assistance hearings in 1965, AID director David Bell sketched the rationale for OPS:

"Plainly, the United States has very great interests in the creation and maintenance of an atmosphere of law and order under humane, civil concepts and control. When there is a need, technical assistance to the police of developing nations to meet their responsibilities promotes and protects these U.S. interests."

The "humane, civil concepts" advocated by AID are purely utilitarian. During the recent "election" campaign in the Dominican Republic, dozens were killed on the streets by the police. Last month the Organization of American States meeting was moved to Washington because of the propensity of the Dominican police to shoot into crowds, violating the Public Safety maxim against providing "martyrs" to the Left. In Colombia, on the other hand, sophisticated telecommunications and gifts, including police helicopters, helped prevent opposition crowds from getting out of hand in a "professional" manner. Volatile situations around an election were handled effectively to accomplish the same political end: the preservation of the U.S.-supported regime and the maintenance of a "favorable investment climate." Out in the countryside, official violence operates discreetly with the help of human sensors, mobile strike units and other Vietnam spin-offs to eliminate the burgeoning guerrilla movement. (Caring enough to use the very best, the Justice Department is already employing the human sensors along the Mexican border in the campaign against pot smuggling and illegal immigration.)

More typical than Colombia is Guatemala, where the prime beneficiaries of law and order are United Fruit and assorted comprador elites. A Mexican journalist describes the Guatemalan police as "aggressive and incompetent," with a basic repertoire of tortures including electric shocks and rubber truncheons. The new Minister of "Gobernación" commented recently that new AID agreements would be welcome in "strengthening our security system and combating delinquency." Under the rubric of Public Safety, AID would have the police become aggressive and competent, and in Venezuela OPS successfully overcame a local tradition that made the police subject to manslaughter charges for shooting students and other "communists."

The strategic import of the Public Safety program is reflected in the Operations Report submitted to Congress after every fiscal year, one of the few documents available to the public which even suggests the existence of the Office of Public Safety. Although the figures given are known to understate the actual expenditures, due to covert funding by the Department of Defense and the CIA, in 1969 (the last year for which figures are available), $35 million was spent by the Office of Public Safety. Of that, $29 million was spent in East Asia. More than half of the rest was spent in Latin America, in the countries most crucial to U.S. corporate interests: Brazil, Dominican Republic, Venezuela, Colombia and Guatemala. In Africa, the pattern is the same, with the Congo, Liberia and Ethiopia getting most of the assistance. The Ethiopian figure is deceptively low, nonetheless, since most of its military and police assistance is channeled by the United States through Israel.

In Brazil, former Public Safety trainees hold positions such as Director of Training or Director of Investigations in several large states. The scope of the program has increased enormously since the pro-U.S. coup in 1964. AID boasts that it has trained over 100,000 police over the same period that the Brazilian economy has been ripped off by U.S. firms, including Hanna Mining, Pfizer Drugs, and Standard Oil. Brazil has been and continues to be one of the largest recipients of Public Safety funds, nearly $8 million since 1959, or more than 20 percent of the total spent in Latin America. The International Commission of Jurists recently accused the regime of "systematic and scientifically developed torture," including "plunging a prisoner's head into buckets of excrement until near suffocation and electric shocks on sensitive parts of the body." While AID claims that "support is not given to dictatorships," former AID administrator Bell considered it "desirable and proper to continue to assist in the improvement of the efficiency of the civilian police force. The police are a strongly anti-communist force right now. For that reason, it is a very important force for us."

In the event of political crisis, large amounts of highly sophisticated equipment, especially telecommunications, vehicles, and lethal and non-lethal armaments, are rushed to Third World countries, sometimes funded by the Department of Defense or the CIA. ("In order to deal with the dynamics of internal security situations." AID administrator Bell explained at another point in his congressional testimony, "the Public Safety program has developed and utilized methods to deliver to threatened countries, in a matter of days, urgently needed assistance, including training, equipment, and technical advice.") This capacity has been exercised several times over the past few months. In both Colombia and the Dominican Republic, rush orders of vehicles and arms were sent down just before their respective elections, in which the United States had a special interest in seeing who won. In the Dominican Republic, Balaguer even used AID trucks to transport his campaign around the country. In South Korea in 1968, demonstrations against the third-term decision of Pres. Chung Hee Park were met with national police vehicles that still had the AID stickers on them.

In actual practice, OPS stresses the need for developing countries to have large amounts of the latest gadgetry. According to a report from a Chief (U.S.) Public Safety Advisor in Venezuela, the host country had spent over a five-year period "the equivalent of some $6 million for U.S.-manufactured items recommended specifically by the Public Safety Advisors." OPS has, in fact, helped to set up a police-industrial network. The Technical Services Division constitutes an important part of OPS's mandate: "the responsibility for developing new equipment and for modifying existing items to meet special field needs." OPS cites its real strategy at congressional hearings: not to give equipment to recipient countries, but to train foreign personnel to need U.S. equipment by standardizing vehicles and electronic gear to require purchases from the United States even after the advisors leave.

Venezuela also affords a glimpse into another feature of the symbiosis between OPS and U.S. business interests overseas. According to a paper written by a former Public Safety Advisor, "The Chief and Deputy Chief Public Safety Advisors meet monthly with security officers of all major oil companies operating in the country and the security officer for the leading mine company." OPS trains Liberian police, who are actually security employees of Firestone Rubber. In Indonesia, any Public Safety assistance is hidden in a general technical assistance budget, but it is worth mentioning that fortunate political prisoners are hired out as chattel labor to the Goodyear plantations there. Last fall in the Dominican Republic, a strike by sugarcane cutters was brutally suppressed by the national police at the behest of the La Romana fields, owned and operated by the Gulf and Western conglomerate.

* * *

One important asset in the campaign to orient Third World police to the United States in ideology — and supplies — is the International Police Academy in Washington, D.C. Due to Robert Kennedy's benevolence after the Bay of Pigs and the independent status of OPS, a special school, the Inter-American Police Academy, was set up in Panama in 1962 (by classified presidential directive), near the Green Beret base at Fort Gulick. The next year it was moved to Washington and appropriately renamed. To date, more than 3,000 carefully screened ranking police officers have gone through a variety of courses that all contain a high dosage of "Marxism" as interpreted by the FBI, as well as technical and administrative training: from setting up a beat system to running through mock riots and demonstrations in the game room known as the Police Operations Control Center.

The general course that most candidates take lasts about three months, is given in English and Spanish, and culminates in an elaborately banal graduation ceremony with the Marine Corps band, celebrities like Maxwell Taylor and William Bundy, and valedictory exhortations to support your international police. Each class presents a trophy or plaque to the academy director as a class memento. The course includes arms training in the basement in one of the finest ranges in the world, according to connoisseurs, CBW training at "a nearby Army installation," three days at the John F. Kennedy School of Special Warfare at Fort Bragg, N.C., and a tour of Washington's own Con Son, Lorton Reformatory. Each student submits a "thesis," which is kept in the IPA library. Like most information about the academy or OPS, such documents, even when unclassified, are unavailable to anyone not working within police circles. The theses are declared inviolable on the grounds of "academic freedom"; it would violate the students' confidences to open them to the public.

Another 2,000 higher-ranking officers have come for special courses, either at IPA, the FBI Academy in Quantico, Va., or specialized university courses in criminalistics, ballistics, and the like. All visitors end their stay with an eight-day bus tour of Middle America. AID assures everyone that "the best majority of the visiting officers find America-in-the-raw of irresistible warmth." Indeed, one of the selling points of the Public Safety program is the claim that 90 percent of the participants come away strongly pro-American. This figure, no doubt, is a statistical average, including one Colombian participant who claimed that he was a "200 percent supporter of the United States."

The director of the International Police Academy is Michael McCann, a former assistant professor in police administration at Indiana University, until he joined the Public Safety program in Iran for several years beginning in 1951. He was in Teheran for the CIA's first successful attempt to subvert a nationalist government. One of the organizers of the coup against Mossadeq was Gen. Norman Schwartzkopf, former head of the New Jersey state police. McCann regards the IPA as an "international forum" for police. A more effusive but accurate AID blurb calls it the "West Point of the police of the non-communist arising world."

McCann's boss is Public Safety Director Byron Engle, a former advertising man turned cop. His first overseas position was with the MacArthur regime in Tokyo, where he was chief police administrator from 1946 to 1955 except for two years in Ankara, Turkey.

Basic direction and overview of OPS and IPA comes from an inter-agency board; besides Engle, it consists of Gen. William Du Puy, special advisor to the Joint Chiefs of Staff on counter-insurgency, representatives from the FBI and the CIA, and the State Department's officer in charge of internal defense policy and politico-military affairs.

Besides channeling ideological and technical training to Third World police, the whole OPS program has provided a laboratory for testing concepts, programs and weapons. General Du Puy, in a graduation address in October 1968, pointed out how well the police-military coordination stressed by the academy has come to be practiced at home: The military now share intelligence on "subversive groups" with the police, he said. After Martin Luther King's assassination, military command posts were set up, in every case, at metropolitan or precinct police stations in the United States. He also cited the incentives of shortened Armed Forces service used to recruit military personnel to join local police forces, and the way that police departments are giving week-long Army training courses in civil disturbance control. Another example of the OPS-fostered police-military partnership is the Civil

Disturbance Steering Committee, which has been meeting weekly after Newark and Detroit in 1967, and is made up of officials from all the military services and the Justice Department. Army teams have been sent to several hundred cities to study with local police street layouts and vital installations. This and other information is stored in the Pentagon's "domestic war room."

The International Police Academy itself has been directly involved in domestic policing. According to a former student, in-service training once included mingling with local and federal counterparts in controlling the "counter-inaugural" demonstrations in Washington in January 1969. Mayor Daley reportedly turned down a request of the State Department to send IPA trainees to Chicago for the Democratic Convention. Another report has it that IPA's Police Operations Control Center was put to domestic use to plot strategy for the Washington police and National Guard during the disorders in response to the closing of Resurrection City (called Insurrection City by OPS officials). In his recommendations to the Kerner Commission in September 1967, Byron Engle recommended the use of chemical munitions as one of "the most effective weapons . . . *if used properly and in quantity*" (his emphasis).

One need not go farther afield than the International Police Academy itself to find a mutually supporting relationship between OPS and a successful corporate elite. The building which houses IPA in Georgetown is rented from O. Roy Chalk for $220,000 per year. (Chalk owns the D.C. Transit Company and built his domestic and foreign business operations on the backs of the capital colony's bus riders—most of them poor and black. The *IPA Review* sometimes donates a commercial to Roy by suggesting that "the participants can ride inexpensive public buses—itself an orientation into American life." Until recently, Chalk owned Trans-Caribbean Airlines. He is a director of International Railways of Central America, which transports the produce of United Fruit Company.)

These ties, while important in their own right, strikingly point up the common interest of the military, the national-security-conscious New Frontiersman, and the traditional robber-businessman in maintaining an identical kind of law and order at home and overseas. Maintenance of the empire demands the same vigilance toward "internal security" in Washington, D.C., Rio de Janeiro, Saigon, Seoul and Santo Domingo. The threat of liberation to one is a threat to all, and the repression of one has lessons for the repression of all. The Kennedys wanted to enforce the stability of the status quo on all the Third World. They succeeded in bringing the tensions and threats of revolution home to the United States.

August 10–17, 1970

Pan Am: Victory Through Air Power

Angus W. McDonald and A. W. McCoy

Without superior air power America is a bound and throttled giant; impotent and easy prey to any yellow dwarf with a pocket knife.　　— LYNDON JOHNSON

Nineteen Pan Am jet clippers plied the skies between the North American mainland and South Vietnam last summer, up to fifty flights a week. Each all-cargo carrier lifts more than 70,000 tons of military cargo to the war zone. On their return, they bring the bodies of the American dead in aluminum caskets.

Most of the top fifty defense contractors sell planes, ships and ammunition to the American military. Pan Am services the machine with transportation. It is the only American line with scheduled service to Vietnam, the largest airline contractor for the Defense Department, and an airline whose experience with imperial adventure is unmatched.

Vietnam is a war of air power. SAC, Air Force and Navy bombers drop the ordnance, but equally important is the lo-

178

gistics. Modern aviation has made it possible for a field commander to receive a high priority item from the factory within seventy-two hours. The Military Air Command (MAC) and "the world's most experienced airline" cooperate closely to link the supply pipeline in the United States with the distant battlefield, for they are mutually supporting parts of a greater whole. Built into the structure of MAC is logistic domination of the Western world. Built into the structure of Pan American World Airways is the will to dominate air routes.

Pan Am has made substantial profits from the war. In 1968 it had $205.7 million in military contracts. Its Pacific division has produced 50 percent of its corporate profit from 1962 to the present, largely because of Pan Am's substantial airlift of troops, cargo, and mail to Vietnam. Military charter accounts directly for about 12 percent of its operating revenues and for a much higher percentage of its profits, since aircraft utilization is higher and expenses lower for military work.

Pan American World Airways is all about air power. Air power was envisioned in 1907 by the prophetic H. G. Wells, nurtured in the minds of biplane fighter pilots like Billy Mitchell, developed by men like Eddie Rickenbacker and Juan Trippe, "proved" in the Battle of Britain, and established by the Enola Gay.

America's control of the air since Hiroshima and its continual planning for another air war have gone hand in hand with development of the Pan Am system into an instrument and participant in that strategy. Pan Am represents the principal instrument of America's international aviation (vastly larger than its nearest competitor, Pan Am serves 111 cities abroad to TWA's 25).

Why is it Pan Am which brings home the bodies? Why is Pan Am consistently able to style itself "the Department of Defense's major civil-commercial airline partner?" Since its earliest days as an outgrowth of the Yale Flying Club, Pan Am has been America's dominant international airline and a major power in U.S. foreign relations.

Juan Terry Trippe, the key figure in the development of Pan Am, was the son of a prominent New York stockbroker. When America entered World War I he became a Navy

pilot. Like Dink Stover, he returned to Yale after the war to
star on the football team, edit the *Graphic*, and found the
Yale Flying Club. In 1922 he quit a job in a brokerage house,
and with some friends from the Yale Flying Club founded
Long Island Airways to fly wealthy New Yorkers to weekend
at their summer estates in the Hamptons. Soon the company's two war surplus aircraft collapsed, and with Cornelius
Vanderbilt Whitney (Yale '22), Trippe gained the backing of
some Boston bankers, created Colonial Airways and won the
first domestic mail contract.

In 1927 Trippe began to realize the potential of the multi-
engine long-distance aircraft for trans-oceanic travel, envision-
ing a New York-to-Florida route linking with a trans-Carib-
bean and Latin American network. It was not a particularly
new idea. As early as 1925 the president of a Colombian
airline had come to Washington to ask permission to fly mail
through the Canal Zone to the United States. The American
official who reviewed the plans found them so promising that
he flatly rejected the Colombian proposal, left public office,
and started a Caribbean airline himself.

Trippe was faced with the problem of three American airlines competing with each other for the same route. When
conservative Boston bankers refused to go beyond New
Haven, Trippe and C. V. Whitney quit Colonial and began to
build Pan Am. They scurried around the New York financial
district and forged an alliance between financiers such as W.
Averell Harriman, John Hay Whitney, William S. Rockefeller, William Vanderbilt, and Robert Lehman (of Lehman
Brothers and United Fruit Co.)—who wanted communications for their growing interests in Latin America—and aircraft manufacturers such as Sherman A. Fairchild, William
A. Boeing and O. M. Keyes of Curtis Aircraft, who needed a
source of growth for their infant industry.

It was Juan Trippe's idea that Pan Am would be the community instrument which would unite all American aviation
interests for international expansion. He flew to Havana and
won exclusive landing rights from dictator Machado. He then
received the first international mail contract, and in October
1927 launched Pan Am's first flight.

Once Trippe had gained a monopoly over the Key West–Havana crossroads and consolidated most of New York's potential airline capital behind him, Pan Am's rise was fast. Trippe married the daughter of Edward R. Stettinius, a J. P. Morgan partner. He then managed to convince the Hoover administration that Pan Am should be "America's chosen instrument" in international air travel.

The government made Pan Am. In 1938, for example, Pan Am's Pacific operations received 78 percent of their revenue from the U.S. Post Office; the Latin American region, 68 percent. Mail contracts were an indirect subsidy. Pan Am also received more than $220 million in direct government subsidies. Hoover's Postmaster-General let it be known that he would tolerate no competition with Pan Am; he forced two U.S. airlines in Latin American to trade valuable equipment to Pan Am for the firm's bloated stock. In Peru, Pan Am put up $500,000 for a 50 percent ownership in Pan American–Grace Airways (now Panagra), with the huge imperial combine W. R. Grace. Pan Am's air rights in Colombia were confirmed in the Kellogg-Olaya pact, the first bilateral air treaty, hastily written one afternoon by Juan Trippe and a helpful State Department official.

In three years, Pan Am had built a vast network of airlines encompassing all of Latin America, purchased vast amounts of expensive equipment, destroyed all of its rivals, and was beginning to make money. In 1934, when the Depression had most domestic airlines on the verge of bankruptcy, Pan Am made a $1.1 million profit. Its Latin American operations were returning a profit of 31 percent on its investment and were financing its push into the Atlantic and Pacific.

But strong American financial control and frequent military intervention had built up tremendous hostility in Latin America. To resolve this problem, Roosevelt replaced direct political control with the indirect economic manipulation of the "Good Neighbor Policy." Indirect controls necessitated much more sophisticated manipulation. As *Fortune* magazine put it (in 1936):

If you want to sell shoes in Ecuador or Brazil or Uruguay, Pan American will collect data for you on prices, competitors, politics and shoe consumption, will offer suggestions as to the best way to exploit the market, and hold your hand when you get into trouble. The imperialist attitude, the world view of things, is no artificial creation on the part of Pan American's management. It rises realistically enough from the fact that Pan Am's business is entirely foreign.

Such spectacular successes did not go unnoticed. Hostile congressional investigations were held, and when they were done, every American airline lost its airmail contracts and had to be reorganized — except Pan Am, which quietly accepted a 10 percent reduction of its rates. Pan Am had broken all the rules, had been the highest bidder for every route, had used its influence to wipe out competitors, and had gotten away with it. Pan Am was now a "great American institution."

* * *

Having conquered Latin America, Pan Am turned to the Pacific. In 1933 it purchased the China National Airways Corporation, formed in 1929 by Curtis-Wright and Chiang Kai-shek's Kuomintang government to save China for American aviation, against British and Dutch competition. Pan Am now began construction of its own transpacific route to integrate the Chinese network into its growing international system. With the assistance of the U.S. Navy, it discovered the existence of two islands the United States was not even sure it owned: Midway and Wake. Pan Am was given landing rights in Hawaii, the Philippines, and Guam; British BOAC was denied them for "reasons of military security." It would have been a violation of the Five-Power Washington Treaty of 1922 for the U.S. Navy to construct airfields on these islands, but Pan Am was not so restricted. On November 22, 1935, the first transpacific flight — by Pan Am — took off from San Francisco Bay, loaded with mail and heavy government subsidy.

The war ripped apart the old limits on American aviation. National and colonial boundaries which had been closed to Pan Am before the war were erased. Pan Am built fifty-three air bases in Latin America and around the world. It expanded its payroll from 4,400 to more than 80,000. In 1943 it earned $126 million for its war services, doing more than 50 percent of all military transport flying. But that success implied dangerous contradictions.

In the pre-war era, air power was the tool of economic interests closely allied with the Department of State, which served as both a helpful partner and an employment service. After the war, Americans were not only worried about international competition but also about international communism, the threat of borders closed and of a great power rising to challenge the American dominion.

Juan Trippe had grandiose plans, but he was willing to compromise Pan Am's monopoly in a special way. He wanted to make Pan Am the core of a "national flag airlines" which would take aggressively to the airways, dominating them with technical achievement and capital investment. Among his spokesmen in the government were Rep. Clare Boothe Luce (R., Conn.), Maine's Sen. Brewster ("the senator from Pan Am") and Sen. Patrick McCarran (R., Nev.), author of the 1938 Civil Aeronautics Act and later a close ally of Sen. Joseph McCarthy. These were the apostles of air power, the narrow nationalist opponents of men like Vice-President Henry Wallace and the coterie of liberal anglophiles surrounding FDR who favored "partnership" in the post-war air.

In her maiden congressional speech in February 1943, Mrs. Luce attacked Wallace's "partnership" approach as "globaloney." Rep. J. William Fulbright, Mrs. Luce's main antagonist in the House, counter-attacked: "The narrow imperialist policy of grab, advocated by the honorable lady, carries with it the seeds of its own destruction."

McCarran introduced the "All-American Flag Line" bill in 1945. Opposition by our British allies and by all the other U.S. airlines eventually caused the bill to be tabled, but the problem became so divisive that it was necessary to call an international aviation conference. The fifty United Nations, members met in Chicago in November 1944, to wrangle over post-war air rights. Juan Trippe's brother-in-law, Edward

Stettinius, Jr., the president of U.S. Steel before the war, became Secretary of State and sabotaged the conference to
Trippe's delight and the dismay of all other airlines. The one
result of Chicago was the creation of the International Air
Transport Association, providing that all international air
pacts have to be unanimously agreed upon. In October 1945,
Pan Am tried to sabotage even that by suddenly announcing a
drastic cut in fares, from $572, New York – London, to $275.
This kind of price cut is standard practice for a company
trying to gain a monopoly. Pan Am would not long fly at
those rates, but no foreign or domestic competitor could fly at
all. The move so badly damaged international harmony that a
second conference was called in 1946 at Bermuda; Pan Am
was boxed by the other seventeen American lines and all foreign ones. A series of fairly strong international air agreements resulted, but were later weakened in Congress by Senators Brewster and McCarran. Pan Am fought on, though
denied by the forces that had brought it into being, the U.S.
government. TWA and American Overseas Airlines (later
absorbed by Pan Am) got European routes, Braniff was given
a competing route in Latin America, and two-bit Northwest-
Orient got a valuable route to Japan via Alaska. In 1947, a
House anti-trust subcommittee heard testimony that Pan Am
had used every means to deny Braniff landing facilities in Latin America: The Mexican army had to be brought in on one
occasion to let Braniff passengers deplane – at an airport con-
structed by the U.S. government. On several occasions in the
late forties and early fifties Pan Am blacked out entire airports when its competitors' aircraft approached for emergency landings.

* * *

The Pacific is Pan Am's mud puddle. Its untapped potential
provided growth when traffic in the rest of the world was
stagnating. Pan American is a future-oriented company, and
growth – not pure profit – is its most important product. Profits are regulated by the CAB, but loose regulations on depre-
ciation and reinvestment leave growth open-ended, especially
if banks are willing to underwrite such expansion. With the
Korean War the promise of the Pacific was revealed, and Pan

Am began to plan for long-range jet aircraft, which were most profitable over the long Pacific distances.

Air power is big business, but it is not only the airline business. Since 1953 Pan Am's Aero-space Division has been prime contractor for the guided missile range at Patrick Air Force Base in Florida (now Cape Kennedy). Not only did Pan Am assume responsibility for the operation of the base cafeteria, police department, and fire squad, but also it ran the down-range intermediate stations stretching along its Latin American routes, across the South Atlantic and the Union of South Africa (Pan Am flies twice weekly to Johannesburg) and into the Indian Ocean. It now employs more than 6,700 on the job.

Some 600 more employees have been engaged in systems work for the Atomic Energy Commission's "Project Rover" at Jackass Flats, Nev. Others worked at Fort MacGregor, Tex., on telemetry and radar communications for anti-aircraft drones. Another 256 work at the Upper Atmosphere Experiment site at Fort Churchill, Canada, and an undetermined number work at the secret "electronic weapons testing station" at Fort Huachuca, Ariz.

While these military contracts were able to satisfy Pan Am in the early fifties, by 1957 Pan Am's directors had committed it to a vast outlay of capital for the purchase of a fleet of Boeing 707 jets large enough to replace all of its piston planes on major routes and to expand Pan Am's passenger capacity far beyond the projected growth of international civil air travel. The company's management was in a crisis; it failed to introduce the jets gradually to get full return on piston investment; and it greatly over-expanded its capacity and thus seriously risked financial collapse—a pattern now repeated almost exactly with the purchase of the new monster, the Boeing 747.

The reason for this "miscalculation" lies in the relationship between Pan Am, the major investment banks, and the aircraft manufacturers. Pan Am was formed as a "community company" which combined the interests of major New York financiers and the largest aircraft manufacturers, who were seeking new outlets for their venture capital and production capacity; it has continued to serve these two interests. When the aircraft industry grew to produce more than 10 percent of the nation's national income during World War II, the means of absorbing this capacity and maintaining its steady growth was no longer just the problem of manufacturers, but became a major concern for America's financial leadership as well.

Part of that solution is Pan American World Airways. Pan Am has a uniquely advantageous credit arrangement with thirty eight banks across the country, led by Chase Manhattan and First National City. These two banks make sure that Pan Am's $350 million "slush fund" is always filled, and it was they who arranged the loan for Pan Am's $525 million deposit on twenty-five 747s, which enabled Boeing to start production.

Boeing has a friend at Chase Manhattan. Chase Manhattan Bank own 8.7 percent of Boeing's stock and conveniently also owns 6.7 percent of Pan Am's stock (5 percent is considered a controlling interest under U.S. law). Under the Civil Aeronautics Act, it seems to be illegal for one company to have a controlling interest in both the manufacturing and operating sides of the industry: Chase Manhattan has not been prosecuted. These banks are more than neutral investors seeking profitable holdings. In many cases they stimulate the purchase of aircraft that the airlines industry cannot really afford, and often wind up actually owning the jets and leasing them to the airlines. Consider the 747.

In 1965 Pan Am announced that since it was introducing the 747 on all its routes, it could reduce its costs by almost a third and pass on the savings to its customers. Competitors scrambled to place orders for their fleets of 747s. Conveniently, all of Pan Am's American-flag international competitors have domestic routes as well, so that eventually even the entirely domestic airlines were forced to buy the 747 to remain "competitive."

* * *

The only possible source of passengers and freight capable of filling aircraft capacity and promising a guaranteed source of growth was the U.S. Air Force. Pan Am's formal relationship with the service came via the Civil Reserve Air Fleet

(CRAF), a doomsday scheme devised by Air Force planners to supply assaults for a post-nuclear war invasion of foreign countries or large-scale conventional engagements.

It was under these weird auspices that Pan Am had applied for military traffic in 1954. Gen. Curtis LeMay and others had opposed any weakening of the Air Force transport capacity until the civil carriers secured "no-strike" union agreements for military duty, increased their cargo capacity, and proved their military abilities. Pan Am alone among civilian carriers began meeting these criteria from 1956–1958, when it conducted a series of five major "war games" sessions with Military Air Transport Service (MATS); it increased its cargo capacity based on military specifications. Today Pan Am's "Air Pak" cargo loading system is essentially the Air Force's 463L system.

In July 1958, Gen. Nathan F. Twining, chairman of the Joint Chiefs of Staff, informed the Senate Armed Services Sub-committee that one of the major foci of these "war games" was the airlift of ground troops in "an operations plan calling for U.S. military participation in the defense of a Far Eastern country."

In apparent violation of the anti-trust laws, Pan Am organized all of the international carriers in January 1958 to win the right to fly military personnel and to adapt their jet fleets to military needs. In 1960, Rep. Mendel Rivers convened a special congressional hearing to get Pan Am and others Air Force business. In one bit of testimony, Juan Trippe explained AFL-CIO president George Meany's support for the military no-strike agreements with the unions and expressed Pan Am's committment to counter-insurgency:

"The other day at a formal dinner here in Washington I had the pleasure of talking with President Meany. Organized labor has approached the problem of work stoppages in a statesmanlike way, and now, with Mr. Meany's support, the military can count on us at all times."

Pan Am quickly became involved in comprehensive planning for a Southeast Asian war, and helped construct a jet fleet capable of supplying such a conflict. In 1961 the U.S. transported 500 Marines and their helicopters to Udorn Base in Thailand to provide transportation for the Royal Laotian Army. Since Pan Am was the sole American airline to fly to Thailand, it began lifting cargo and civilian personnel. The next year, Pan Am's charter cargo load in the Pacific region increased 500 percent, to 4.9 million ton-miles.

It came just in time. In 1961 the long-predicted crunch hit the Atlantic. Pan Am's Atlantic service ran at a loss. But the growing Pacific revenues were large enough to give the company an overall 6.3 percent profit. All other airlines were deeply in the red.

Pan Am began to reinforce its Pacific holdings: Juan Trippe's son Charles (Yale '57) became director of Pan Am's Intercontinental Hotels subsidiary; Pan Am began to dot the South Pacific and Asia with luxury hotels—in the "exciting fun capitals of Asia and the Pacific" to which Pan Am ferries its R&R passengers. These hotels themselves represent a novel form of exploitation: while tourists are drawn by their interest in Asian cultures, the bulk of the money they spend can be safely returned to America as long as they stay at an Intercontinental.

The assassination of President Kennedy meant a temporary setback to the company. Johnson began helping his wheeler-dealer cronies, ignoring New York–based Pan Am. Robert Six of Continental Airlines, collector of Oriental art and American actresses, was a loyal LBJ Democrat, as was Jimmy Ling of the Houston-based Ling-Temco-Vought, owner of Braniff Airlines. In 1964, Continental was picked by the CIA to supplement its own airlines, Air America, whose cover was about to be blown. Continental took over Pan Am's charter business in Micronesia. Six hired Pierre Salinger out of the White House to run his publicity campaign, and took on a former governor of Guam to ease the way with the Pacific bureaucrats.

In 1962, Continental charter operations had flown fewer than 4 million passenger-miles (one passenger flown one mile: a basic airline yardstick). In 1965 it flew 253 million, and in 1966 it rose 390 percent to 1.25 billion passenger-miles of charter. Continental's charter freight operations rose from nothing in 1962 to 93 million ton-miles in 1967. Braniff's rise was from just over half a million charter passenger-miles in 1963 to over a billion in 1967. In 1968 it leaped to 2 billion. Other airlines also prospered.

Pan Am was strong, but the trends were bad for a growth company. Pan Am was being cut to size by Northwest, Continental, Braniff and TWA—and by LBJ. So Juan Trippe hired Najeeb Halaby to rescue the situation.

Najeeb Elias Halaby, Yale Law '40, Los Angeles attorney, test pilot of the first Lockheed jet, was chief of the Intelligence Division for the Department of State and Assistant Secretary of Defense for International Security Affairs during the formative years of the colossus (1946–1953). He was a founder of Aerospace Corp. (the chief Air Force think tank, which among other tasks, is in charge of satellite communications for Vietnam), a leader of Kennedy's 1960 Los Angeles campaign, appointed administrator of the Federal Aviation Administration, the prime architect of the supersonic transport (SST).

For Pan Am, Halaby adopted a simple strategy: if others could get into the charter business through the White House, he could get his company back into it through the military. But what did the military need that Pan Am, and no one else, could give? Answer: fun.

Greater by far than the invention of B-52 blind raids, helicopter gunships and airborne chemical defoliation is Rest and Recuperation (R&R): Vietnam's new aspect of air power. On the wings of 707s, R&R has reduced pervasive alienation. It has saved depreciated aircraft from the scrap heap and put them in the service of the national interest. And in the interest of Pan Am as well: in the first few months of service there was a perceptible turnabout in Pan Am's Pacific charters. As the months lengthened into a year, Pan Am's service to the nation was up a measurable 358 percent, once again the largest charter operator of the bunch, carrying over live matériel and bringing back dead bodies—at a profit. Now fifty Boeing 707 321B flights go each week, each loaded with 70,000 lb of war matériel, computers and equipment of the man's technology. No "profiteering"; Pan Am doesn't run R&R for profit. It doesn't need to. It got back its charters.

It got its routes too. When the long-anticipated Pacific route hearings finally were called in 1967, every line applied for its share. Mountains of documents were submitted, but the case was decided less by the CAB than by those who hired the carriers, and then according to the maxim: "Them that got, gets." The recommendations of the examiner were considered by most observers a fair allocation of the applicants. Pan Am got its coveted Great Circle routes from New York to Tokyo and from San Francisco–L.A. to Tokyo.

The CAB, a Democratically appointed body, tipped the balance in favor of Democratic lines, Continental and Braniff, but allowed Republican Eastern (Rockefeller) and Pan Am their fair share. It passed its decision on to President Johnson, who insisted that Continental and Braniff get Eastern's routes—but did not touch Pan Am. The subsequent maneuvering under Nixon has left Pan Am safe, too. To be sure, a monopoly has been transformed into an oligopoly, but Pan Am will manage—so long as the market in the Pacific continues to grow.

But tourist trade is not enough. Government, military, and businessmen must continue to travel in increasing numbers, for Pan Am will have to fill its gargantuan 747s with them. If government turns toward solving America's domestic problems, if the military traffic were reduced, if American business were hit by the latent anti-Americanism now restrained by American client governments in the area, if disorder and change scare away the tourists—the market will not grow as planned.

For Pan Am to continue to grow, the attention of America must continue to be focused on Asia; Americans must continue to fly in increasing numbers. Paradoxically, Pan Am needs the specter of communism, the looming image of malignant China—it draws the tourists and it draws American concern. Pan American began with government aid. It is only with government aid of a newer sort that it will remain as it is—on the firm foundations of American interventionism.

* * *

As scholars of Asia we originally turned our attention to Pan Am as an example of American business-as-usual during what we considered a bloody, unnecessary and wholly inexcusable war. Our eye was caught by the statistic that Pan Am was paid $99.8 million for Military Air Command work during the fiscal year 1968 and that reduced yields from government services were reported to stockholders to have reduced Pan Am's revenues by $26.4 million. We learned that "your company's transpacific airlift provides up to six flights a day to Vietnam," up to forty-two a week (in August it was up to fifty). We determined that our essay should expose profiteering by a member of the military-industrial complex and should provide solid factual background for a worldwide boycott of Pan American World Airways.

Pan Am's simple beginnings in the banana republics were transformed by the foresighted, well-connected and ambitious Juan Trippe and his friends with the aid of luck and the U.S. government; what had begun as a communications system for a sophisticated Latin American empire graduated into the trunk line for a worldwide system.

It was in Korea that the colossus came together at last: the logic of air power, the exaggerated, paranoic fear of communism, the newly unified military services and their civilian suppliers working in cozy and profitable proximity. The whole was synergistic, more than the sum of its parts: a colossus checked only by a few remaining shreds of dissent in a complex America. The logic of Juan Trippe, of Billy Mitchell and the Battle of Britain have reached a climax on the battlefield of Vietnam. When a ragged peasant wearing sandals can ride his bicycle to a North Vietnamese hilltop and shoot his rifle directly into the maw of a jet approaching at twice the speed of sound—and shoot it down—the logic is exhausted.

January 26 – February 2, 1970

Why Are We in Alaska?

Robb Burlage

Yeah, the boys is up in the boreal-montane coniferous forest biome (dig . . . ecologist big university librarian groper) and that biome may run from Labrador to western Alaska, but it about ready to give out, it's had it, all that three-to-four-thousand-mile patch of balsam fir and black spruce . . . wolverines, we ain't seeing much more of the tamarack on stream sides, and the willows, the birch, the alder and the poplars . . . no, the boys are stepping up the south slopes. . . .

Says Rusty, "I didn't come to Alaska to debate the merits and vices of technological infiltration. . . ."

Texas will carries Texas cowards to places they never dreamed of being. —NORMAN MAILER,
Why Are We in Vietnam?

Anchorage

"Take me away, away . . . out of this world," sings lank

192

Johnny from Talkeetna. It's Saturday night at the Malamute Saloon on Fourth Avenue, the great drunken white way of this jerry-built, bungalow north metropole around which reside or flop about a third of Alaska's 275,000 censused people. Moustache and manner like a Buffalo Springfield refugee (band, not bulldozer), he articulates a crisp C&W loudspeaker sound over the refrains of his electric guitar. Next to him, Western-clad, gum-chewing all the while, yodels Corinna Carson, for two decades the Texas Rose of the Anchorage strip.

The Malamute's wildly appreciative clientele through the years has consisted most heartily of both Alaska natives (Eskimo, Indian, and Aleut) and WASP expatriates with Nashville or Waco memories somewhere in their heads. There are Air Force and Army enlisted men, guardians of the DEW Line (Distant Early Warning anti-missile radar) to make Seattle safe for Boeing. At least a fourth of the state's population are thus militarized and world-restless. Eskimo "Scout" National Guardsmen and other native seekers are down for the latest natural disaster: forest fire, flood, earthquake, change of political office, military investment shift, economic extraction boom-bust (furs, gold, whales and salmon, timber; now, oil). Loners are by, going up or down to the Lower forty-eight states on the latest round of construction or fire-fighting work. GS-9 federal field bureaucrats are here guzzling and eyeballing their native wards, of whom some of their best friends are. But at some point even midnight-sun cowboys must choose between nostalgia and progress.

Big Oil has hit town. The au-go-go parlors are reviving, even with transvestite talent to fill the womanpower shortage. Oil company executive credit cards and charge accounts have top billing for airlines, hotels, restaurants, even taxicabs, barbershops, and cleaners. Alaska Airlines, itself now financially interlocked with oil, has extra peekaboo tourist flights to see the Eskimos and to wink across the Bering Strait at Red Siberia.

All talk of oil stocks, retainers, sub-contracts, franchises, windfall jobs from pipeline welder to computer programmer. Consumer prices are rising even more than their usual 40 percent above ordinary U.S. indices. Beers may go to a buck. Coke machines are retooling for a quarter. A Tulsa development firm is planning a weatherproof, 5,000-person, skyscraper-centered, oil-company-headquartered new town under a Plexiglas astrodome near Anchorage. Oilmen can then jet from Houston by Alaska Airlines, with gay nineties decor and Robert Service ballads about fastening your seatbelt and enjoying your sandwiches. They can live in a totally air-conditioned new town. They can drive to and from the jetports in bubble-top, air-conditioned limos. They can see Mt. Mc-Kinley through their Plexiglas picture roof. They can jet air-conditioned to air-conditioned oil rig quarters on the North Slope. They can see the Brooks Range through airplane picture windows. They never leave Houston.

Norman Mailer's Texans-in-Alaska anti-war fantasy is prophecy, not allegory. When his book was published in 1967, there were Texans already stepping up the slopes north of the Brooks Range. They were pursuing not grizzly bears but seismic and drilling gambles on land they had purchased from the state of Alaska (and some from the Feds directly) for a few songs.

Early in 1967, incoming Gov. Walter J. Hickel (now Nixon's Protector of the Interior) had been pressured by Big Oil to hold another oil lands lease sale for the North Slope. Otherwise, the story goes, Oil would withdraw its troops. Until then, the companies said, it had been unhappy enclaves, dry holes, although there were "Texas towers" pumping away moderately well offshore and inland along the Cook Inlet and Kenai Peninsula below Anchorage. Most petroleum geologists knew there was a lot of it somewhere, someday up there. The Navy had grabbed and pumped some oil and gas out of its Petroleum Reserve No. 4 two or three decades before in the Alaskan Arctic Northwest above the Brooks Range.

There were reports known—at least to the Alaska statehouse—as early as 1966 that something was already happening up there. But the state held another "competitive" lease sale quickly in 1967, and, as in 1964–1965 and before, three giants in single and joint ventures had been the main players. They are Atlantic-Richfield (ARCO); Humble, largest division, Texas-based, of Jersey Standard (the Rockefellers with Stetsons); and British Petroleum. BP brings a new clipped accent to the American oil scene, riding joint ventures, options, and mergers, including its recent anti-trust-challenged hookup with Standard of Ohio. Between them, after the 1967 Hickel sale, they had accumulated cheap leases on almost a million state acres for only $12 million. These had been given over to the state as part of the ultimate 103-million-acre promise (of Alaska's total 375 million acres, previously mostly federal land) under the 1958 statehood act.

Then, in January 1968, the big news blew in with Atlantic-Richfield and Humble's joint venture strike at Prudhoe Bay State 1 and more decisively, in mid-1968, with another Arco-Humble strike at Sag River 1. Soon thereafter, BP came in with Put River 1. Now the estimate runs as much as 50 to 100 billion barrels, almost as much as all North American recoverable discoveries up until then.

By this past summer there were more than a dozen companies doing Big Oil wildcatting along a 150-mile stretch of the North Slope in a total area the size of Massachusetts. It is the central part of a world "play" by the industry along a 720-mile capitalistic Arctic "front" including western Canada, parallel to some similar, though so far less spectacular, developments across the Bering Strait in Russia.

* * *

On September 10 in Anchorage at a patriotic state-leasing-bids festival at Sidney Lawrence Auditorium, Big Oil plunked down slightly less than a cool billion to win the hearts and minds of the Alaska middle class (who now seek no taxes, dividends if they can, while it lasts) to assure its foothold on the hottest petroleum real estate in American history. Presiding over World Oil Lease-a-Rama was young, tall, Texas A& M-trained geologist Tom Kelly. Kelly was Hickel's hand-picked State Natural Resources Commissioner and is now associated with "acting" Republican Gov. Keith Miller, while Wally's away in Washington. Kelly is probably more politically powerful now than Miller. Kelly was once with Conoco and has major Slope-playing oil stocks of his own in his family portfolio.

President Nixon is directly interested in the Alaska question. Not only did he give the Interior portfolio to Hickel on the advice of Big Oil; then, until the interest-conflict backlash seemed too obvious, he had chosen his own brother to be head of federal Alaskan regional development. Nixon may also be trying to use "public partnership" in merchant marine development and continental shelf and ocean frontiering: one expects him to have an Astronoid banquet for Humble Oil's SS *Manhattan*–Northwest Passage project. The benefit to defense contractors—worried about peacetime business—is obvious. Alaska's Arctic natural wealth and turf opening up also means a new battle or bargaining ground with the Russians and the Japanese.

Big Oil has thus negotiated a major lease-sale "treaty" with the Hickel-ite Republican state government: a major security beachhead against general U.S.—and world—public demands, including the native-Alaskan "Third World." It is digging into all available political and economic enclaves in the state to prevent it from being another overturned domino. After all, it could lead to more public expropriation, ownership, regulation, environmental projection, taxation, international free trade, vulgar competition and cut-throat price slashing, and other forms of anarchy and subversion of the "Private World Government of Oil and Energy."

At the September state lease sale, the previous Big Three North Slope oil giants consolidated their positions and gave a foot in the action to other giants and joint ventures. Of course, "Free World Oil" is essentially in the business of purchasing governments, markets and land, not necessarily producing oil. There are even strong feelings that most of Big Oil doesn't really want that much new domestic oil coming along at the same time as a national taxpayers revolt. But once the early supply and extra-market-share seekers have really stumbled on it, the whole thing has to be put under their private world government.

Nevertheless, the frantic exploration and potential production of its technological infiltration does proceed apace for the benefit of its tax status and world audience. This melodrama, more theatrically competitive just before the big September lease sale, has been accelerating over the last eighteen months or so on the stark stage of the North Slope. Any cutting into the 1,000-feet-plus deep, eternally frozen permafrost such as for drill tower supports or dock installations must use gravel or refrigerant material to keep the holes from melting during the year, or all will go askew. A hotel in Nome which failed to properly account for this effect is now affectionately referred to as the Tiltin' Hilton. The state just abandoned the new Walter J. Hickel Highway to the Slope.

* * *

The tundra area is just below the ice-filled Arctic Ocean and above a seemingly endless expanse of snow-engulfed mountains, the Brooks Range, forming an overwhelming east-west natural barrier across northern Alaska, around perhaps the world's — and certainly America's — last great wilderness.

For the tourists, as well as the capitalists and managers, it's an air-conditioned, jet-set war against nature. From an Interior Airlines Prudhoe Bay jet special out of frontier-city Fairbanks one can see much of the panoramic show without ever landing at one of the gravel oil company jetports. Even before one approaches the most concentrated activity areas of this Danang-on-the-Artic, the indelible tracks and cat scratches of oil-exploring seismic crews — tractors and lines of seismic dynamite testing explosions — mar the vast white tundra. In most places it is flat as a billiard table, a seemingly endless vista, totally lacking in contrast. Some crews on contract to the big companies have left their own names, arrows, and company names kilroyed onto the earth.

Waste material lasts practically forever in the deep-freeze environment without eroding. Abandoned oil drums and pyramids of garbage are the major monuments to explorations three decades ago or more at the Navy's Pet 4 Reserve southwest of the prime Prudhoe area. Drums, garbage, and untreated human waste lagoons have accumulated in the recent rush, as well.

Then one begins from the air to see one, two, three . . . many oil company perimeters, each with "Christmas tree" oil

drilling rigs, gravel airstrips, oil and equipment storage landings, cranes and derricks, trucks and helicopters, and quonset
storage buildings, arrays of prefabricated, motel-like living
units connected as instant new towns for the crews. Many
also have direct access to their own bay docking facilities.

The total human population of the entire area, except for
hunters and migrants, including the only substantial coastal
Eskimo city, Barrow, was about 3,000 before the oil invasion,
less than two years ago. Now this original number is being
approached by the new working inhabitants of the oil development perimeters. No more than 5 percent of the actual
direct new employment has gone to the natives, although
there may be more cold-weather construction jobs for natives
on the pipeline, with federal pressure, as there were on the
DEW line.

As Appalachians have discovered with coal and East Texans with oil, most of these billions accrue to imperial capital
and even to labor outside the area—and there are no local
private landowners here. Most of the direct labor—exploration, drilling, construction, transportation—will be transient
or imported, and most of the refining and product development will probably be done elsewhere. Perhaps the latter is
sparing to the air and water, but not income-producing for the
local people. Therefore, except for the public lease-sale revenues and low-rate tax and royalty returns and the transitory
boom-town concessions, the payoffs may be quite limited for
Alaskans. This is especially true for the natives, who by both
history and morality are the true primary landholders. The
costs, on the other hand, may be mounting for generations to
come.

As in the delta marshes of Vietnam, the resistance to imperial technology is expressed in the uniquely prohibitive soil,
environment, and habitat as well as directly by the native
people. It is an epochal war on turf. They are directly attacking the tortoiseshell ice pockets and endless permafrost of the
deltas of North Slope's Big Sag and Coleville. They are cutting north around the great Arctic mixing bowl of mankind's
climate with a winter freeze-in covering four and a half million square nautical miles, separating the Eurasian from the

North American land mass. By a billion-dollar pipeline with numerous access roads they are digging south 800 miles to year-round port estuaries on the southern coast, through two ranges of the Rocky Mountains, mighty rivers such as the Yukon, massive glaciers, and permafrosted soil much of the way. One big *Torrey Canyon* oil tanker spill or one Santa Barbara offshore oil leak way up there, scientists say, could so darken the Arctic ice surface and so capture solar energy to raise temperatures enough to melt all polar ice within a decade. Then all that weird, cold heavy stuff would be in Houston for real, not on television.

Who are these ice warriors? The driver, based with British Petroleum, who took us around in early September just before the big lease sale was friendly, athletic, in his mid-twenties, from northwest Colorado: he had come from being a truck driver in the Army in Vietnam for two years to the big money lure of oil in Colorado and Wyoming and then on to the North Slope. He was being paid as much as $2,000 a month to work in six-week stints, with a paid R&R of two weeks in between when he hops to Colorado to see his wife and his new baby son. He figures five years of Vietnam and Alaska away from his family and then he's home free. He's saving enough to be able to build a home in the mountain country of Colorado and have a lot of time for the rest of his life to work seasonally and get in lots of good trout fishing.

Life in an Arctic oil outpost, even in the frenzy of big corporate exploration and drilling before the big "competitive" sales, is generally dead-simple, slow-paced, but *macho*. It is mainly a bet by the well-paid male migrant that the work interruptions will outnumber the actual engagements of hard energy—a skill obviously learned in the Army.

The drama around the actual drilling towers is often intensive, of course. During the feverish weeks before the lease sale, when companies were compiling information on which to base bids, everything was spychase. Drilling depths were described in code on the company truck intercoms. Our driver reported that a crewman had been discovered trying to sell information to another company for more than $100,000 and "was sent up fast."

The highlight of our tour to the North Slope was the driver proudly showing off his motel, a welding together of dozens of prefab units brought in by barge, lifted by helicopter, and laid down by giant crane. It was one big, connected, weather-tight tunnel, a yellow plastic submarine inside, with all the conveniences—fancy chow (the chef had 45 different spices in his built-in kitchen), ice cream and brownie snacks always available in the hall, billiards and movies (John Wayne twice a week), Muzak, *Playboy* centerfolds on every wall. Our young veteran claimed that there was a minimum of heavy drinking or grass smoking in close quarters like that, although the code in such a "dry camp" is: Don't bother anyone, do your job, and booze is okay. Firearms are also outlawed, but there have already been potshots taken at the few curious or hungry animals, caribou, foxes, and wolves, that have ventured near. As for sex in these all-male ice submarines, there is none; people wait for R&R rather than couple in prison.

Naturalists are deeply worried about the effects of oil development on the soil, streams, landscape, and the often rare wildlife. It is already great sport for rich hunters (with two airplanes, in case one goes down) to go after polar bear on the ice; the new oil crowd may add to this sport. Polar bears are already showing deadly signs of DDT fallout from the world's use atmospherically dumped on the Arctic.

Eskimo settlements, especially Barrow, are being so disrupted by the huge new migration, the ups and downs of cash and employment, some observers expect native riots before long. Only one lonesome, abandoned Eskimo hut could be seen around the actual oil perimeters in the Prudhoe area, but the effect on natural habitat, hunting, trapping, fishing, and migration areas will undoubtedly be fantastic.

* * *

So who else is on the scene besides the imperialists, the soldiers of fortune, the contract grabbers, the camp followers, the puppet government, the honky village chiefs? Besides the Alaska natives, there is not a clearly identifiable social base of even potential resistance, and the natives are yet mostly restless for a billion-dollar federal payoff and hunk of the action. But some other people talk, sometimes vote, but seldom dare to struggle.

A sizable urban, middle-class, liberal-moderate population exists, especially in Anchorage, Fairbanks, Juneau, and Sitka, to give some alternative to the growing cocktail-party Republicanism and Birchism and some handle for tackling issues like conservation, urban blight, and the Amchitka nuclear tests. They huddle around the few liberal state legislators.

Organized labor, in its own co-business form, especially teamsters, construction workers, operating engineers, and the like, has a lot of inflationary political and economic clout in the state. A consortium of construction unions recently concluded a major agreement with TAPS, a consortium of Humble, ARCO, BP and others, that included large percentage bonuses for workers staying to the pipeline's completion. Labor in these terms is largely a transient, fickle, and business-oriented array of the well-paid, many of whom are not actually voting residents of the state and are only around to hit paydirt and run. The incredible cost of living for working people is a major reason, and the treadmill goes on. There is some concern on the part of the new Alaskan oil management that the militant labor spirit now sweeping western Canadian oil workers, using general strikes for pioneering demands for new safety and health and welfare funds, as well as escalating wages and bonuses, will turn the Alaskan oilfields into new international labor battlegrounds. But, as in the U.S.A. below, with blacks and browns, the Alaska natives are generally shut out of major oil, construction, and industrial work, and they see unions more as racist social enemies than as potential political-struggle allies. So much for the New Deal, let alone the New Left, in Alaska.

* * *

Two weeks before the lease sale, what passes for Alaska's liberal intellectual establishment held a conference at the University of Alaska, near Fairbanks. The conference was oiled by the Alaska Oil and Gas Association and the National Academy of Science as some kind of effort to give a hint of rationality to the oil rush, with some liberal academics, legislators, lawyers, and planners trying to make something of it. Oil was well represented. Atlantic-Richfield community relations representative Joseph Fitzgerald (recently grabbed up a fancy price from chairmanship of the presidentially appointed Federal Field Committee for Alaska) said that no new towns or urban planning were needed in the oil development areas of the north but everything except profitmaking was probably up to government. Fitzgerald is probably the most prominent government, academic, or journalistic figure among many who have already been plucked up by Big Oil to be their direct representatives and rationalizers. And almost the entire University of Alaska Arctic specialty, geology, engineering, and environmental staffs appear to be on retainer to the oil industry for developing the extraction or pipeline systems.

The new Hickel-ite Republican U.S. Senator, appointee Ted Stevens, saw his opportunity at the conference on statewide TV to make a speech attacking the egghead outside agitators. Pointing out that old Alaskan sourdoughs know more about wilderness than any San Francisco parlor pink Sierra Clubber, he said that the ecological nuts are out to take sprayguns away from the people to deal with mosquitoes, and, he said, if private enterprise promises to build a road free, "you should get down on your knees."

A petition for delaying the oil lease sale was circulated at the conference and was signed by a couple hundred persons. But all such points were clearly too late and too esoteric to generate broad political support for putting brakes on the rush. The potential coalition of liberal reasonables—a few urban legislators and their pro-public-expenditure supporters, the Alaska Federation of Natives, citizen conservation groups and advocates, and academic or bureaucratic planning types—thus far has been kept at bay by Big Oil. The issues of native claims, wilderness protection, and positive urban and economic development have been kept apart, and there are no statesmen who can yet link them.

* * *

By the time the Russians conned Secretary of State Seward in 1867 (because the furs were running out and they wanted to keep Alaska away from the British Empire), they had not

even communicated with most of the interior native population, let alone claimed to have conquered their land for sale to
the United States. Big Oil, therefore, even today has to deal
separately, through the U.S. government and on its own, with
the "native question." It does not come neatly packaged with
domination of the economy and politics of the state.

The Eskimos, Aleuts, and Indians in the mid-19th century
and late into that century had the population majority. Today
they are about one-fifth of the Alaska population. They claim
by rights 90 percent of the land in the state, including many of
the wealthy North Slope oil lands, based on "aboriginal use
and occupancy." More than 70 percent of the natives still live
in primitive rural and town conditions. Most, even the urban
dwellers, are dirt-poor in a very middle-class and high-priced
territory. They are now appealing to Congress, under an 1884
statute, to settle the land-claims issue. They are asking for a
billion dollars, community control of a development fund, 40
million choice acres, and royalties on oil and other mineral
development.

The natives of many locales and leaderships have become
increasingly ignited and united about the claims—they call
them rights—as the oil prospects and international visibility
of the issue has become more obvious. Some militants like
young Eskimo-born Charlie (Etok) Edwardson—brilliant, self
-styled jet-set ecologist and former federal poverty warrior
from Barrow—"marred" the television coverage and cham-
pagne atmosphere of the September lease sale by picketing in
front of the auditorium: "$2,000,000,000 Native Land Rob-
bery," "Eskimos Own the North Slope."

Native bitterness goes back through the generations of
white men's destruction of their own natural environment for
fishing, hunting, trapping, migrating and dwelling—and of
their own peace with the harsh environment of the Far North
and the rich surroundings of the Aleutians, the Southeast and
Panhandle. They cumulatively resent all the white man's
blessings of tuberculosis, venereal disease, social disruption
causing mental illness, alcoholism, gunshot and mechanized
"dogsled" accidents, dependence on doctors for infant deliv-
ery and then greater mortality without sufficient attention, all

adding up to a life expectancy of about thirty-five.

They resent the uncertain external employment cycles and dependence on the cash economy of military and economic extraction investments over which they have no control; the robbery of pelts and fishing areas or imperial pricing domination by monopoly traders; prohibition of trade and development arrangements with foreigners such as Russians and Japanese. Outrageous is the exploitative tourism like the Alaska Airline jets that hit Kotzebue for a few hours, look at the natives, and leave no real income or social control with the native people. Despised are the business and welfare imperialism of the company stores, the homestead and reservation rules that prohibit effective native landowning, the federal small-business and housing loan programs that prohibit "unstable" enterprise and "primitive" village-dwelling building or improvement applications. Characteristic are the marked-up prices for natives for gallons of pure water and kerosene in some cities and villages, when Alaska has the hemisphere's greatest supply of pure water and oil.

From the federal claims, the native groups are hoping to build well-heeled and balanced regional and community development organizations that can provide for all natives both "native power" and assimilation options with full political power, social and economic security, and cultural pride.

However, despite the ripe populist Big Oil target, the visible native "Third World" demands, and a transplanted California veneer culture for the young, there are yet few New Left signs in the North Country. A few self-styled militants such as Edwardson and people around the *Tundra Times* hint that a new breed of college-educated early-SNCC types might be emerging among the natives, but this is still only a barely discernible gleam in the usual "tom-tom" leaders' eyes.

A late-fifties-style folk and rock festival, even with a lot of late-sixties Woodstock totality, could probably lure thousands of youth who are here already or who come up to Alaska to "camp" for the summer for the inevitable fire-fighting jobs. A military base outside Fairbanks put up some of the underemployed overflow for awhile this summer until the more golden smoke became too embarrassingly thick. There are even a couple of wilderness youth communes between Anchorage and Fairbanks, but "hippie" youth have also been shot, *Easy Rider* style, by tougher, older homesteaders in the interior. Plenty of pot is permeating the younger generation here, as everywhere, in contrast to their alcoholics-unanimous elders, but it has thus far had less noticeable cultural and political expressions.

But most of the youth-haired customers at the Deli spend their time watching the likes of Dick Clark on "delayed" color TV. Fairbanks has a youth loft club (no hard liquor or dope, nobody over twenty-one) with usually the only live hard-rock music in the state, but it is more an adult get-'em-off-the-streets effort than a Movement center. There are no New Left GI coffeehouses for the thousands who get shipped up here (some because they are anti-Vietnam, organizing troublemakers at bases in the Lower forty-eight).

While the natives grow more restless, the 10,000 or so blacks are peacefully caught in between, most quietly escaping into lower-level government, maintenance, and clerical jobs and sub-contract black petit capitalism, most dwelling in and around Anchorage. The nearest thing to a young Black United-Fronter at the University of Alaska in the last few years now has his own personnel firm seeking "qualified" natives and blacks for token North Slope construction jobs.

There is no rush to put money on the slim white hopes of liberal reforms on this frantic frontier. The more likely question is what particular style will the state assume as only the brightest new pawn of the international energy industry, led by Big Oil.

An "Appalachia"? — back to being a Federal reservation when the big boom runs out or all the big returns are draining outside the state, the rest of the natural and economic potential has been ruined, and all institutions have been tailored to the needs of one extractive industry?

A "Texas"? — with its own regional oil politics (Wally Hickel as LBJ and Tom Kelly as a one-man, oil-self-regulating Texas Railroad Commission), commercial and cultural pollution, poverty midst plenty, but a lot of big spending, hell-raising, and military-industrial spin-offs before it's all over?

A "British Columbia" (Canada)? — with a quasi-fascist "social credit" system in which every patriotic "homeowner" (read WASP) is a coupon-clipper of the fiscal-juggling state, enmeshed in its own oil strikes and playing games with private big capital on many fronts?

Or a "Vietnam"? — was Mailer allegorically prophetic in reverse? Where Texas oilmen hold oilfield and urban enclaves, while the natives hold the interior, Arctic rimland, and the Indian panhandle "delta," holding out for reparations and rights, always threatening the vital installations such as pipelines, airstrips, tanker depots, railheads, and DEW lines, subversively attempting to make alliances with the wildcat construction and oil-rig workers, many of whom worked their last trick in Indochina? Could the war be brought home at last — driving the Texans back another frontier, back to stew in their own juices of Houston astrodomes, aero-space, and local SDS and SNCC chapters? One, two, many . . . or one too many Alaskas?

November 17–24, 1969

Talking
High School Blues

Joan Biren

We schoolchildren, preparing for society,
Being blinded by lies and inadequate lighting.
— NANCY ERNST,
from The South Dakota Seditionist Monthly

DuVal Senior High School sprawls across a large unwooded lot in Prince Georges County, Md., a section of suburban Washington, D.C. The many wings of the rambling flat-faced structure are identical and successfully conceal the main entrance. Inside, the cinderblock walls are painted in pastel shades. There is a jukebox in the senior cafeteria and Muzak in the administrative offices: "Bad Moon Rising" to "Smoke Gets in Your Eyes." At the main desk are slips for everything: locker repair, schedule change, leave early, walk in the hall. On the wall of the office is a time sheet where the teachers sign in and out of work.

DuVal is conventional if not typical. There is a wide distribution of income and occupation among the students' families. The students score squarely on the fiftieth percentile in College Boards and about half go on to college. The school staff is liberal and well qualified, as those things go. And the school is in trouble. Parents are upset; students fight. The teachers teach less; the principal demands more authority.

DuVal, ten years old, with a student body of 1,800, is located in the middle of a rapidly expanding area outside Washington. Despite "open-housing" legislation, neighborhoods in DuVal's area remain almost entirely segregated. The school serves at least five distinctive communities—one of which is black. Housing ranges from urban-renewal public to $50,000 single-family private. The school is situated between government space and spy installations, and a high proportion of the students have parents who work for the government: jobs vary from NASA scientist to NSA file clerk. People in the school tell you that they are representative of the full spectrum of society, America in miniature. And, like the country, the school is self-consciously middle-class.

Until 1965, nearly all the schools in Prince Georges remained segregated. Since then, the percentage of black students in the white high schools has been gradually increasing. The county still has two all-black high shcools, which are now threatened with loss of federal aid unless the school authorities obey a HEW order to integrate by next autumn. Four years ago 8 percent of the students at DuVal were black; this year the figure is 25 percent. The increase is the result of the gradual desegregation of schools and—most important—the growth of the black community within the school "catchment area," because of out-migration from the inner city. Most of the school's students have received all their prior education in segregated schools. It is not until they are about fifteen years old that they are introduced to racially mixed classrooms and corridors.

When they leave DuVal, most of the students carry on, for however brief a time, with their education. About a quarter of each graduating class starts at regular four-year colleges, mostly at the University of Maryland (whence many flunk out). Another 25 percent go to the two-year county community college. The rest of the approximately 60 percent of the class in "higher" education is scattered among colleges, commercial courses and trade schools. The Armed Forces claim a twentieth of each graduating class. The remainder, mostly women, work. They work for employers like the telephone company and Montgomery Ward, as secretaries and salesclerks.

* * *

The appearance of the DuVal students as they jog and stroll through the corridors of their school is striking: girls in trousers, boys in ruffles, everything in between — and in reverse. The dress code was withdrawn last year after a tough protest battle, and now manner of dress, more than ever before, is a distinguishing characteristic of the various groups who compose the informal power structure of the school. The conventionally well-dressed students form the old guard of the school known as "The Clique." Membership in this self-perpetuating group is awarded almost exclusively to boys in varsity athletics and girls who are pom-poms, cheerleaders or majorettes. The Clique, historically, controlled the student government and was generally recognized by the other kids as a social elite. A couple of years ago all that began changing. Blacks in the school meant blacks on the teams. Blacks on the teams meant blacks on the cheerleader squad. For a jockstrap school, where sports are the most important activity conducted with official blessing, these changes alone required a lot of adjustment. But the position of The Clique was challenged in more subtle ways as well.

The arrival of the blacks precipitated the emergence of a distinct group known as the Rednecks. Unlike the Greasers — the traditional hoody element — the Rednecks were a new challenge on the "Right-of-center." They disturbed the equanimity of The Clique by daring them to join in expressions of overt racism. On the "Left," the Niggers, a group composed of hippie freaks and militants, both black and white, took over the student government. At the moment, the Niggers seem to be clearly in the ascendancy as the school hotshots. Several members of the student government, including the president, are former members of The Clique.

"Sure I hung around with those guys for awhile. But then I quit — after I was elected."

"Yeah man, you should have seen this guy when he came

back from the summer, hair all long and everything, spent the summer tripping."

"Oh, I was queen of the school last year, really big with The Clique. We have pajama parties, you know, decide who'll be in or out. But those kids are so dumb, so boring. This year has been unbelievably interesting."

"Let's see, I don't think student government has sponsored any dances at all or stuff like that. We've been working on getting information on contraception and abortion available."

"Then there was organizing for the Mobe. That was terrific."

These students are bright, attractive, active and, in fact, exactly the sort of students one would expect to find in student government, getting good grades and going along with the school administration all down the line. But they have turned off the school's stereotype of what they should be and turned on to themselves. They are clearly seeking to substitute personal experience for arbitrary authority as a method of formulating values and learning about life. A "bill of rights" produced at DuVal demands that students should be allowed to learn by experience even when this means learning by mistakes. As long as there is no harm to others, a student should be permitted to act to his own detriment without the intervention of the school, students say. But responsibility for one's own action is precisely what the school administrators deny the students — while complaining that all "the youngsters" are interested in is rights without responsibilities.

* * *

There was a fight in the halls on a Tuesday last month. This was a planned fight. It was planned to settle a few scores between The Clique and the Niggers. Both sides were ready; slights of various sorts had been accumulating and there hadn't been a big fight for months. The individual leaders cleverly stayed out of the actual fisticuffs. They merely sent out the word — when and where. The fighting — in the corridors during school hours — was between blacks and whites. But the planning, a process unrecognized by parents and administration, was carried out by an integrated group. The worst injury in Tuesday's fight was the loss of some teeth by a young man just completing orthodontia treatment. He was an outsider to the quarrel and tried to intervene between the two fighting gangs. There are four or five gangs of fighters in the school, with about ten boys in each, which correspond with the larger social groupings.

On the Friday night after the Tuesday fight there was another skirmish at a local drive-in restaurant. The Greasers were included in this one. Then, on Sunday, a group of white parents met to discuss the "problem of violence." The meeting was held in the high school, illegally, but apparently with the principal's permission. The assistant state's attorney was present. No black parents were invited. The meeting was marked by crude racial outbursts on the part of some parents, harsh criticism of the principal by others, and suggestions of "citizen support" for the school by others. Word of the meeting spread quickly through the black community, which heard that the whites were preparing vigilante groups. Black parents decided to organize themselves. Unable on short notice to obtain permission to meet in the high school, they converted a local "citizen's association" meeting set for Wednesday into a meeting about the school. In the meantime, the white citizen support group produced several fathers to patrol the halls on Monday. This let them see another punch-up in the school.

On Monday the blacks were surprised and provoked by another group, the Nazis. Somebody set off a tear gas pen. Nobody was hurt beyond scrapes and bruises, but the administration arranged for eleven white kids and eleven black kids to be busted by the police. Two plainclothes detectives were already wandering around the school in a followup to the Friday night fight. Neither the detectives, the parents, nor the administration, whose offices formed a backdrop to the scuffle, were able to prevent the violence. Uniformed police were brought in to patrol the halls for the rest of the day.

Thursday was the birthday of Martin Luther King, Jr., and the school decided hurriedly to put together a commemorative assembly. There have been few assemblies in the past, for fear of bringing the student body together in explosive conditions. Attendance at this one was optional. Thursday morning about 95 percent of the black population of the school and about 50 white students filed into the gym. The students sat, for the most part, in racially separate sections — just as students do at all school athletic events. Next door, at the VFW building, more than a dozen police cars waited for trouble to start. There was band and choral music, modern dance, and speeches and no trouble.

The emergency meeting of black and white parents the same evening presented some startling contrasts. The meeting opened with an explanation from the principal. The school board bureaucracy had been persuaded to bend enough to allow a meeting on short notice in the school, he said, on the conditions that it was not to be an official PTA meeting and that no students were to be invited. He did not explain that the PTA president, who thought he was running the meeting, had already invited members of the student government to come and address the parents. The principal neglected to revoke the invitations until the students showed up. When at first they resisted the suggestion that they leave the meeting, the principal privately threatened the students with arrest.

Now the microphone was turned over to a "chairman" selected in advance by the principal. The chairman, with no further reference to the assembled gathering, proceeded to announce an agenda and a time limit for speakers. The question for the meeting as he saw it was: "Do teachers have the authority to discipline students under their command?" The 800 parents in the hall, almost as many black as white, fell into a morass of self-congratulatory speeches swearing that they would be willing to have their children expelled from school if the children seriously misbehaved. One parent shouted: "We must not bow to student rule. If there are chronic trouble-makers, shove 'em out!" Cheers.

The meeting had moved on to consideration of the formation of an investigating committee when the place was suddenly thrown into total turmoil. The student government kids entered the front of the hall and stood solidly before the parents.

The parents screamed, shook their fists, stomped their feet, jumped up on chairs, raced to the front of the hall and pushed out the back. Nobody was in command of the meeting, and very few parents were in control of themselves. "They acted like all the white kids had hair down to their ankles and all the black kids had hair six feet high," one of the students said later. Most parents were shrieking: "Throw them out, get them out of here." "They think they can run everything; who invited them?" A few hundred parents walked out and never came back. One mother screamed, "They don't represent my child. My child looks like a boy." On a hand vote, about seven parents were in favor of hearing what the students had come to say. The next day there were stories going around the school that the students had been toting machine guns and rifles. However, the students never even spoke a word to the audience, never gained access to the microphone, and, fifteen minutes after entering the auditorium, they turned and left. They went because they realized the futility of achieving anything with the adult group and because they were afraid of being attacked by the parents or arrested by the police.

Having expelled the "intruders," the parents settled down to see if they could determine what the problem in the school was. They argued about whether Item C, Article 4, in the PTA Code prohibited the association from lobbying the governor. They attacked the principal for his leniency with the students. There was an almost unanimous show of hands in favor of the principal's exercising more power. The principal, obviously exasperated with the evening's events, decided to lay it squarely on the parents:

"I'm trying to be practical and honest," he said. "The parents of the troublemakers are not here. These troublemakers, who compose about 2 percent of the school, take time away from your children. They have psychological or emotional hang-ups. It would be better for everyone if they were not in the regular schools. But at the moment, because of school board regulations, the principal does not have the power to expel troublemakers from his school. You ask me what I want to restore discipline. Absolute authority. No appeals. No running to make telephone calls. No conferences. When I say something in the school, that's it. That's the authority I want." Applause. The meeting concluded with an exhortation to the silent majority to speak out to the school board for a return of authority to the school.

The next day the students abolished the student government. The meeting of the representative council opened with a "word of inspiration" from the SGA chaplain—a poem from *Soul on Ice* (a book not available in the school's library). A resolution was offered: "To support the New Left in its wars of liberation to return 'All Power to the People.'" Motion seconded. Point of information: What is the New Left? Answer: Everything you're not. Question: What will the New Left do? Answer: Kick the ass of the ruling class. Debate: The New Left is bullshit. "All Power to the People" is a bullshit slogan because the people aren't liberated. Furthermore, Student Government Association is the biggest bullshit of all. Motion defeated.

Another motion was offered: "Whereas, students are puppets of the school board and have absolutely no power to govern themselves and absolutely no control over the important issues of education; whereas, student governments are designed by this country only to be used as a playground where students can play government in a manner in which children play cops and robbers; whereas, most students view student government as an excuse to get out of classes: Therefore, be it resolved that the SGA be dissolved until the educational situation in this country has been changed so that the students have a significant voice."

No debate. Voice vote. Motion carried. The student government president, smiling benignly (it was all his idea), said: "Well, the meeting's over, you can all go." The shock of what they had done had almost passed over the students when the executive committee started spreading the word that, naturally, all clubs and societies chartered by the SGA had also been abolished. One distraught majorette went dashing to the staff lounge to seek out her club adviser. "Do you know what they've done? Do you know? They've abolished all the clubs."

"How did you vote?"

"Oh, I voted in favor, but that's just when I thought it meant getting rid of those kids on the executive committee."

* * *

Most students laugh off the description of themselves as disruptive and hung-up. They will tell you that the schools are falling apart through internal rot; where the kids are helping to tear them down it is less through any destructive urge than through boredom. "There's nothing else interesting to do around this place," I was told. "They don't control anything and we just don't listen." "The parents want to know what the problem is. Well they're the problem." Now students are carrying guns to school, and it seems to be only a question of time before they are used. In the week before the fighting at DuVal, a fifteen-year-old student was accidentally shot and killed in a Washington junior high.

Black and white parents alike live in fear of the city coming to the suburbs: violence sweeping out like a firestorm. In Washington, Chicago, New York and Philadelphia, on-duty police with guns patrol school halls all day, every day. In Baltimore, Los Angeles and many other cities, armed "security agents," often off-duty or retired policemen, guard the halls of senior and junior high schools. Parents say their goal is an orderly school. So some arm their children, "defensively," and then call for more effective policing. One boy told me his father gave him a can of pressurized Mace: "Use it in good health," daddy said. While the courts ponder the question of whether or not lockers can be searched without a warrant, the principal works on the assumption that it is irresponsible not to search when searches consistently turn up blackjacks, razors and other weapons: "If you have to shake them down, you do it whether it's legal or not," he said.

The principal boasts of a close working relationship between his school and the juvenile and vice squads of the police department. He also relies on student informers. But in one respect—drugs—the informers are silent. The administration is sure that the majority of students in the school involved in the drug scene are "popping pills." The kids, contemptuous of pills because that's what their parents are doing, are heavily into acid. Student dealers say that all kinds of straight kids ask them for tabs—right in the halls of the school.

Not all the kids are on the same kind of trip, of course, The school has both "hippies" and "Nazis." Some students spend their time in the school halls passing out cards bearing swastikas and the phone number to call for the "White Power Message." The tape-recorded voice on the phone announces:

"Now we all know that one of the biggest reasons for this abominable increase in crime in our schools is racial integration. Whenever Negroes move into a white school or a white neighborhood, the crime rate begins going up. Much of the crime in integrated schools is simply black students assaulting, robbing and raping white students and teachers. But the problem is really a lot worse than that. White kids themselves are committing many more crimes than they used to. White kids in ever-larger numbers are becoming anti-social. They are turning against the entire white establishment, rejecting it, lashing out at it. And who can really blame them for rejecting the rotten thing that the present system in this country has become? How can a kid have any respect or sympathy for a system which subjects him every day to the black terror which rages in our integrated schools and then shuts its ears to his calls for help?"

No solutions are offered, but listeners are invited to contact the National Socialist White People's Party, a Virginia-based group that is the successor to Rockwell's American Nazi Party.

Moderate and liberal parents and administrators blame Supreme Court decisions for destroying the public school system—not by integration orders but rather with decisions restricting the authority of the school to deal with troublemakers. *Tinker* v. *Des Moines* is the most offensive case for these people. Last year it set out the principle that a student's freedom of speech can be curbed only when his conduct materially and substantially interferes with the maintenance of appropriate discipline. Abe Fortas wrote the decision, which arose from a case of students wearing black armbands to school in protest against the war in Vietnam. "In our system," Fortas wrote, "state-operated schools may not be enclaves of totalitarianism. School officials do not possess absolute authority over their students. Students in school as well as out of school are 'persons' under our Constitution." The principal at DuVal, puzzled, has gone back to reading the Constitution.

As their problems seem to grow, school administrators feel less and less able to cope with them and their major grievance is against the courts who have "eroded authority." One administrator said: "To keep a taut ship these days, we'd have to be Perry Mason and James Bond together. The students learn a negative lesson here: 'If I break rules, I won't get into trouble.' So they start to make their own moral judgments. There is no respect for law and authority because criminals are protected. You can live as an animal with no penalty. For a juvenile the maximum sentence for murder is five years. Kids don't learn from experience because they don't get into severe trouble. Used to be a time when if someone told you, 'Report to the principal's office,' you'd be scared. Not anymore." He favored the congressional move to lower the age of responsibility to sixteen years, so that most high school students would fall into the jurisdiction of the adult courts.

The administrators, and not the teachers, spoke of the question of professionalism. "Outfits like the ACLU are causing chaos and destruction. They'd let the schools fall into the hands of teenagers and untrained parents. If they had their way with curriculum, we'd end up without any technically trained or professional people."

"Professionalism" in the schools was often mentioned in contrast to "community control." The principal: "My frustration turns to disgust because I can see what should be done, but I can't do it. Interference from the community is hampering the school's operation. A plumber or a bricklayer comes in here and tells me what to do—it's nonsense! I've spent my whole life in education. They must leave it to the trained people."

By his own admission, the principal thought little of the teachers' training. The teaching staff is bogged down in petty gossip, gross rumor and escapist busywork. The teachers prefer to keep their distance and discuss the students as though they were some sort of strange exhibit, like trained apes or visitors from Saturn. Overheard in the staff lounge (a plastic affair with vending machines for Cokes, coffee, candy bars): "There's so much sex in the halls I wonder what those kids do in private."

"The ones that aren't doing sex are smoking pot."

"Two girls in my room got into a fight and, boy, did I learn a few filthy words."

Teachers in Prince Georges County get a starting salary of $6,800. They may go on strike if salary negotiations don't go well for them this year. But their militancy does not extend to dealings with the students. They are frightened and admit it: "Well, I'm afraid to go into the halls. If there's going to be trouble tomorrow, I think I'll be sick and stay home."

"I keep watching the bulletin board with Martin Luther King on it. If it gets defaced, I'm not coming into school."

* * *

A principal function of the public schools historically has been to keep kids off the streets, away from the labor markets, and out of their parents' hair: to babysit. The babysitters now have to function as active jailers; the streets have come into the schools. Compulsory schooling may be on the way out. In the South, the move toward private academies is already gaining great strength as a result of court-ordered immediate integration. In the rest of the country there is a growing feeling that school is dangerous to the bodies as well as the minds of the people who must, for more than ten years of their lives, sit in them.

Many parents prefer no formal schooling for their children to public schooling as it exists today, based on fear and guilt and aimed at the production of dependence, insecurity and self-hate. Locking students in such a death system resulted in what Peter Marin calls a "gentle violence," violence turned inward against oneself, violence which destroys all life instincts. What is happening today in more and more schools is that the life instincts are being set free, the gentle violence has ceased to be gentle. The breakdown of authority has removed fear as a motivating force. Students who have their own definition of failure cannot be intimidated by threats of punishment, bad grades or comments on the "permanent record card." As the "authority figures" are more and more obviously revealed as dishonest, incompetent and ineffectual, students feel increasingly free to express their alienation. When some students within the system rebel, they then threaten the others who begin to suspect the foolishness of a course of action which continues to conform to outmoded, overturned authority patterns.

Some students undoubtedly agree with the administration, teachers and parents who want a "stable" situation in the school, who want to eliminate troublemakers from the environment. Schools teach attitudes toward the self which allow exploitation, but more and more students are failing that course and loving it.

A sign on the wall of the administrative office at DuVal explains as well as anything the outbreak of violence in the school: "Children learn what they live: If a child lives with hostility he learns to fight."

February 16 – 23, 1970

White on Black

Andrew Kopkind

"As America gets worse and worse," Murray Kempton once wrote, "its reports get better and better." No report of a commission investigating America's recent crises has found so warm a public welcome as the Kerner Commission's study of the season of civil disorders in the summer of 1967. In its official and private editions the Riot Commission Report has sold almost 2 million copies. Countless critiques and analyses have greeted it in the press, and it has turned to grist for thesis mills in the nation's graduate schools and colleges. The careers of several commissioners, staff officials and consultants have been considerably enhanced by their association with the report (and only a few reputations have suffered). All in all, the report has become a basic document in the platform of American liberals for social reform, a catalogue of problems and a program of solutions.

But by and large, those who were cheered by the report's solemn platitudes or impressed by its torrent of statistics missed its essential political functions and its crucial social consequences. It presented – and legitimized – a specific view of the riots and a particular understanding of America that now constitutes the standard approach to the treatment of social ills. The commission was able to do that job because of the way it was set up, staffed, manipulated and terminated; because of the promises and rewards it offered those who worked for it; because of its punishments for criticism and dissension; and because of its calculated presentation to the public through press and mass media.

Reportage and analysis of the commission's work have largely failed, and for the same reasons: Reporters and analysts became deeply implicated in the "success" of the report. Although there was an unusual amount of reportable conflicts during the commission's seven months of operation, reporters never got past the vague rumors of friction between liberal and conservative forces, or the whispered hints of White House interference. The firing of 120 staff members in late 1967 was never explained; the substantial hostility of black staffers toward the commission's own "institutional" racism was never mentioned; the "underground" commission document, "The Harvest of American Racism," was never examined; the White House veto on employment of staff and consultants active in anti-war work was never disclosed; the tacit agreement to "forget" the war in Vietnam throughout the commission's investigations and its report was overlooked; and the secret plan of Commissioner Charles ("Tex") Thornton to torpedo the report just before launching is still an untold story.

In similar ways, the political analysts who pored over the long document never got past its liberal rhetoric and its profuse programmatics to see its political role. No one has yet detailed the report's lasting effect on the set of signals it delivered to corporations, foundations and government planners to manage urban affairs on the model of foreign aid and counterinsurgency programs of the early sixties.

For the report does not exist outside of its political context. It can logically escape neither the conflicts which informed its operations, nor the uses to which it will be put. Strictures on thinking "unthinkable" thoughts about Vietnam (among other unthinkables) made impossible a realistic assessment of the nature of riotous America. Total concern for the way resources of the society are allocated—rather than control of the allocation process—eliminated discussion of the possibilities of serious social change. Acceptance of pluralistic myths about the operation of American institutions limited the report to the exposition of a narrow ideology. Failure to analyze in any way the "white racism" asserted by the commissioners in the report's summary transformed that critical category into a cheap slogan. And overall, the report's mindless attention to documenting conventional perceptions and drowning them in conventional wisdom made meaningless the commissioners' demands for social reconstruction.

The very acceptance—and acceptability—of the report is a clue to its emptiness. It threatens no real, commanding interests. It demands, by implication or explication, no real shifts in the way power and wealth are apportioned among classes; it assumes that the political and social elites now in control will (and should) remain in their positions. By avoiding an approach to the riots as events of political insurrection, or as part of a worldwide response to an overbearing U.S. empire, the report makes sure that social therapy will be applied only to surface effects, not systemic faults.

President Johnson chose eleven members for his National Advisory Commission on Civil Disorders, a collection remarkable chiefly for its predictable moderation. There could, and would, be no surprises. The list was comprised of men (and one woman) representing various aspects of economic and political elites in the United States: expansive corporatism (Charles B. Thornton, the president, director and chairman of Litton Industries); bureaucratic labor (I. W. Abel, president of the United Steel Workers); the pre-1965 civil rights establishment (Roy Wilkins, executive director of the NAACP); Republicans (Rep. William M. McCulloch of Ohio and Sen. Edward W. Brooke of Massachusetts); Democrats (Rep. James Corman of California and Sen. Fred Harris of Oklahoma); old-style machine politics (Chairman Otto Kerner, governor of Illinois); new-style urban politics (Vice-Chairman John Lindsay, mayor of New York City); the police

(Chief Herbert Jenkins, of Atlanta); and women-in-politics (Katherine Graham Peden, then Commerce Commissioner of the state of Kentucky).

Like all presidential commissions, the Kerner panel was designed not to study questions but state them, not conduct investigations but accept them, not formulate policy but confirm it. Although the commission conducted hundreds of hours of official "hearings" and traveled in groups of two and three commissioners to riot cities, the basic work was done by the staff—and by the scores of outside consultants, specialists and experts who were directed into the really critical policymaking roles. Together, the outsiders made up the elite of professional "urbanists" which has become the command group for the management of social crises.

Staff Director David Ginsburg was chief political cadre for the Administration. His assignment was to manipulate the internal and external operations of the commission so as to produce a forward-looking report and avoid the worst pitfalls of controversy, bickering and career damage. President Johnson himself appointed Ginsburg as the director, shortly after he announced the names of the commissioners. It was an unusual move, and a source of some suspicion afterward; commissions like to hire their own hands. But the job of political organizer was too important to be left to any old bureaucrat. The White House had to keep control of the commission, even indirectly—*preferably* indirectly. David Ginsburg filled the required role to perfection. A quiet, commanding West Virginia lawyer, he had first met Johnson in New Deal days, and became one of his pool of Jewish lawyers (cf. Abe Fortas, Edwin Weisl), who are always available for odd jobs, big deals and general counsel (myths of ethnic attributes grow tall in Texas).

As Ginsburg was the political manager and manipulator of the commission, his deputy Victor Palmieri was the administrator and theoretician. Palmieri was a young Southern California lawyer, very much in the hard-living, aggressive Kennedy style. By the time he was thirty-five he had become president of the Janss Corporation, one of the West's biggest landholding and development corporations.

If Ginsburg had a broad rhetorical view of the commission's purposes, Palmieri had a much more specific notion of what it was supposed to do: "We thought we had a damn good chance of moving to a major racial conflagration. . . . The most important thing was what the response would be in the white police forces. The objective was to affect the posture of local authorities in the next summer."

President Johnson had called for two separate products from the commission: an "interim" document in March 1968, and a final report by August 1. But Palmieri and Ginsburg came to believe that the schedule of separate reports would have to be discarded, if the commission was to influence events in the summer of 1968.

It fell to Palmieri to assemble a crew of social scientists to document and analyze the "causes" of the riots, on which everyone had agreed before the commission's work ever started. President Johnson's television speech on July 27 — written in part and edited by Justice Abe Fortas — asserted that the riots then engulfing scores of cities were "caused" by "ignorance, discrimination, slums, poverty, disease, not enough jobs."

It should not have been difficult to find social scientists who accepted the commission's premises. Until very recently, there has been no tradition of radical analysis in the social sciences. Many of the most important figures in academic and political social science in the United States came of age in the late forties and fifties, when the "end of ideology" was proclaimed. But while many social science stars agreed to "consult" with the commission, none would undertake a full-time commitment. The staff finally had to settle for a National Institute of Mental Health psychologist, Robert Shellow, who was a commissioned officer in the Public Health Service.

There was also some question about the acceptability to the Administration of those academics who agreed to work in any capacity on the report. Herbert Gans, for instance, was "vetoed" by the White House as a regular consultant because he had indulged in anti-war activities. Palmieri (who was personally very much against the war, too) succeeded in hiring Gans on a "contract" basis. The White House veto operation was run by presidential assistant Marvin Watson, the notorious hatchet man of the late Johnson years, who kept names of anti-war activists in a computer file in the basement of the executive offices. Gans's name turned up as a member of a group of artists, writers and academics who declared that they would refuse tax payments as a protest against the war in Vietnam.

Within the commission staff, Palmieri tried a management device designed to provide alternate circuits and prevent overloading of the "social science input." He laid out his system of "fail-safes" in an attempt to treat conclusively the data received from field researchers. According to Palmieri's plan, the investigative and research material would be worked over in three ways: sociologically, by Robert Shellow; journalistically, by Robert Conot, co-author of a book on the Watts riots of 1965; and practical-politically, by staff lawyers, such as Ginsburg, Palmieri and Stephen Kurzman.

What happened in the end, as Palmieri once said, was that the system had an "abort" in its critical center—the social scientific, "intellectual" effort. The fail-safe failed. To Palmieri's way of thinking, that failure gutted the whole report. The journalistic accounts, the statistical tables and the political suggestions were never bound in a coherent analytical structure.

* * *

It was more than a month after the commissioners were appointed that the "critical" social scientific staff began its work. Having failed to enlist the undivided attentions of the top men at the universities and research centers around the country, Director Robert Shellow called for their recommendations for bright young assistants to round out his department. In time, he was provided with a half-dozen full- and part-time men, three undergraduate "interns" from Antioch College, and scores of consultants who would fly to Washington at $100 or $150 per diem.

Like many government agencies, bureaus and departments plowing the new fields of "social technology"—education, urban development, anti-poverty, welfare, health and civil rights—the commission drew to it every academic entrepreneur with a scheme to sell. Some were more successful than others: Washington is full of small research firms where returned VISTAs, Peace Corpsmen or Appalachian Volunteers can earn $12 or $15 thousand a year trading on their brief associations with the poor, black and oppressed. Such operations are often run by the returnees' old bosses at the various government agencies which funded the volunteer projects in the first place.

The commission signed a contract, quite early in the game, with the Trans-Century Corporation, a Washington-based research, training and job-placement company run by Warren Wiggins, a former deputy director of the Peace Corps, and staffed in large measure by returned volunteers and their friends. Several Trans-Centurions joined the commission staff. The company itself won its $18,000 contract to recruit staff.

Hundreds of thousands of dollars went into research contracts. The Bureau of Applied Social Science Research at Columbia (where several commission contractors and consultants, including Herbert Gans, now work) got $45,540 for a study of arrest records of rioters. A University of Michigan spin-off research department got $45,488 for a study of the life habits of rioters. The International Association of Chiefs of Police won a $38,000 contract for a study of police preparedness.

One of the most important commission research contracts was given to Systemetrics, a subsidiary of the Real Estate Research Corporation, of Chicago. Systemetrics is run by Anthony G. Downs, an old friend of Palmieri's. Downs is on the "new breed" side of a family connected with Mayor Daley's Chicago. He is a major ideologist of "downtownism" and "urban land reform."

Systemetrics was assigned two jobs: to design research and management programs for the commission, and to combine and summarize the field research reports on twenty-four riots in twenty-three cities. The way the Systemetrics researchers perceived the riots in the twenty-four summaries could profoundly affect the commissioners' understanding of the processes of conflict. If the summaries portrayed ghetto blacks as pitiable victims, surrounded by rats and roaches and put upon by evil and prejudiced predators, that would be how the commissioners ultimately would perceive the situation.

Systemetrics did use that approach, of course, and it was the theme of the final report. That theme grows out of the "middle position" between reactionary and revolutionary ideologies. It expresses the notion that since the conflicts of black and white America are non-ideological, no real shifts of power are needed to correct them. The problems which were seen in the American cities in the summer of 1967 did not represent contradictions within the whole political economy, but malfunctions of one or another institution—the failure to get food or money or jobs to the black people and whites in the same income group, to establish lines of communication between "control authorities" and the people they "serve." Racial prejudice, practiced by individuals alone or in groups, compounds the problems. But there is no real answer to prejudice; the "solution" to racial and urban problems must always be put in technical terms. And although it may be extremely difficult, solutions can be produced by the existing political elites.

Much of the foundation for that "middle position" was laid in an early paper written for the commission by Howard Margolis, of the Institute for Defense Analysis, the secret war-research corporation. The memorandum—never made public—reportedly laid out three possible perspectives for the commissioners to ponder: (1) the "Right-wing" theory that a conspiracy lay behind the riots, and that program recommendations should emphasize the restoration of "law and order"; (2) the "Left-wing" theory that the riots represented a para-political rebellion of the black poor in America, and that only radical social change could integrate that rebellion into a new American "system"; and (3) the "middle position," focussing on the presumably "neutral" problems of migration, urban over-population, and historical Negro underprivilege. Programs designed to deal with those problems implied no threat to the current organization of corporate capitalism in America.

The central contradiction of the entire commission operation was embedded in the "middle position." As Margolis — and other staff assistants who read it in the first months of the commission's autumn — understood, the position did not fit the realities of the black rebellions of the summer. The problem was not that it was "wrong," but that it didn't represent the forces at work in the country. Its presentation was meant to serve a single political purpose.

For that reason, its unquestioned reception created a constellation of problems for the commission staff, for the commissioners themselves, and for final report. The contradiction between theory and reality hampered the work of the field investigators, who felt themselves pulled apart between the blacks they were interviewing and the commission they were serving. It created fatal tensions within the social science section, which was charged with integrating research materials and historical perspectives in a framework which was abstracted from real conditions. It made the official "hearings" before the full commission quite irrelevant, for it gave values to the parameters of testimony before anyone ever was heard. And finally, it denied meaning to the report, for it based programs on unrealistic theories.

The field investigation teams were the first to feel the tensions. Teams of six investigators were sent to each of twenty-three cities. In each city, "sub-teams" of two people would speak with officials, private citizens in positions of power, and ghetto residents and activists. The teams were organized on racial lines. According to a memorandum from David Ginsburg to the commission staff, it was to be assumed that "only Negroes would be able to obtain information from residents in the ghetto areas." Whites, Ginsburg added, would be sent to interview officials and private citizens.

It was not long, however, before the black investigators began to sense that they were being used for purposes of which they were at least partly suspicious; specifically, they were worried that the reports of their interviews would be misrepresented when shown to the higher levels of the commission staff, or that information on militants might ultimately be passed on to law-enforcement agencies, despite official assurances that it would go only as far as the National Archives.

Many black staffers remained convinced that "the whole thing was a racist operation," as one of the field investigators put it. All the top policymaking jobs were held by whites, except for the post of general counsel, which had been given to a black man, Merle McCurdy. There were only a few "token" black consultants in the long list appended to the report. Overall, the report was always thought of as a white document written by white writers and aimed at a white audience — *about* black people. It was primarily a response to the white response to the riots. It was supposed to prescribe policy for black people, not for whites. Although it named "white racism," it did not describe white-racist society.

The central contradiction of the commission — between what was politic and what was real — was felt most strongly by the social science section, under research director Robert Shellow. It was expressed primarily in the drafting of the document, "The Harvest of American Racism," and the word "Harvest's" eventual rejection by Palmieri; and by the firing of Shellow and his entire staff in late December 1967. Although perceptions of the reasons for the firings differ widely, the context of contradictions is hardly arguable: the report was intended to serve particular political ends, and "Harvest" and the social scientists interfered.

Shellow had four assistants working on "Harvest": David Boesel, Louis Goldberg, Gary T. Marx and David Sears. All of them were young social scientists with liberal or radical tendencies. To them, the riots were not incoherent freakouts, but rather specific (though unplanned) responses to oppression. They could not be understood without a conception of black struggle against white domination; and the "causes" could not be found in the obviously bad living conditions, but in the distribution of power in the total system. In other words, the riots were rebellions.

By early November, the Shellow section began to feel the critical press of time. No underlings had yet been told that there would be only one report — instead of the March interim document and the August final version — so the summary analysis of the whole summer of riots would have to be finished by the end of November to meet the interim deadline. "We were working around the clock," Boesel said. "We slept in our offices—they brought in cots—and we never left. It was crazy. We'd be found in our underwear darting across the hall in the mornings, just before people came to work. But we were really excited. We thought our case studies would be the guts of the report. We thought our original doubts about how the commission would operate were proving unfounded, and that we'd be able to say what we wanted."

What they wanted to say was contained in a 176-page document of forceful impressions, if somewhat limited analysis. "The Harvest of American Racism" was hardly the kind of work that a government agency would be happy to endorse. It did not couch its ideology in the conventions of "neutrality," but stated its positions boldly. It also was confused and inconsistent even in its own terms, and mixed traditional liberal assumptions which even the commission would find perfectly acceptable with radical notions about the nature of oppression and the development of rebellion. The most extraordinary part was the last chapter: "America on the Brink: White Racism and Black Rebellion." Written in rather heated language, it went further than most top staff officials thought prudent in charging that racism infused all American institutions, and characterized the riots as a first step in a developing black revolution, in which Negroes will "feel it is legitimate and necessary to use violence against the social order. A truly revolutionary spirit has begun to take hold . . . an unwillingness to compromise or wait any longer, to risk death rather than have their people continue in a subordinate status."

Both Palmieri and Ginsburg admit that they were appalled when they read "Harvest." Ginsburg, who was thought to be the soul of genteel manners and quiet control, spoke of the document in four-letter words. Palmieri said he fairly threw it across the room when Shellow gave it to him. The real problem was not that it was poorly done (it was no worse a job than much of the finished report) but that it defied the categories that the top officials had established for the "social science input."

Palmieri "fired" Shellow on the spot, although the actual process of separation was much more ambiguous and drawn out. But from that point on, Shellow was excluded from all important commission activities. "Harvest" was popped down a memory hold.

At length, Palmieri gave up entirely on "social science input," a notion in which he once placed so much confidence, and gave the analysis section of the report to Stephen Kurzman, a lawyer who was a deputy director of the commission, to complete. Kurzman turned out a quick, lawyerlike job, incorporating those notions in the "Harvest" thesis which were acceptable from the start, but removing the more threatening ideas.

Many of the 120 investigators and social scientists "released" from the commission staff in December 1967 will always believe that the firings were ordered by the Johnson administration. But there is every reason to believe that the action was undertaken by Palmieri (with Ginsburg concurring) because of the failure of Shellow's group to produce an "acceptable" analytical section.

The commissioners themselves knew little of the firings, or of the controversy surrounding them, until the few speculative reports in the press were seen. On December 8, Ginsburg gave the commission the news: "It was simply flabbergasting," a staff member reported. "Ginsburg said that the publication of the report in March wouldn't really mean the end of the commission, that there would be supplemental reports and such. And the commissioners allowed themselves to be deluded. 'Oh, well,' Kerner said, 'if it's not really going to be the end of the commission, then I guess it's all right.' He fell right in line, then Harris behind him, then Brooke. The rest of them sort of looked at one another. The decision was made in just fourteen minutes."

* * *

From the beginning, it was clear that John Lindsay was the chief spokesman for the liberal position, and Tex Thornton was the heavy for the conservatives. Lindsay's closest allies were Senator Harris, Chief Jenkins, and Roy Wilkins. Thornton had only Mrs. Peden as a full-time cohort. The others roamed around the middle or, like Brooke, who had the worst attendance record, roamed elsewhere.

What the "liberal" side meant first of all was a full acceptance of the "middle position" as laid out long before in the Margolis memo. Beyond that, it entailed a rhetorical emphasis on the horrors of life for ghetto blacks, and a sense — as Hubert Humphrey once expressed it — that things were bad enough to explain (but not excuse) rioting. There was no agreement, however, that the riots were a positive or beneficial political act (as "Harvest" had proposed); nor, of course, was there any idea that the failure of black Americans to achieve equality with whites was a structural failure of the American political and economic system.

The "conservative" side grudgingly accepted that same "middle position" thesis but emphasized the bad character of the criminal element in the ghettoes rather than the conditions of life there. Secret minutes of a commission meeting of November 10, 1967, taken by a staff member, illustrate Thornton's attitudes; in this instance, he was responding to a discussion on "what causes riots":

> In re "bitterness and despair": We're playing right into the hands of the militants who will use it as justification for violence. Maybe bitterness and an element of despair; but only 2 or 3 percent actually start the riots. It's also the rewards, the benefit from free burglary. Put in . . . "an increasing lack of respect for the law": that's what it is, and the report has to bring this out loud and clear. There's little restraint to participation in disorders. . . . Improve the police departments: the military should train soldiers about to come out of the service in law-enforcement work. Help solve big recruitment problem. There are up to 60,000 coming out per year. . . . No question that show of restraining force, quickly applied, actually has restraining effect. Show of military force (even with no bullets or bayonets fixed) quickly stopped militants. We should provide maybe that federal troops be made available on standby basis as a precautionary measure.
>
> Let's not mention about the slave background and the poor Negro. Sins of forefathers idea will fall on deaf ears. Only 10 to 15 percent of whites had slave-owning forefathers.

No law and no courts will change the attitude of the whites. Labor unions have this very bad attitude, as does the so-called establishment. . . . Open housing helps force Negroes onto whites and releases hostile attitudes. . . . If we voice poverty, etc., as a cause of riots, 30 million poor people will use it as an excuse to riot.

On the other hand, Lindsay thought that the report, even in its finished form, was "wishy-washy." He was particularly angry that no mention was made of the war in Vietnam as a contributing factor to the riot process. But in a meeting of the commission to debate the point of "mentioning" the war, Lindsay was voted down. Although there is no reason to think that President Johnson directed Ginsburg to avoid mention of the war, it is clear that Ginsburg was doing Johnson's bidding: that, indeed, was his function, and the reason he was picked to head the commission staff—by the President himself. Early fears that Lindsay entertained about Ginsburg's "daily" contact with Johnson were irrelevant. Ginsburg didn't *have* to see Johnson.

There was, however, one exception. Late in 1967, Thornton grew anxious about the final report's "liberalism." He was particularly worried that it would suggest legislation for enormous federal expenditures; and, more than that, that it would generate "expectations" in the black community which could never be fulfilled, and which would lead to more rioting. Thornton went to George Mahon, the Texas Democrat who heads the House Appropriations Committee, and asked him to intercede with the White House on behalf of the "conservative" side of the commission. Mahon, Thornton and the President were, of course, all Texans. Mahon and Thornton were also allied through Litton Industries' intense interest in government appropriations.

On the night before the final meeting, Lindsay and his personal staff put together what he describes as an "end game." The plan was that Lindsay would "assume" at the next day's meeting that a summary would precede the full report. He would then read just such a summary—written in an all-night session by his aides. In promoting the summary, Lindsay would tell how deeply he felt about the issues it raised. The implication was that he would not sign the report if the summary were not included. The move had three objectives. First, Lindsay's "support" of the report (with summary) would put the burden of "dissent" on the conservative side. Second, Lindsay got his own summary into the hopper before any others. Finally, the gambit would lay the emotional and intellectual basis for Lindsay's personal dissent, should his summary be defeated, or if the conservatives won their points.

But the game worked smoothly. At first, Thornton and Corman argued against Lindsay's summary, but Thornton's attempt to put together a majority against it (and, by implication, against the report as it stood) came to nothing.

Could the report have gone either way? Palmieri, for instance, thought there was a real danger that it could turn into an obviously illiberal document. But the structure of the commission and the context in which it operated suggest that its tone could hardly have been other than "liberal." The finished product almost exactly reproduced the ideological sense given it by President Johnson more than half a year earlier. The choice of commissioners, staff, consultants and contractors led in the same direction. The political constituency foremost in the directors' minds—the audience to which the report was played—had been conditioned to expect and accept a catalogue of ills and a list of reforms.

According to the directors, the real fights in the commission came over the introduction to the "Recommendations for National Action." That 70-page chapter was supposed to outline the scope of a national program of social reforms, in employment, education, welfare and housing, with no "price tag" attached.

The chapter was based on a thorough memorandum of program recommendations drawn up for the commission by Anthony Downs of Systemetrics.

The importance of the Downs strategy is not in the specifics of its programs, which in many cases are considered desirable by most right-thinking people, but in the nature of its political demands. Continuing, reinforcing—and to some degree, setting—the ideology of the commission, it assumes the dominance of the same elites now in power, minus the old fogeys and plus the new technocrats. While its theory of programming may be dynamic, its theory of power is static.

September 15–22, 1969

Law and Power in Washington

Andrew Kopkind and James Ridgeway

Abe Fortas's progress from New Deal to wheeler-deal is not only the story of one man's travels but can serve as a parable for the epic of a generation. The New Dealers have done extremely well by doing a little good. Washington is full of hucksters, hustlers and high-priced hangers-on who have built powerful roles for themselves on a base of free-enterprise liberalism. Not all of them command the heights of power and profit as securely as Fortas and his old law firm of Arnold, Fortas & Porter, but then few have commanded comparable resources: the capital of great corporations, the minds of fine law schools, the friendship of influential men, and the ear of a President.

All told – if all could ever be told – the top Washington law firms occupy a political position far from the traditional concept of legal counsel and advocacy. Together, they constitute a new "estate" of government, all the more powerful because of its isolation from inspection and its insulation from criticism. At least in theory, the other political estates – federal bureaucracies, legislatures, corporations, foundations, the military—are subject in some degree to public scrutiny. The law estate is locked in privacy and shrouded in the canons of an ethical code which makes exposure of its secrets a mortal sin, or worse.

The great Washington firms stand as brokers between their corporate clients and agencies of government. Their lawyers do not plead cases so much as they negotiate interests. An hour's lunch with a powerful senator or the chairman of a regulatory commission can be more useful than a month's work on a brief. But firms like Arnold & Porter (Fortas's name was dropped when he went to the Supreme Court) can afford both approaches. The top dogs have the lunches; the bottom ones write the briefs.

The big black Cadillacs pull up every day at the Arnold & Porter *palazzi* astride the kitty-corner of Nineteenth and N Streets, in the heart of Washington's forest of regulatory agencies and welfare bureaus. The Office of Economic Opportunity, the Federal Communications Commission, bureaus of HUD, Labor and Transportation are within walking distance of A & P, and on any given workday it's easy to see little delegations of the firm's lawyers scurrying to or from one or another of them. It is more difficult to see just who it is the limousines bring, for the client list is relatively well-guarded, except for the obvious stars: Philip Morris, Coca-Cola, Federated Department Stores, Braniff Airways, the Commonwealth of Puerto Rico. In the heyday of the Johnson administration, famous losers like Bobby Baker and Walter Jenkins would show up at the A & P corner, too; Fortas negotiated both their misfortunes.

* * *

Inside the old houses converted to A & P offices, thirty-two partners and twenty-three associates divvy up the work and the profits. At present, the firm's gross income is between $6 and $7 million annually, of which 55 or 60 percent is distributed as profit to the partners. In the 1965 distribution of income, for instance, the top partners' shares were worth $325,000 apiece; those on the next level got $216,000 each; and the third-level partners made about $125,000 each.

Thurman Arnold, Paul Porter and Fortas were at the top, of course (except that Fortas's share was prorated under the others' that year because he had left in midyear for the Court). Fortas's wife, Carolyn Agger, the head of A & P's tax law section, was at the second level of income. The third-level types were junior partners, usually in their late thirties. (By comparison, the top men at Covington & Burling—another fortress of the law estate—made only as much as the third-level people at A & P that year.) Young associates in their twenties make $25,000 or more, a few years after they leave Harvard or Yale law schools and their court clerkships; and even summertime clerks get $250 a week.

Many lawyers join A & P not only for the money but for the good feeling that comes from working for an institution with a social conscience. But they soon come to understand how much that feeling is illusion. "They don't even *let* you sell out," one former A & P lawyer said recently. "They don't give you the salve for your conscience. It's pure business and nothing else."

For the crusades of the New Deal have become the cautions of the wheeler-deal. Thurman Arnold was a pioneer trust buster as FDR's Assistant Attorney General, but now he advises the trusts on how to beat the busters. He is well liked on Capitol Hill for his earnest defenses of Coca-Cola against proposed anti-monopoly legislation; he charms the legislators with tales of Coke's advantages for small business.

Fortas's championship of liberal and civil libertarian causes did not stop him from participating in the smear job on Leland Olds, a federal power commissioner denied reappointment during the Truman administration because of his support of public power systems; Fortas engaged in that campaign on behalf of private power interests. The firm has consistently been on the side of monopolies in anti-trust actions: it represented Bank of America, Lever Brothers and the First Security National Bank of Lexington, Ky., in notorious cases. The firm has also fought unionization on behalf of its corporate clients: Fortas handled a famous action of the Southern Newspaper Publishers Association against the International Typographical Union. Dennis Lyons, the firm's brilliant young hotshot, argued a Supreme Court brief for one of the most anti-labor railroads in the country, Florida East Coast.

One of the convenient myths of the law game is that lawyers have no ethical connection with the alleged crimes of their clients. But that category of ethics (like many others) was developed in the days when lawyers stood in a totally different relationship to their clients than they do now. Firms like Arnold & Porter make their enormous profits precisely because they do share in their clients' business. The more exploitative the clients, the bigger the A & P percentage distribution will be.

* * *

Paul Porter once told a young liberal lawyer in the firm that A F & P had "paid its dues" to civil rights and liberties in the early days; it was time now to get on with the business of making money. In those early days, Fortas and the firm defended some celebrated innocents (Owen Lattimore, for one) against McCarthyist attacks. Some business was lost on that account: it is said around the office that the Pew family (Sun Oil) withdrew as a client. Later, Fortas was appointed by high courts to argue one or another case for which judges had staked out constitutional issues. He did the landmark *Durham* (insanity test) and *Gideon* (right to counsel) arguments as a court appointee.

Younger lawyers in the firm still handle work for moderate black and liberal-radical organizations in Washington. A & P represents the Institute for Policy Studies, and the firm half-heartedly agreed to take the case of IPS' director, Marcus Raskin, when he was indicted for conspiracy in the Spock-Coffin group. But the conditions A & P imposed on Raskin — to withdraw completely from protest politics — were so strict that Raskin chose another firm. But one A & P partner is still on IPS' board.

For the most part, the "conscience" cases made icing on a very rich cake, and it all served some useful purposes as well. The famous trials attracted the good young lawyers, and the firm's liberalism legitimized its share of the profits in the system whose victims Fortas defended.

Increasingly, A & P has stopped playing even those inex-

pensive liberal games. When many more "conservative" firms
were sending out their lawyers for legal aid work or paying
expenses for their lawyers to go South in the civil rights campaigns, A F & P employees had to go during their vacations
at their own expense. Privately, Fortas would argue vigorously against such volunteer services; in public, he took credit
for his lawyers' defense of the poor, black and downtrodden.
And the $20,000 he took from—and returned to—Louis
Wolfson was for civil rights "research."

The firm's uptightness in that area was the result of several
coincident problems. First, there was real "panic" (in one
lawyer's word) when Fortas split for the Supreme Court. Fortas was unquestionably the key man. From the beginning,
Arnold was the figurehead, Porter was the charmer, but Fortas
was the brains and the organizer. He had run things single-
handedly—some say tyrannically—and it was feared that
profits would measurably decline. (They didn't.)

Second, some of the older partners were much less sympathetic toward the darker races than were the younger associates. For years, the only visible Negro around the firm was
the old man who polished up the handle on the big front door
on the mansion house at the southeast angle of the corner.
(He occasionally opened and shut limousine doors, for variety.) There has never been a Negro lawyer in the firm, although the first is supposedly arriving this summer; and until
a few years ago, there was an unwritten law against hiring
Negro secretaries. (One civil rightsy associate broke the law
and hired an "imported" black lady from a foreign country,
but she was kept well hidden in one of the outbuildings of the
office complex.)

But there were business reasons, too, for laying off the liberal causes. Once, a small group of Arnold & Porter lawyers
who had been active in mid-sixties civil rights work developed a plan to bring stockholders' lawsuits against big corporations that discriminated against Negroes in employment
in their Southern branch facilities. The target company would
be Continental Can—not an A F & P client—which had a
plant in Louisiana. The lawyers found a Washington man of
means named Robert Eichholz, a longtime stockholder in

Continental, to put up $40,000 for the suit, which would be done on non-firm time. But A F & P's management commit-tee — G. Duane ("Bud") Veith, Dennis Lyons and Carolyn Agger Fortas — vetoed the idea. Their principal objection, they told the lawyers, was that the firm had a primary respon-sibility to its clients, and it was not in their clients' interests to establish a legal precedent that might be applied against them. As the lawyers knew, several client corporations had South-ern operations that might run afoul of fair employment laws. What was bad for Continental Can might be bad for Federat-ed Department Stores or Philip Morris. And as it happened, the first adjudicated fair employment case was in fact against Philip Morris' Richmond, Va., facilities. (A & P did not han-dle it.)

* * *

As institutions, the great Washington law firms incorporate the deals made by their several partners along the way. His-toric friendships, old favors and current contracts are com-bined, juggled and manipulated for maximum power and prof-it. A classic example was A F & P's nose-deep involvement in Puerto Rico:

Abe Fortas had been Undersecretary of the Interior in FDR's last cabinet. One of his duties was to manage Puerto Rico's affairs in Washington. He also was a member of a presidential commission appointed in 1943 to redefine the colony's relationship to the United States. In the context of Puerto Rican – U.S. politics at the time, the commission's es-sential job was to provide some form of limited "home rule" in order to abort a growing movement for full independence.

Fortas felt strongly that the federal government — not pri-vate lawyers — should represent the interests of U.S. territo-ries in Washington; in a well-known letter to Puerto Rico's Gov. Rex Tugwell, he argued that very theory. Whereupon, a few days after leaving Interior in 1946, he "lifted" Puerto Rico out of the department and plopped it into his new pri-vate law practice — for a $12,000 retainer.

Fortas and his firm represented the Commonwealth for twenty-three years, until the association was terminated this spring with the removal of Fortas's old pals in both San Juan and Washington. But in those decades, Fortas and Puerto Rico's ruling elites did well by and for each other. Fortas was instrumental in getting the Commonwealth included in all sorts of deals he considered good for the islanders—not excluding welfare legislation and protection. At the same time, Fortas would argue vigorously against statehood or independence for the colony. Any alteration of the colonial status, of course, would put obstacles in the way of Puerto Rico's operation as a tax haven and an advantageous trading post for U.S. corporations; and at the same time it would displace Fortas's contacts in power in the Commonwealth.

When other dealers wanted a piece of the Puerto Rican action, they came to Fortas. Thus, a few years ago, when Phillips Petroleum sought to build a huge petrochemical complex on the island, Arnold, Fortas & Porter (with Fortas the principal mover) argued Phillips's case on behalf of the Commonwealth before the Interior Department. The deal was particularly luscious in Phillips's eyes, because it would allow the company to import large quantities of Venezuelan crude oil above its previous import quota allotment. (By a curious irony—or something—A F & P also represented a trade association of small oil companies seeking to block the Phillips deal.) Phillips won. Interior Secretary Udall reshuffled the oil quotas and granted permission for the installation. More curious but less ironic was the fact that the three principals in the action—Fortas, Udall and Phillips's Board Chairman K. S. Adams—were closely tied to the Johnson administration. Fortas was LBJ's No. 1 Boy; Udall was in his cabinet; and Adams was a major Democratic party contributor and a member of the "President's Club" of moneybags.

Fortas's interests in the Caribbean went farther afield. For two decades he was a director of the Sucrest Corporation, the third-largest East Coast sugar refiner, with extensive general interests in both Puerto Rico and the Dominican Republic. (Former New Deal adviser A. A. Berle, Jr., was Sucrest's chairman.) Arnold & Porter partner William D. Rogers—a former AID and Alianza administrator—worked on the Puerto Rico account, and now handles El Salto, a Guatemalan sugar company, as well as Braniff Airways' tourist services and hotel chain in Latin America. Braniff is now part of the Ling-Temco-Vought conglomeration.

Within one law firm, a whole network of Caribbean interests—from Venezuela to Texas—interlocked. When Lyndon Johnson sent Abe Fortas on a secret mission to Puerto Rico to save America's face in the 1965 Dominican invasion, he was sending more than an "adviser." Fortas worked through his old friends Luis Muñoz Marin and Jaimé Benitez—the colony's old elite guards—both of them his close personal friends and associates. (Fortas is godfather to Benitez's daughter; she once worked briefly for Fortas's firm.) So Fortas had an independent base of influence in Caribbean affairs and significant power in the formulation of basic attitudes of U.S. policy in that region.

* * *

"There is a mystique," one lawyer said recently, "that Arnold & Porter lawyers are not owned by their clients. But that's nostalgia." In some ways it may still be true: In its role as power broker, A & P has more leeway than the great Wall Street firms that act purely as mouthpieces for their biggest corporate accounts or form "legal departments" for their clients' companies. But the leeway has been reduced as the stakes are raised—for the clients as well as for the firm's income. The firm's association with the tobacco lobby is a case in point:

Late in 1963, shortly before the Public Health Service released its report linking smoking with cancer, Fortas turned up representing Philip Morris. During the next two years the lawyers at Arnold, Fortas & Porter played a major role in helping the tobacco companies fend off the government and avoid warning the public about the dangers of smoking. Philip Morris paid them an estimated annual retainer of $1 million.

The fight over cigarettes was extensive and resulted in an extraordinary piece of special-interest legislation favoring the tobacco companies. Overall strategy was planned through a committee of the general counsels of the different companies. They ironed out company differences and settled on an industrywide attack. Then, policy was carried out in Washington by a network of lawyers and lobbyists. Chief among them was Earle C. Clements, the former U.S. Senate Democratic whip from Kentucky who runs the Tobacco Institute, the industry's lobby. Clements was a friend of Johnson's and an experienced operator with Congress. Arnold, Fortas & Porter did work for the Tobacco Institute as well as Philip Morris. The firm mapped strategy and handled most of the tedious legal and political details during the fight. Fortas himself, who got the account to begin with and who was advising the President informally at the time, stayed in the background, surfacing only when key problems required his presence, but he was always very much under the thumb of Paul Smith, the general counsel of Philip Morris. Paul Porter was assigned the role of front man for the firm in the tobacco fight; Fortas could not afford to be seen in the foreground.

After the PHS made its report, the Federal Trade Commission took the unusually bold step of proposing rules requiring tobacco companies to place health warnings on packages of cigarettes. More important, the FTC insisted tobacco companies insert some sort of warning in advertising.

The industry laid out a counter-strategy: First, shift the fight from the FTC to Congress, where the chairman of the House Commerce Committee was Oren Harris, a local tobacco man from Arkansas. Clements could work his contacts to best advantage in Congress. Second, keep the White House out of the picture. Both Fortas and Clements were friends of the President. Moreover, there was ample precedent for his remaining out of the picture: John Kennedy had also made it policy to stay clear of the tobacco and health issue. Finally, while opposing any sort of legislation or regulation in principle, the tobacco companies were prepared to accept a compromise: in return for putting a health warning on the package, Congress would promise to keep the government from meddling in advertising. Television advertising aimed at young people is what sells cigarettes, and above all else, the industry didn't want to give it up. As for the label, it might actually work to the industry's benefit by serving as a legal defense in medical suits.

Things moved right along as the industry had planned:

Oren Harris wrote a nasty letter to Paul Rand Dixon, chairman of the FTC, and told him to leave cigarettes alone until Congress looked at the matter; Dixon dropped the issue. Harris began hearings before the House Commerce Committee. Meanwhile the lawyers at Arnold & Porter had been busy writing up an advertising code for the industry. This was a gimmick to persuade the public and the Congress that the industry itself could police advertising. An "independent" organization would be set up, headed by Robert B. Meyner, the former governor of New Jersey. He would look out for unseemly ads, i.e., baseball players dragging on butts as they hurl no-hitters, naked women smoking Kents, etc. It was thought necessary to get Justice Department clearance before going ahead with the code, and at that point, Fortas showed up in person to put in a good word for the industry.

Then Arnold, Fortas & Porter set about building a congressional campaign. There was no trouble in the House committee, which was pro-industry. The House dutifully endorsed the label law and at the same time voted to prevent the FTC from ever regulating advertising. Things were not quite so simple in the Senate, where Warren Magnuson, chairman of the Commerce Committee, had to contend with a small group of liberals, led by Maurine Neuberger, who wanted to get a warning in advertising. The lawyers at Arnold, Fortas & Porter wrote testimony for the witnesses, including the testimony for the main industry spokesman, Bowman Gray, then chairman of Reynolds. In addition, they added frills such as bringing in professors to give their independent scholarly opinions on smoking. For instance, A F & P asked Darrell B. Lucas, chairman of the marketing department at NYU, to say something about cigarettes. He sent in a statement for the record, and was paid $3,200 for the trouble. The Senate committee eventually reported out, and the Senate voted a bill which provided for a label on the package but stayed the FTC from acting for only four years, not forever. The issue then went to conference, and Fortas started making telephone calls on behalf of the House bill. There was one recorded at Magnuson's office, June 24, 1965. "He [Fortas] hopes you will go along with provisions of the House-passed bill." Magnuson didn't follow Fortas's advice, and the final legislation tied the FTC's hands for only four years.

The four years are now up, and the industry is back lobbying hard, using the same strategy as before. This time its chances of winning are less sure. Arnold & Porter still represents Philip Morris, although the lawyers' enthusiasm is said to be flagging. The firm also represents Philip Morris and the Tobacco Institute in battles before the Federal Communications Commission. There, the industry has been opposing the application of the "fairness" doctrine to pro- and anti-smoking advertising.

* * *

The cigarette case is not an isolated example of Arnold & Porter's interest brokerage. For another example, the firm represented the Florida East Coast Railway when it sought to prevent the railway brotherhoods from striking terminals in Florida. (A & P lost the case.) Fortas represented the Murchisons in the great proxy battle for control of Alleghany Corp. in the early sixties; and last year Paul Porter appeared at the FCC on behalf of WLBT, a Jackson, Miss., television station controlled by the Murchisons. A church group opposed renewal of the station's license on the grounds it discriminated in its news coverage against blacks. Porter argued for the station and won in the commission. The case is now in the U.S. Court of Appeals. It was Arnold & Porter which represented the First Security National Bank in Lexington before the courts, in its efforts to avoid the anti-trust laws and merge with another bank. After the Supreme Court struck down this merger on two different occasions, the bankers got together and rammed special legislation through Congress, exempting six big banks from anti-trust laws. The Lexington bank was one of them.

Among its other clients, Arnold & Porter has represented the Swiss watch cartel, organized baseball, Lever Brothers, Federated Department Stores (where Fortas was a director and vice-president before going to the Court), the Parvin Foundation (dropped like a hot potato a couple of weeks ago), Allis-Chalmers and *Playboy*. Also, Chesebrough-Pond's, maker of Measurin, a heavy-duty aspirin allowed on the market by the Food and Drug Administration after heavy lobbying from Arnold & Porter, despite test data which the FDA said was "phony" (people cited in the tests were dead or fictitious); and Unimed, Inc., maker of Serc, anti-vertigo medicine for people afflicted with Ménière's syndrome. Serc is on the market, although evidence to show its effectiveness is slim. Again, Arnold & Porter pushed hard. One reason: the company's stock rose on news of the drug's release and ran from $15 to more than $80.

But Arnold & Porter is best known for its wheeler-dealer clients from the South and Southwest. It is a kind of advocacy and protection center for the new moneymen who have built up conglomerates which are now raiding older corporations based in the Republican hinterlands.

Until his appointment to the Supreme Court, Fortas was general counsel and director of Greatamerica Corp., a sprawling financial conglomerate with $2 billion in assets controlled by Troy V. Post. Post is a Dallas operator who shied away from oil and built an empire on insurance instead. Post was one of the first who caught on to the idea that the steady flow of insurance premiums could be used to buy other companies and pyramid an empire. Fortas, who had helped Post in some of his early dealings, is credited with fashioning the complicated legal structures on which Greatamerica rested. Eventually, Greatamerica controlled a handful of insurance companies and a bank. In addition, Post bought Braniff Airways, and he last year merged the whole into Ling-Temco-Vought, which is run by his former business associate James Ling. Post helped bankroll Ling's original merger of Chance-Vought into L-T-V, and the two men have been in and out of deals together for some time. L-T-V has since sold off the insurance company but retained Braniff.

Fortas also has helped represent Ling. On one occasion several years ago, when Ling's Electro-Science Shares, Inc., was under scrutiny by the Securities and Exchange Commission, Fortas intervened directly with commission chairman

William Carey. He told Carey to leave Ling alone because he was a big contributor to the Democratic party. Carey got furious and spread the story around Washington.

More recently A & P represented Braniff in its quest for a Pacific air route. Under Johnson's decision (which benefited his friends), Braniff got a run to the South Pacific via Acapulco. For its work in the case in 1968, Arnold & Porter got $408,636. Then Nixon came along and threw Braniff out; the airline now has no Pacific route.

* * *

Fortas was well on the way to creating his own little Washington financial combine, à la Post and Ling, through the Madison National Bank. He and his wife helped start the bank, and she remains a director. Arnold & Porter is counsel. The Madison Bank is a clubhouse for the Antonelli & Gould realty operation, a $10 million affair—peanuts in Texas, but a hefty operation for Washington. Dominic Antonelli is the son of an Italian immigrant, and Kingdon Gould (recently elevated by Nixon to be ambassador to Luxembourg) is the grandson of railroad robber baron Jay Gould. The two of them have converted downtown commercial Washington to a sea of parking lots. They buy old buildings, rip them down, turn the lot into a parking lot to produce income, and then wait for the opportune moment when enough land is assembled to build an office structure, which likely as not is let to the government. Antonelli & Gould run the Madison Bank along with their building partners, who include a Maryland garbage king, a Greek restaurateur, and a prominent builder called Charles E. Smith. Smith is chairman of the bank. He runs a slew of realty syndicates in Washington and Virginia. The membership of any one of them reads like a Georgetown cocktail party guest list. Members of recent syndicates in Washington and Virginia include Fortas and his wife; former U.N. Ambassador and Supreme Court Justice Arthur Goldberg; Justice William Brennan; David L. Bazelon, chief judge of the U.S. Court of Appeals for the District of Columbia; J. Skelly Wright, another judge on the same Court of Appeals; Simon E. Sobeloff, of the Court of Appeals for the Fourth Circuit; Milton E. Kronheim, Jr., scion of Washington's biggest liquor-dealing family and now judge of the Court of General Sessions in Washington; Sen. Ribicoff; and former Internal Revenue Service Director Mortimer Caplin. Even jaded tongues wagged and cynical eyebrows lifted in Washington at the prospect of Fortas's business partnership with judges before whose courts his firm practiced. But that seemed no more (though no less) suspect than Fortas's continued connection—through marriage—to a firm that practiced before his own Supreme Court. Nor, for that matter, was it worse than Fortas's continuing and intimate relationship with the President—again, on matters which had Constitutional as well as political implications.

Since the hearings last summer on Fortas's abortive nomination to be Chief Justice, it has been known that he kept close to the White House during his associate justiceship. But much of the extent of that relationship has never been detailed. Last week, a former Administration official disclosed that Fortas did more than "advise" the President in an informal way, as the Justice claimed last summer. One some occasions, he sent over memos to the White House or the Justice Department concerning government actions. One or two of them were prepared, in part, by his law clerks.

For example, during a steel price dispute, Fortas fixed up a memo on the possibilities for executive action to set price ceilings, under World War II emergency powers still in effect. During the Detroit riots in 1967, he not only became Johnson's principal adviser on the deployment of federal troops, he wrote the President's television speech, according to one of the other advisers in the meetings at that time. (To return the favor, A & P wrote a long memo on Fortas's Court decisions, to be used for the Chief Justiceship hearings; the Justice Department then promulgated it, as its own work.)

Fortas's closeness to Johnson was both his triumph and his undoing. It was as if he were attached to some mad mephistophelean creature which fed him power and glory and, at length, reclaimed his soul. What bargain had been struck first became known in 1948, when Fortas helped Johnson liquidate the legal proceedings resulting from his 87-vote "victory" over Coke Stevenson in the Texas senatorial primary.

Fortas succeeded in convincing Justice Hugo Black to quash an injunction over voting frauds; that allowed Johnson to get his name on the ballot and, ultimately, to go to the Senate. Fortas later represented George Parr, the "Duke of Duval County" — where major irregularities were said to have occurred in the 1948 election — when Parr was appealing to the Supreme Court on a federal mail-fraud indictment in the fifties. (Parr won.)

No one can tell just how much money came to Fortas and his firm from the Johnson connection. Philip Morris obviously came to his office because of his importance in high politics. In the same way, A F & P got the case of the Chicago & North Western Railway's corporate contest with the Union Pacific over control of the Rock Island Railroad. Chicago & North Western was owned by Ben Heineman, a Chicago entrepreneur in Johnson's entourage. The merger fight will prove to be the most complicated administrative proceedings in the history of American law, costing $55 million.

Fortas had an impact on that deal, although he had left the firm. On the Supreme Court, he wrote the decision in the Pennsylvania Railroad – New York Central merger case and included language which sought to guide government policy in future railroad mergers — such as Chicago & North Western's. Fortas's prominence in the Penn-Central decision saddened Justice Department anti-trust lawyers. One former high official there said recently that he thought Fortas "never should have participated" in the case. Fortas's continuing connection to A & P was also seen in the list of contributors to his "seminar" fund at American University: all were clients. And he intervened to change a moderate "anti-war" position of the Business Council by calling its chairman — who happened to be a member of the Lazarus family of Federated Stores.

The fact of the matter is that the impropriety of his role never even occurred to Fortas. One of his old friends, who now teaches law, remarked the other day that Fortas and Arnold "began to believe that the rules that apply to ordinary mortals don't apply to them." But Fortas, at least, seems never to have believed in the rules in the first place. He was a

Washington Mr. Fix-it, asserting judgments without regard for moral values. He once told a clerk, "I'm a Supreme Court justice. I don't argue. I decide."

* * *

Arnold & Porter—and Fortas—are big, and they will fall hard. In a sense, they are all victims of the contradictions in a system that they did much to establish. Fortas fell from attacks of his competitors in Washington's highest political elites: as the amount of power available at the top begins to diminish—as it flows to the suburban McCarthy campaigners, the student rebels, the blacks, the poor (and the Vietcong)—the scramble for power becomes more bitter. When there's enough to go around, the various sectors of Republicans and Democrats, corporate liberals and middle-managers, Texas *mafiosi* and Wall Street bankers, can let each other lie like sleeping dogs. But now the dogfights are beginning.

The firm is also vulnerable to an insurgent society. A & P's lasting, stable resource is its smart staff. But now young people either eschew law "careerism," or else they go into one of the many centers for "social action law" springing up around the country. Two of the brightest recent A & P lawyers—one still at the firm and another who left for full-time civil rights work a few years ago—both are planning to join such outfits this year. In one way, the exposure of Abe Fortas's corruption and the mindless profiteering of his firm has advanced the process of dissolution. The rot finally begins to smell, the rats are heard in the walls. The big Cadillacs come with men's money, but they leave with men's souls.

June 16–23, 1969

Part Five
The Crisis of Consciousness

In the end, the "revolution" in American life that has grown out of the crises of the sixties begins in individual consciousness, in a context of the reality which society imposes. Woodstock, Weatherman, the underground, the drug culture, the sexual revolution: all are uniquely American, because they connect with the reality of American life in this historical moment. What hope they have of development — in their own terms and against increasingly severe repression — derives from their unique origins, not from older, other-worldly models.

Coming of Age in Aquarius

Andrew Kopkind

The Woodstock Music and Art Fair wasn't held in Wood-stock; the music was secondarily important and the art was for the most part unproduced; and it was as much of a fair as the French Revolution or the San Francisco earthquake. What went down on Max Yasgur's farm in the low Catskills last weekend defied casual categories and conventional per-ceptions. Some monstrous and marvelous metaphor had come alive, revealing itself only in terms of its contradictions: para-dise and concentration camp, sharing and profiteering, sky and mud, love and death. The urges of the ten years' genera-tion roamed the woods and pastures, and who could tell whether it was some rough beast or a speckled bird slouching toward its Day-Glo manger to be born?

* * *

The road from the Hudson River west to White Lake runs through hills like green knishes, soft inside with good earth, and crusty with rock and wood on top. What works of man remain are rural expressions of an Other East Village, where the Mothers were little old ladies with *sheitls*, not hip radicals with guns. There's Esther Manor and Siegel's Motor Court and Elfenbaum's Grocery: no crash communes or head shops. Along that route, a long march of freaks in microbuses, shit cars and bikes—or on thumb and foot—passed like movie extras in front of a process screen. On the roadside, holidaymakers from the Bronx looked up from their pinochle games and afghan knitting and knew that the season of the witch had come.

"Beatniks out to make it rich": Woodstock was, first of all, an environment created by a couple of hip entrepreneurs to consolidate the culture revolution and (in order to?) extract the money of its troops. Michael Lang, a twenty-five-year-old former heavy dealer from Bensonhurt dreamed it up; he then organized the large inheritance of John Roberts, twenty-six, for a financial base and brought in several more operatives and financiers. Lang does not distinguish between hip culture and hip capital; he vowed to make a million before he was twenty-five, beat his deadline by two years, and didn't stop. With his Village/Durango clothes, a white Porsche and a gleaming BSA, he looks, acts and *is* hip; his interest in capital accumulation is an extension of every hippie's desire to rip off a bunch of stuff from the A&P. It's a gas.

The place-name "Woodstock" was meant only to evoke cultural-revolutionary images of Dylan, whose home base is in that Hudson River village. Woodstock is where The Band hangs out and the culture heroes congregate; it's where Mick Jagger (they say) once ate an acid-infused Baby Ruth right inside the crotch of a famous groupie. A legend like that is good for ticket sales, but the festival was always meant to be held in Wallkill, forty miles away.

By early summer, Woodstock looked to be the super rock festival of all time, and promoters of a dozen other summertime festivals were feverishly hyping up their own projects to catch the overflow of publicity and enthusiasm: Rock music (al fresco or recorded) is still one of the easiest ways to make money off the new culture, along with boutique clothes and jewelry, posters, drugs and trip equipment, *Esquire* magazine, Zig-Zag papers and Sara Lee cakes. But the Woodstock hype

worried the burghers of Wallkill, and the law implemented
their fears by kicking the bash out of town. Other communities, however, were either less uptight or more greedy; six
hard offers for sites came to the promoters the day Wallkill
gave them the boot. With less than a month to get ready,
Woodstock Ventures, Inc., chose the 600-acre Yasgur farm
(with some other parcels thrown in) at White Lake, N.Y.

Locals there were divided on the idea, and Yasgur was attacked by some neighbors for renting (for a reported $50,000)
to Woodstock. But in the end, the profit motive drove the
deal home. One townsman wrote to the Monticello newspaper: "It's none of their business how Max uses his land. If
they are so worried about Max making a few dollars from his
land they should try to take advantage of this chance to make
a few dollars themselves. They can rent camping space or
even sell water or lemonade." Against fears of hippie horrors,
businessmen set promises of rich rewards: "Some of these
people are shortsighted and don't understand what these children are doing," one said. "The results will bring an economic boost to the county, without it costing the taxpayer a
cent."

* * *

The vanguard of freaks started coming a week or more before opening day, and by Wednesday they were moving
steadily down Route 17B, like a busy day on the Ho Chi
Minh Trail. The early-comers were mostly hard-core, permanent dropouts: Their hair or their manner or their rap indicat-
ed that they had long ago dug into their communes or radical
politics or simply into oppositional life-styles. In the cool and
clear night they played music and danced, and sat around
fires toasting joints and smoking hashish on a pinpoint. No
busts, pigs or hassle; everything cool, together, outasight.

By the end of the next day, Thursday, the ambience had
changed from splendor in the grass to explosive urban sprawl.
Light and low fences erected to channel the crowds without
actually seeming to oppress them were toppled or ignored;
cars and trucks bounced over the meadows; tents sprung up
between stone outcroppings and cow plop. Construction went

on through the night, and already the Johnny-on-the-Spot la-trines were smelly and out of toilet paper, the food supply was spotty, and long lines were forming at the water tank. And on Friday morning, when the population explosion was upon us all, a sense of siege took hold: difficult as it was to get in, it would be almost impossible to leave for days.

* * *

From the beginning, the managers of the festival were faced with the practical problem of control. Berkeley and Chicago and Zap, N.D., were the functional models for youth mobs rampaging at the slightest provocation—or no provoca-tion at all. The promoters interviewed 800 off-duty New York City policemen for a security guard (Sample question: "What would you do if a kid walked up and blew marijuana smoke in your face?" Incorrect answer: "Bust him." Correct answer: "Inhale deeply and smile."), chose 300 or so, and fitted them with mod uniforms. But at the last minute they were withdrawn under pressure from the Police Department, and the managers had to hire camp counselors, phys ed teach-ers and stray straights from the surrounding area.

The guards had no license to use force or arrest people; they merely were to be "present," in their red Day-Glo shirts emblazoned with the peace symbol, and could direct traffic and help out in emergencies if need be. The real work of keeping order, if not law, was to be done by members of the Hog Farm commune, who had been brought from New Mexi-co, along with people from other hippie retreats, in a chartered airplane (at $16,000) and psychedelic buses from Kennedy Airport.

Beneath the practical problem of maintaining order was the principal contradiction of the festival: how to stimulate the energies of the new culture and profit thereby, and at the same time control them. In a way, the Woodstock venture was a test of the ability of avant-garde capitalism at once to profit from and control the insurgencies which its system spawns. "Black capitalism," the media industry, educational technology, and Third World economic development are other models, but more diffuse. Here it was in one field during one weekend: The microcosmic system would "fail" if Wood-stock Ventures lost its shirt, or if the control mechanisms broke down.

The promoters must have sensed the responsibility they carried. They tried every aspect of cooptation theory. SDS, Newsreel and underground newspapers were handed thou-sands of dollars to participate in the festival, and they were given a choice spot for a "Movement City"; the idea was that they would give hip legitimacy to the weekend and channel their activities "within the system." (They bought the idea.) Real cops were specifically barred from the campgrounds, and the word went out that there would be no busts for ordi-nary tripping, although big dealers were discouraged. There would be free food, water, camping facilities — and, in the end, free music, when attempts at crowd channeling failed. But the Hog Farmers were the critical element. Hip beyond any doubt, they spread the love/groove ethic throughout the farm, breaking up incipient actions against "the system" with cool, low-key hippie talk about making love not war, the mystical integrity of earth, and the importance of doing your *own* thing, preferably alone. On the other hand — actually, on the same hand — they were the only good organizers in camp. They ran the free food operation (oats, rice and bulgar), helped acid freaks through bad trips without thorazine, and (with Abbie Hoffman) ran the medical system when that be-came necessary.

The several dozen Movement organizers at the festival had nothing to do. After Friday night's rain there was a theory that revolt was brewing on a mass scale, but the SDS people found themselves unable to organize around the issue of in-clement weather. People were objectively trapped; and in that partial aspect, the Yasgur farm *was* a concentration camp — or a hippie reservation — but almost everyone was stoned and happy. Then the rain stopped, the music blared, food and water arrived, and everyone shared what he had. Dope be-came plentiful and entirely legitimate; in a soft cool forest, where craftsmen had set up their portable head shops, dealers sat on tree stumps selling their wares: "acid, mesc, psilocy-bin, hash. . . . " No one among the half million could not have turned on if he wanted to; joints were passed from blanket to blanket, lumps of hashish materialized like manna, and there was Blue Cheer, Sunshine acid and pink mescaline to spare.

Seen from any edge or angle, the army strung out against the hillside sloping from the stage created scenes almost unimaginable in commonplace terms. No day's demonstration or political action had brought these troops together; no congress or cultural event before produced such urgent need for in-gathering and self-inspection. The ambiguities and contradictions of the imposed environment were worrisome; but to miss the exhilaration of a generation's arrival at its own campsite was to define the world in only one dimension.

Although the outside press saw only masses, inside the differentiation was more impressive. Maybe half the crowd was weekend hip, out from Long Island for a quick dip in the compelling sea of freaks. The other half had longer been immersed. It was composed of tribes dedicated to whatever gods now seem effective and whatever myths produce the energy needed to survive: Meher Baba, Mother Earth, street-fighting man, Janis Joplin, Atlantis, Jimi Hendrix, Che.

The hillside was their home. Early Saturday morning, after the long night of rain—from Ravi Shankar through Joan Baez—they still had not abandoned the turf. Twenty or forty thousand people (exactitude lost its meaning: it was that sight, not the knowledge of the numbers that was so staggering) sat stonily silent on the muddy ground, staring at a stage where no one played: petrified playgoers in the marble stands at Epidaurus, thousands of years after the chorus had left for the last time.

No one in this country in this century had ever seen a "society" so free of repression. Everyone swam nude in the lake, balling was easier than getting breakfast, and the "pigs" just smiled and passed out the oats. For people who had never glimpsed the intense communitarian closeness of a militant struggle—People's Park or Paris in the month of May or Cuba—Woodstock must always be their model of how good we will all feel after the revolution.

So it was an illusion and it wasn't. For all but the hard core, the ball and the balling is over; the hassles begin again at Monticello. The repression-free weekend was provided by promoters as a way to increase their take, and it will not be repeated unless future profits are guaranteed (it's almost certain now that Woodstock Ventures lost its wad). The media nonsense about death and O.D.s has already enraged the guardians of the old culture. The system didn't change; it just accommodated the freaks for the weekend.

What is not illusionary is the reality of the new culture of opposition. It grows out of the disintegration of the old forms, the vinyl and aerosol institutions that carry all the insane and destructive values of privatism, competition, commercialism, profitability and elitism. The new culture has yet to produce its own institutions on a mass scale; it controls none of the resources to do so. For the moment, it must be content — or discontent — to feed the swinging sectors of the old system with new ideas, with rock and dope and love and openness. Then it all comes back, from Columbia Records or Hollywood or Bloomingdale's, in perverted and degraded forms. But something will survive, because there's no drug on earth to dispel the nausea. It's not a "youth thing" now but a generational event; chronological age is only the current phase. Mass politics, it's clear, can't yet be organized around the nausea; political radicals have to see the cultural revolution as a sea in which they can swim, like black militants in "black culture." But the urges are roaming, and when the dope freaks and nude swimmers and loveniks and ecological cultists and music groovers find out that they have to fight for love, all fucking hell will break loose.

August 25 – September 1, 1969

A Sense
of Crisis
Andrew Kopkind

But you see, we all believe in what Bakunin and Na-chaev said: that a revolutionary is a doomed man. . . . So you come to terms with the idea that you may be killed. And when you have to live with the prospect of being wiped out in a flash, you either stop doing what you're doing and remove yourself from that situation, or else you have to accept it and kind of repress it, and get it off your mind. Otherwise, you'll be nonfunctional. You can't walk around afraid and watching and looking over your shoulder. Anyway, I think many people these days have learned to live with that understanding. I learned to live with it somehow. —ELDRIDGE CLEAVER

Ralph Featherstone lived in Neshoba County, Miss., for two years, off and on. He had first come there one day in the summer of 1964 to meet three fellow civil rights workers in a church in the county seat of Philadelphia. The three had left Featherstone in Meridian in the morning; he was to catch up

261

with them in Neshoba later in the afternoon. Featherstone waited all afternoon in the church in Philadelphia. Micky Schwerner, James Chaney and Andy Goodman never did come.

Black folds in Philadelphia gave Featherstone a place to sleep and food to eat, and he'd pay them a few dollars every now and then with money he'd get from Northern white contributions to SNCC. Then the money stopped, and Featherstone began working on economic development projects which might make the Southern movement, and the black community, self-sustaining. I spent some time with Ralph in Neshoba, and the one day I remember most vividly was framed by two visits: by the FBI in the morning and by the notorious sheriffs Rainey and Price in the late afternoon. Neither visit was pleasant; the FBI was polite and menacing and the sheriffs were rude and menacing, but Ralph dealt coolly and good-naturedly with both. At the end of the day he drank a lot of milk and took medicine for his stomach. He kept a shotgun next to the medicine.

The economic development project didn't work, and Featherstone came back to Washington, where he had grown up and had gone to college, to try a similar scheme. That one came to little, too, and he went back to Mississippi for a spell. As the movements of the sixties progressed, he went to Japan to talk to young people there, and he traveled to Cuba to see what that was like, and to Africa. SNCC pretty much stopped functioning as an organization, but Featherstone and some of the best of the SNCC people kept working. In the months before he was blown to bits by a bomb in Bel Air, Md., Featherstone and several others were running a bookstore, a publishing house and a school in Washington. Ralph lived a few blocks from me, and we'd bump into each other every few weeks, chat briefly, and make vague plans to get together for a meal or a longer talk. As we both knew, the plans would not be followed. Somewhat mindlessly, I would slip Ralph into a category called "the black thing," which was a locked box decorated with exotic Benin artifacts, and a tag: "Do Not Open Until. . . . " I shudder now at the thought of the tag on the bag he had for me.

I don't doubt that the road from Meridian ended, in many more ways than one, last week. Ralph's progression in the last six years was, like the road itself, an attenuated metaphor. Strung out along the way were the mileposts of a generation, the markings of a movement, passed as soon as they were come upon, quickly out of sight. It's hard to say how one or another man or woman is bound to travel, and it can't be known where anyone is going to stop. Ralph missed a meeting in Neshoba; but then he kept his appointment in Bel Air.

* * *

A desperate irony of history, a dialectical pun, put Featherstone's death next to the explosions in the Wilkerson house in Greenwich Village and the bombings a few nights later of three corporations' offices in Manhattan. In evidentiary terms the events of that week seem totally disconnected. Featherstone and his companion, Che Payne, were most probably murdered by persons who believed that Rap Brown was in their car. Featherstone had gone to Bel Air on the eve of Brown's scheduled appearance at the trial to make security arrangements; Brown had good reason to fear for his safety in that red neck of the woods. No one who knew the kinds of politics Featherstone was practicing, or the mission he was on in Bel Air, or the quality of his judgment, believes that he was transporting a bomb—in the front seat of a car, leaving Bel Air, at midnight, in hostile territory, with police everywhere.

The police and newspaper accounts of the goings-on in the Wilkerson house on West Eleventh Street seem—in outline, at least—consistent within themselves and probable in the (dim) light of developments after the recent breakup of a formal Weatherman organization. The tensions within Weatherman, both organizationally and politically, were always as explosive as any bomb; Weathermen were experimenting not only with new tactics and ideas but with new styles of living, new ways of loving, and new values of existence. They changed their course almost fortnightly: puritanical one week, totally uninhibited the next; druggy and orgiastic, then ascetic and celibate; concerned with a mass line and liberal movements, then deep into guerrilla training. And all the time they were dealing—not very successfully—with open repression from the Man and open hostility from most other radicals. It was clear at the Weatherman convention at Flint in December that the organization was not going to grow in size and legitimacy, and as early Weathersymps and cadre from the collectives dropped out of contact, the core hardened. In a few months, the distance between the guerrilla center and the discarded cadre and the lost sympathizers could be measured in light-years; people who had once worked closely with the women who were, reportedly, in the Eleventh Street house knew nothing of those recent activities, and could not begin to find out.

The bombings in Manhattan on the night of March 11 appear to be the work of people with politics quite different from the post-Weathermen of Eleventh Street. The obvious differences can be seen in the messages the bombers left; even a cursory *explication du texte* indicates that the bombers were of the same anarchist strain as those who hit similar targets last November, and quite distinct from the specific line of Weatherman. The notes spoke in terms of "death culture" and life forces, but contained few of the internationalist, anti-police, anti-racism and pro-Viet Cong references which mark the Weather ethic.

But although the three events are disconnected in all particulars, they are at the same time tied at some radical bottom. Guerrilla attacks by the revolutionary Left and counter-attacks by the extreme Right seem almost natural in America this winter. When students demonstrate, they do not merely sit in but burn up: they fire-bomb a bank in Santa Barbara, snipe at policemen in Buffalo. Few peaceful marches end peacefully; both marchers and police are ready to fight.

The newspapers have begun calling the current crop of radicals "revolutionaries," but they have removed the quotation marks and have dropped such skeptical qualifiers as "self-styled" or "so-called" before the word. For the first time in half a century, at least—and perhaps since 1776—there is a generalized revolutionary movement in the United States. It is not directed at organizing labor or winning civil rights for minorities or gaining power for students in the administration of universities. Wholly unorganized and utterly undirected, the revolutionary movement exists not because it is planned but because it is logical: not because a handful of young blacks or dissident middle-class whites will it, but because the conditions of American life create it: not because the Left is so strong, but because the center is so weak.

It's worth saying what the revolutionary movement is *not*. First of all, it's not big—at least the active part. All the people who are into demolitions this year could gather in a town-house or two in the Village—and probably did. There have been scores of bombings in the past six months—in New York, Seattle, the San Francisco Bay Area, Colorado and scattered college towns. In Madison, Wis., for instance, someone predicted *Zabriskie Point* and bombed an ROTC building from an airplane (the bombs did not go off). But a hundred or two hundred people could have done all that, and there is no reason to believe that there are vast divisions preparing for the next assaults.

Second, it's not yet a revolution. A bomb in Standard Oil's headquarters in Manhattan does as much material damage to Standard Oil as a tick does to a tiger. Universities have not ground to a halt, draft boards have not been shut down, the war in Indochina hardly has ended. The resources of the corporations and the government that make public decisions and social policy are complete.

But then, the revolutionary movement is not isolated in its few activists, not confined to its few acts of violence. There was a general sense of depression in the liberal Left when the Eleventh Street house blew up; and there was a genuine sense of exhilaration when the bombings followed. People who could not, in their weirdest fantasies, ever see themselves lighting a fuse were lifted for a moment from their set of dull futility. For that reason, the guerrilla acts cannot be dismissed as "isolated terror" by a "lunatic fringe"; they draw a positive response from a surprisingly large number of ordinary people—even those who venture out of their conventional lives for nothing more exciting than a Moratorium rally, and who will tell you before you ask that they "deplore" violence. The contradictions of the society as a whole exist within each of them as well.

Finally, the revolutionary movement is not professional, nor is it politically mature, nor tactically consistent. Nor is there much chance that it will get itself together in the coming months. If it was a "tragic accident" that killed three young people in the Eleventh Street house, it was in one sense no accident: those who seek to build a revolution from scratch must inevitably make such mistakes. (For a description of how amatuerish revolutionaries can be, read Che's diaries). The politics of the guerrilla acts are not always self-explanatory, even to committed radicals; in what kind of political demands were the Manhattan bombings set? One New York radical activist said recently that those acts could have contextual meaning only if the messages demanded U.S. withdrawal from Vietnam and Laos, say, or freedom for Black Panthers in jail. A note, which threatened continued attacks until the war ended, for example, would make sense to many more people than the seemingly "nihilist" statements made last week.

At this stage, tactics can be crucial. Attacks against property — in which care is taken to avoid injuries to people — are much more easily understood than terrorist acts against police, much less "innocent" bystanders. It's necessary, too, to think through any action to avoid bringing retaliation down against those who are not responsible: for example, the firebombing of Judge Murtagh's house in New York (in protest against the trial of the Panther Twenty-one) was obviously prejudicial to the Panthers' case and their cause. If whites did that act, they should have made it their own responsibility — and they should have set its political meaning straight. Explanations are necessary, but they are hard to make by the underground guerrillas, in the absence of an overground mass movement — tied in sympathy but not in fact to those below.

* * *

The escalation of radical protest into revolutionary action will produce two major social effects: a sense of crisis in the society as a whole, and a need for repression by the authorities. The two effects are inextricably related. If there is crisis, there will be an appropriate response to it. The sense of crisis is not the work of the bombers or bank burners or demonstrators or Panthers alone. It develops easily when the phones don't work, the beaches are oil-slicked, the blacks are bussed to white schools, the priests are marrying, the redwoods are toppling, the teenagers are shooting-up, the women are liberating themselves, the stock market is falling and the Viet Cong is winning.

Neither does repression happen in a single tone of voice. Even in the most critical of times (*especially* in the most critical of times) the state acts, as Lenin put it, like hangman and priest. Despite the policy of "benign neglect" which the Nixon administration is following in most matters, the process of buying off black revolution—by accepting black militancy—is continuing at a fast clip. If the government tends to fall behind in the effort, private corporations, foundations and educational institutions keep up the pace. In the same months that Fred Hampton is killed or desegregation is postponed in Mississippi, millions of dollars went to black urban bureaucrats; black students were streaming into previously white colleges and white jobs; and the government made plans to give preferential hiring to blacks in construction jobs. It's easy but unwise to dismiss such methods as "meaningless," or "too little," or "cynical." Of course, the "Philadelphia plan" for hiring black construction workers is also a way to limit the power of labor unions. But in the near and middle distances those measures—the repressive and the cooptive—are reasonably successful in blunting the chopping edge of the black liberation movement.

In the week that Vice-President Agnew is denouncing "kooks" and "social misfits," and conspiracy prosecutor Foran is talking of a "freaking fag revolution," the Nixon administration and a coalition of politicans from (and including) Goldwater to Kennedy are proposing lowering the voting age to eighteen, and plans are going ahead for an all-volunteer Army. Again, the point is not that either of those proposals will accomplish much in the way of changing social values in

America; but those measures are not exactly Nuremburg Laws to be used against a radical force or a distasteful element of society.

In the wake of the bombings and deaths last week, the FBI fanned out to question anyone known to have a connection with the Eleventh Street people. Agents were unusually uptight; one set of FBI visitors called a New York man who declined to speak to them a "motherfucker." There were police agents with walkie-talkies standing around major airports all week long. The newspapers—especially in New York—bannered scare headlines and speculated endlessly, and foolishly, on the connections between the events. Authorities "leaked" word to Richard Starnes, a Scripps-Howard reporter in Washington who often acts as an unofficial flack for the FBI, that both Featherstone and the three Eleventh Street people so far identified had visited Cuba—and that Attorney Leonard Boudin, whose daughter's papers were found in the house, represented the Cuban government in legal matters in the United States. Sen. Eastland has now called for an investigation of the Venceremos Brigade of Americans who have gone to Cuba to harvest sugarcane. No one believes that the natives in America can be restless—all by themselves.

The level of fear (that is, paranoia with good reason) rose to exorbitant heights, but that too affects the general sense of crisis in the society. Seen in relief (if there can by any), that crisis is the most serious organizing effect of the bombings. If the radical movements are to win middle-class people—or those, both black and white, who aspire to middle-class comfort and security—they must devise ways of forcing real existential choices upon them. At one time, marches and rallies or sit-ins or building occupations provided a setting for those choices. But privileged Americans do not easily make the revolutionary choice. Only if their privilege is worthless are they free to act. Now, the sense of crisis is the specific contradiction to privilege: that is, all the things that Americans want to get and spend are without meaning if the world no longer holds together. At such times, people choose to fight—one way or the other. It may be that such a time is now.

March 23–30, 1970

The Changeling

Interview with Don Meinshausen

Don Meinshausen, a nineteen-year-old New Jersey stu-
dent, was called before the House Internal Security
Committee (formerly HUAC) one day in August to tes-
tify as a "friendly" witness on his activities as paid infil-
trator of SDS chapters, conventions, and the National
Office. Several months before, however, Meinshausen
had begun a process of changing allegiances from
HUAC to the Movement. He had come to Washington
to seek the advice of Karl Hess, a former Right-wing ac-
tivist and Goldwater aide, who in the past year had also
begun to think of himself as part of the radical move-
ment. The night before the HUAC hearing, Meinshau-
sen drafted a statement condemning the committee. The
next morning, before Meinshausen—dressed in jeans and
a work shirt, with long hair, a moustache and granny
glasses—had a chance to testify, committee staffers
learned of his change of mind and in a series of baffling
maneuvers (with attempted strong-arm tactics against

269

*the witness), managed to cancel the hearing altogether.
Later in the same week, Meinshausen was interviewed by
Andrew Kopkind, and the following edited version of the
recorded transcript was made:*

I grew up in Nutley, N.J. My parents were German immigrants, Lutherans. My father was a baker till his business
failed. He was conservative, and both my parents were
against communists—we have relatives behind the Iron Curtain who we would send packages to—and they were influenced a lot by the mass media. All sorts of things, like "I Led
Three Lives." We went to church once a week, but the
church was mostly old people. I couldn't identify with it. My
parents' attitude toward Negroes was very weird. It seemed
we liked Negro people all right, and we gave stuff to them as
charity, but we wouldn't want to live next door to them. We
put a lot of money in the house, and, you know, property values go down.

In high school I got caught up in the Goldwater movement.
We had a pretty big group; at the time we thought we wanted
a change. Looking back it all seems pretty romantic. We liked
him because he was an individualist, because he was fighting
the Eastern liberal establishment, because he was talking
about a return to American ideals. And he had guts. You
could just tell that he wasn't a phoney. But most of the people
who were in that group have gone, left. One of them has been
involved in People's Park; another one has been arrested for
selling guns; another's a real Leftist. Others, I guess, have just
gotten sick of politics and left it.

Gradually, I got into politics more seriously. I went
through a stage when I studied Ayn Rand and took a few
courses on Objectivism. I think I needed what they had: a
way to answer everything with a certain formula. And at one
point I went to a civil rights camp sponsored by the National
Conference of Christians and Jews. Most of the kids there
were more liberal than I was. Like, I would say that integration would never work—at the peak of the civil rights movement—or that federal aid to education would lead to federal
control. But I noticed that on a lot of things I was more radi-

cal than the others. They were still sort of hung up in a vague
sort of Christianity while I was coming out with something
like atheism. Once I was arguing with a girl, who was supposed to be liberal, about why two people should be allowed
to live together if they want to. She thought it was horrible; I
thought it was OK. I think I was looking for a radical alternative to liberalism, and the only place I could find it was in
Goldwaterism on the right. At one point I considered joining
the Birch Society and even went to some of their meetings.

In September 1967, I went out to California to a middle-
class junior college, Ventura. There was no YAF [Young
Americans for Freedom] out there, but there was an SDS
chapter. It was a very liberal type of thing. We were just
holding picket signs. I mean, how can you react to that? It
was like nothing. I held a few jobs: one job, at a MacDonald's
hamburger stand, really fucked me over—for $1.40 an hour.
They treated you like a machine. First they checked into my
background, and they found out I had a high IQ. I found this
amazing because I figured, MacDonald's hamburger stand,
why would they want to check my IQ? And you would have
to do something every single second; if you weren't making
hamburgers, you had to go around wiping stuff. They tried to
generate this phoney enthusiasm. "MacDonald's is clean and
neat and courteous" and "smile for the customers" and all
this type of thing. And I found out that it was really bad stuff.
I mean, I don't know if it was inferior meat or anything like
that, but it was just bland; it was not really that good at all.

I held some other jobs and then I came back East to Essex
County College in Newark, in September 1968. I wanted to go
back into politics since I'd really dug the Goldwater thing,
but I didn't want to contradict what I'd already done, so I got
involved in YAF. And what happened was that we were sitting around analyzing what happened to Columbia and saying
we don't want this to happen again, and gradually we got the
idea that if we could find out ahead of time what the radicals
were planning—you know, like the takeover of a building or
something—we'd be better off. We looked at it as a problem
in military strategy; we needed better intelligence. And I figured that since I was new I was the only person not known as

a Right-winger and that I could get into SDS much more easily.

* * *

Essex County is really one of the worst schools in the world. It's in a building right in the middle of Newark that was part of Seton Hall, which sold it to the city. It's old and dingy, and a couple of weeks a year they tear up the street and you can't hear anything that's going on. The halls are always crowded. You go into the cafeteria and it smells like a factory. There's no place you can go to relax. The college was started to keep kids off the streets, prevent riots and to make the city administration look good. A lot of the deans were brought up from places in the South. Only one of about thirty-three administrators was black. Another, the assistant to the dean of students, was a goddamn fascist. At one point he tried to get the Right-wing Italian kids to organize politically against me.

There was no SDS chapter at Essex, and to "infiltrate" I had to organize one. I talked to a lot of kids who looked friendly and said, look, let's organize an SDS or some kind of peace group. People liked the idea and I started to go through the channels, and that's when I got my first hasslings from the administration. They said I couldn't organize SDS because they didn't want any new national organizations on campus, so I said OK, we're going to call it Students for Peace. I wasn't really doing it as a put-on but as a kind of political experiment. I figured I'd just set it in motion and see how it moves along, and this way I could see firsthand what really happens. The first meeting of Students for Peace was OK. There were a lot of people there, and some very radical sponsors from the faculty, and I said, "Well, we're going to do this, this and this, and talk about the war, and see what we can do." Then at the second meeting we had I got a speaker from the National Lawyers Guild to come talk on draft resistance.

In the meantime opposition had developed from some of the Italian immigrant kids on campus. They were very hostile to SDS, because they had heard what happened at Columbia and they looked on Essex County College as their only chance of making it in society. They figured, if their college gets closed down or something like that, they'd get screwed. So they were very angry and showed up at the meeting with the Lawyers Guild speaker, shouting and disrupting and calling him a dirty communist. And all the time I'm trying to keep it down to a very low key, just to let it develop and see what happens, and these kids are fucking it up. Later I was called in by the dean, who accused me of holding a disruptive meeting and inviting an outside speaker without going through channels. He said the administration would hold a trial on the charges. So I went to the Lawyers Guild and one of the guys said, great, we'll represent you, make a big issue out of this. And he wrote a letter to the dean saying that. And the dean caved in because he was afraid of the lawyers, and eventually the charges just disappeared. I got a lot of publicity; I mean, I was interviewed by the school newspaper and all that. Suddenly I found myself cast in this role: SDS organizer on campus. And I thought, insane. This was the most insane possible thing that could happen. But it was cool, you know.

Another weird thing happened. SDS-Rutgers had called for a march through Newark, condemning the elections. So I figured the thing for me to do is get some kids to march, just to see how it goes again. I told the YAF kids about it, and they said they'd try to arrange some counter-demonstration, but that nothing serious would happen. They were wrong. The demonstration got wild. There was a rally inside a park, with SDS and the Panthers and guerrilla theater and everything like that. On the outside were the YAF kids plus these Italian North Ward kids, shouting and screaming at us. And we're trying to leave, and I don't know who started it, but somehow fights break out and more fights and there was a lot of misunderstanding and confusion about what to do, and all of a sudden I see these five guys about to attack me. And a black kid who I made friends with the day before is fighting off one of the kids who is attacking me and draws a knife on him. And all of a sudden the cops come, and they check this black kid who's got the knife and they arrest him. And at the same time the YAF kids are trying to stop the guys from beating me up, yelling, "Don't do it, don't do it, he's on our side." And my mind is going crazy. It was like literally being pulled apart. On one hand, this black kid who I'd just met — he was on probation but he risked himself to try and save me. And on the other side, there was another kid who knew what I was up to who also risked his neck to try and save me. I couldn't figure it all out. I wondered, am I to blame for all this that's happening?

Anyway, I continued as an SDS organizer. Eventually we formed a coalition with the black students and had big rallies leading to a sit-in which eventually closed down the school. It was really amazing. You know, like, for the first time in their lives, guys from opposite sides of town were talking to someone different and really trying to reach an understanding and agreeing on demands. The whites agreed to black demands for black administrators. And I was one of the leaders of it; I was sort of leading the hip people. I was really emotionally involved because, like, what kids were demanding was that certain incompetent people be fired, that we should have freedom of discussion, and make the school more responsive to the people there. And you know I could really dig something like this. Some of the kids in SDS didn't like it. They said: "Well look at your demands. None of them are oriented toward the working class. None of them show the contradictions of our society. They're all student-power demands. You can't build a movement from that." And I was screaming at them, "What the fuck do you know? I mean, you go to some place like Rutgers or Princeton or some place like that, while any day I get my ass kicked in over here." I was really pissed off at them.

I was getting variously hung up. Mostly I found good kids in SDS. Kids that really seemed to be committed to the Movement and really wanted to do good things. They helped me when I got in trouble with the dean. One time I had a talk with Mark Rudd and he really dug what I was doing, you know, organizing at a working-class college, and I felt a sort of superiority to kids who were going to Cornell and Harvard while I was doing working-class organizing. But some things I didn't like. Especially their attitude toward civil liberties.

That was very important to me. I'd talk to them and say, "If Gus Hall was not allowed to speak on campus, would you support or defend the campus position?" And they'd say, "Oh, I'd support it, because Gus Hall presents such a lousy view·of communism." And I've seen times at SDS meetings where they'd say, "Well, we created a civil liberties issue, but it was a good thing anyway." You know, apologizing! And saying that student power isn't really what we're up to. I was pretty far into it, but the farther in I got, the more confused I got. I think I understand some things a little better now, like what civil liberties mean in a society when one class makes the rules. But I don't believe in a manipulative struggle. I think we're going to have to work it up to revolution. Any other way is bad. And I figure if you can really get clear-cut concessions going, get them. Because I think the ruling class can make concessions that will hurt them, too, and eventually sort of maneuver themselves out of the picture.

* * *

Around January of this year I started to work for HUAC. One of the YAF kids told me that a guy from HUAC wanted to get in touch with me. There are a lot of connections between YAF and HUAC—they sort of mutually help each other out—and it was all sort of natural. This particular fellow, Herb Romerstein, was a nice guy. He was a member of the Communist party from 1947 to 1949. We met first in the Pennsylvania Railroad Terminal in Newark, and later we met seven or eight times in various restaurants. Sometimes Reynolds was there, an intelligence guy from the New Jersey state police. I had gotten literature and some names, and they said it looked good, pretty much what they wanted. They said especially to try to find connections between SDS and the CP.

I kept on getting all this stuff—names and leaflets—but I thought it was pretty silly. The names they could have gotten just by asking on a campus who the SDS people were. And the leaflets said things like, there's going to be a meeting somewhere; or else they said things like, America is an imperialist country and we're revolutionaries. I thought: big deal. So they're calling themselves communists. But Romerstein and Reynolds thought it was really something that anybody would call themselves revolutionary communists. What I wanted them to do was expose situations in which SDS was really manipulating people, and I wanted to have HUAC fight them ideologically, but that wasn't what was really going on.

At the same time I was getting more and more into dope. I tried acid, and a few other things. The two things—politics and dope—weren't really contradictory, but they sort of pulled me back and forth. Also at the same time, I began taking their money. Eventually I told them I was willing to go to the SDS convention in Austin, and they said they'd pay for it. I gave them all the resolutions and all the literature that was passed out—there was no security, and anybody could have gotten in. I figured it was all a waste of time, but Romerstein kept saying, "No, it's good stuff, it's good stuff." What it was was piles and piles of shit that no one should have bothered reading. He would ask me: What was happening to SDS? I would talk to a few guys and give him some quotes. Then he'd ask: Did anybody call himself a communist? I think they said that every other sentence. I heard it so much—you know, Marxist, communist and so on—I didn't think it was very impressive. Meanwhile, I was getting kind of involved. The speeches and stuff bored me, but after I got the HUAC stuff out of the way, I'd go off and talk with some people and smoke dope. I developed principles about what I was doing. I figured I was spying against SDS, but I wouldn't tell them about who smoked grass. I mean, if a person smokes dope and he's a communist, cool; I'll tell them he's a communist but I won't tell them that he smokes drugs. And I wouldn't tell on people who were really innocent. But I'd really give it to PL when I could. I hated them.

I went to Chicago twice, once to the SDS convention [in June], once to sort of work there. At the convention I guess I really became involved. I didn't want to work for HUAC, I just wanted to find the people closest to my own type of politics. But Romerstein was there, and he would be standing outside with the pigs and I would go to his hotel room and give the literature and tell him what was happening. But I was becoming more and more reticent to talk. I did find some people in the Anarchist Caucus I felt close to; they said they had a lot of YAF members in their SDS chapters, and I saw some of the former YAF people to talk to myself. I liked that, but I didn't like what I saw happening at the rest of the convention, and a lot of people agreed with me. Like the security guards. I thought they were just pigs. A kind of Gestapo within the movement. In fact, I thought the whole security thing was completely ridiculous, egotistical nonsense. It was like the Democratic convention, hassling people about credentials, and it wasn't doing any good. Anybody could get in who wanted to. I didn't like what I saw (the Ohio and Michigan delegations waving the *Red Book* and shouting "Long live Mao Tse-Tung" and "Ho, Ho, Ho Chi Minh," and I didn't like the thing with the Black Panther when he talked about pussy power and everyone yelled "stop male chauvinism" and I didn't like PL). I began to feel a little guilty because I felt that if I'd joined SDS a few years ago I could have stopped it from becoming what it is becoming.

Later I decided to go to work in the NO [SDS National Office]. Romerstein thought that was good. As it turned out I actually only worked there for one day, because Rudd was the only one I knew and he wasn't there, and they were very uptight about strangers. All I actually did was talk to Mark Rudd. I tried to warn him, tell him about what I was doing. I said, "Look, I know there are spies in SDS and a guy from HUAC has been after me to spy for them." And I told him about YAF — that YAF was becoming more libertarian — and in general I tried to tell him what was going on, and find out where his head was at. Sometime at about that point I decided it was all over.

* * *

I'm not too sure why I eventually changed my mind, but I guess it was building up in me for a long time. Karl Hess was very important to me. I met him at a YAF conference in the spring of '69. He really intrigued me. I talked to him as if I were an SDS person, and he was telling me how all these people like Taft and Webster and Jefferson were really sort of New Leftists, and that they wanted revolution, and things like that. I came to see him in Washington a few times after that, and eventually told him what I was doing. What happened in Newark during the Election Day march and all the things that happened in my school were important. Something in Carl Oglesby's book. Meeting members of SDS who used to belong to YAF. Taking acid. I'm really not sure. At some point my reasons for doing what I was doing came to seem sort of romantic, James Bondish. I wasn't ashamed of what I'd done, but I felt I had to make it right somehow, or rationalize it. But I guess I just wanted to stop. I don't know what I'm going to do, but now I consider myself part of the Movement.

September 29 – October 6, 1969

Underground
Woman

Mary Moylan

Mary Moylan was one of the "Catonsville Nine," who destroyed draft files at a Selective Service office in the suburbs of Baltimore on May 17, 1968. The nine were convicted of two federal and four state crimes; appeals failed, and six were to begin serving their concurrent terms on April 9, 1970 (two others were given brief extensions; the ninth defendant had died). Four of those scheduled to be imprisoned failed to appear at the appointed time. The woman among them—Mary Moylan— recorded the story of her first few days "underground." Hard Times obtained a copy, and is presenting it in Miss Moylan's own words. The editors believe that internal evidence in the story proves its authenticity. At the time she wrote, Miss Moylan was reportedly in an Eastern city.

I've been underground—if you can call it that—for only a short time. I was supposed to show up at the federal mar-

279

shal's offices in Baltimore on Thursday, April 9, at 8:30 A.M.,
to begin serving my sentence, which is two years, I think. We
had gotten together—the remaining eight of us—about a week
or so before that and the decision that came out of that meeting was that we would do our own thing. I hadn't intended at
all to show up, but then neither had I intended to—so to speak
—go underground. To cooperate with such authority is to find
yourself in a kind of weird position to begin with, and I had
just planned to take a walk and smell the flowers, and then
they could come and pick me up when they so desired. But
then, when I realized four men of the group were going underground, that they were not going to show up and were not
going to be available, I did some re-thinking and decided that
because women's liberation is one of the most important issues being raised, I felt I had to do the same thing—and do it
with sisters, and with the help of sisters. So I let a few sisters
know that I did not want to show up, and with their cooperation, I've been sitting around since Thursday.

Being "underground" is strange. I live in an apartment with
one bedroom, a kitchen, living room and hall. I spend my
days reading, drinking, smoking and sleeping. I'm not at all
sure what it means to be underground. I know it means being
out of touch with many people, being inactive. I was thinking
about the two Kathys—Wilkerson and Boudin—and wherever they are I hope they're in good health because I'm sure
they would probably get life sentences if they ever surfaced
again. But then, how do you operate? I don't think we have
the mechanisms set up for that. I think the black community
does, but not the whites. I think there is a growing interest in
the Movement in setting up some kind of an underground
network, and people are trying to get straight in their heads
what exactly "underground" means (we use the term so
easily).

I expect to turn myself in after the four men do. I think that
will be fairly soon, but if it lasts more than six months, say, I
would probably leave the country and go to Canada and see
what's happening with the resisters. I don't think the feds are
looking very hard for us because we're certainly not the ten-
most-wanted, and yet in one sense I think we must be very

irritating to them. And in this perhaps is our greatest impact.

Up until last Thursday I hadn't really decided what I wanted to do, because I'm confused on the whole question of non-violence. I believe in non-violence. There are two groups in the non-violent camp. One of these groups is straight pacifist; the other is much looser and feels that somehow we have to continue to respect human life: and that's probably the only way we hew the pacifist line. The sort of public non-cooperation of pacifists bothers me; most pacifists I know would have told me to go take a walk in the park and smell the flowers, but it just didn't strike me as enough. It would have been such a futile thing because they would have come and picked me up. The other difficulty is that the feds know who my friends in Baltimore are, and I had to consider the question of how much pressure would be brought to bear on them, so I knew I couldn't go to any of the people in Baltimore, and I had to go to other people in another city.

* * *

I have to laugh when I think about the Catonsville action. I don't regret it at all. I'm very content and happy I did it, but it was totally insane. The nine of us drove out to the Catonsville draft board offices around noon. It was a weekday, because we wanted to go when the board was open. Tom Lewis and I went in first, and he had a prepared speech to read to the clerks to reassure them that we were not going to wipe them out. Bureaucracy is fantastic: we walked in and nobody would look at us. Tom came up and started reading: "We are a group of clergymen and laymen concerned about the war." And nobody would look up, they were so busy writing. So we went through our scene—draft files were dumped into our baskets, and the phones were taken care of so the clerks couldn't call for help until we had left the building. The clerks were very upset—one woman kept screaming about us taking *her* files, and she would have to protect *her* files. The other woman in the office was determined to make a phone call, so we went through a wrestling match. But we eventually made it out, and I guess they eventually called. The night before, we had cooked up some homemade napalm, so we put the files on the ground outside and stood around in a circle watching them burn. There were some people from the press there, and some of our people made statements. We stood there and we waited and we waited and we waited, and the people were watching us — the clerks from the second floor — and nobody knew what we were doing. Then a little cop on one of those three-wheel things came up and he stood there and watched us, and we thought, "My God, they're not going to arrest us; what are we going to do?" But eventually they came skidding into the parking lot and they arrested us, and we went through the arrest scene, with the FBI wandering in and out.

Then finally we went to jail — thank God — I was so pooped. We hadn't had anything to eat — those people don't feed you — that was a big shock. I thought I'd always heard about cops giving you mugs of coffee, and I was just dying for a coffee or a Coke or something. We never got anything until 10 o'clock that night.

We had all known we were going to jail, so we all had our toothbrushes. I was just exhausted; I took my little box of clothes and stuck it under the cot and climbed into bed. Now all the women in the Baltimore County jail were black — I think there was only one white. The women were waking me up and saying, "Aren't you going to cry?" I said, "What about?" They said, "You're in jail." And I said, "Yeah, I knew I'd be here." So I lay down again and they kept on waking me up and wanting to know when I was going to cry. I said, "I left this morning knowing I was going to be here — what's there to cry about? I should have cried last night." They were funny; a lot of women in jail are coming off dope, and after they get off the first very bad withdrawal symptoms they have a hard time sleeping. I was sleeping between two of these women, and every morning I'd wake up and they'd be leaning on their elbows watching me. They'd say, "You slept all night." I'd say, "Yeah, and I plan to do that every night." And they couldn't believe it. They were good. We had good times.

* * *

I had a very thorough Catholic upbringing — all the way through nurses' training. I spent some time in Uganda working as a nurse-midwife with the Women Volunteers Association, a Catholic organization. The nuns sent me home in December 1965; they decided they didn't like me either. When I got home, I became, through some insanity, director of the group. Then I met Patrick Aloysius Cardinal O'Boyle, we had a few disagreements, and that finished me. I began working as a nurse in Washington—there's no such thing as working as a midwife in Washington—and met some of the active black people there.

Then George Mische, whom I had known for several years, came to town, and he wanted to start a radical Catholic house. It didn't appeal to me at all. I just didn't want to have anything to do with the Church to begin with and wasn't interested in attacking it or saving it or doing anything with it. I just wanted it to go away quietly.

The establishment press constantly described us, after Catonsville, as "Catholic pacifists," and that's when I stopped believing the establishment press. I'm much too Irish to be a pacifist, and my relationship with the Roman Catholic Church has been off and on, to say the very least, for quite a while. Realizing that that was where I came from, the "Catholic" title bothered me less than the "pacifist" title. But it's even more difficult now because I have no relationship with the Catholic Church, nor do I want any. Everybody in the group, except George and me, was either a priest or a brother or a sister or an ex-one-or-the-other. So everyone assumed when they met me that I was an ex-nun. I've had a lot of problems in my life, but that wasn't one of them.

I suppose the political turning point in my life came while I was in Uganda. I was there when American planes were bombing the Congo, and we were very close to the Congo border. The planes came over and bombed two villages in Uganda (I don't know how the hell anyone figures out where the borders are). But it wasn't that; it was what the hell were American planes doing, piloted by Cubans, bombing the Congo when, as far as I knew, the United Nations was the peace-keeping force in the Congo. Where the hell did the American planes come in?

Later on I was in Dar Es Salaam, and Chou En-lai came to town. The American Embassy sent out letters saying that no

Americans were to be on the street, because this was a dirty communist leader; but I decided this was a man who was making history and I wanted to see him. We did go and Chou waved to us — probably because we were the only white faces there.

When I came home from Africa, I moved to Washington and had to deal with the scene there and the insanity and brutality of the cops and the type of life that was led by most of the citizens of that city — 70 percent black. Nobody believed that the cops were ever brutal — all black people just happened to be lippy and they needed to get a slap in the face once in awhile, and that was just a fact of life.

And then Vietnam and the napalm and the defoliants, and the bombings: it was probably Vietnam last of all, as a matter of fact. All the liberals are running around bleeding all over Vietnam, and I can remember all those people who used to knit bandages for lepers in Africa, and all they prayed was that those lepers never ever came near them. The bandages went, and the lepers were happy, and they were happy, but there was never any desire to really deal with the problem. Sometimes I get the impression from some of the more liberal elements in the Movement that it's enough to keep the Vietnamese happy in Vietnam, but we don't want to be involved in any of the dirt and shit that goes on.

* * *

I got involved with the women's movement about a year ago. I had heard about it and read about it, and the women in Baltimore were forming a women's liberation group. I was in New York, where there were all kinds of women's lib groups, so I got in on some of that. In my relations with men I was becoming more and more aware of the fact that they were chauvinists — I guess that's the nicest thing I can think of to say about them. It struck me that there were all these men running around trying to build a human society who couldn't relate to a woman as a human being. The man-woman relationship is a basic unit of society; even if we have communes or collectives, still men and women are going to be with each other. Unless we can deal with that, I feel that our attempts to relate to the Third World or to any other group of people are going to fail. I began to believe that SDS, before their split, would have their revolution, and I certainly wasn't going to stop them, but that we would just have to do it all over again because they were incapable of building a human society, in large part because they're incapable of dealing with women's liberation.

I think I'm really talking about freeing *people:* men aren't proving anything about themselves as people in saying they've got muscles or that they can rape a woman; or that they're the brains and women are the heart; or that women have certain virtues, all of which are soft. Woman is compassionate, woman is this, that and the other thing, and it's nice to have women around to help men out when they need compassion. I really feel that this is a pivotal issue, and for me it's just a gut reaction; I very definitely would only relate to brothers who, I felt, were trying to deal with the issue—and preferably, only to sisters. If I ever decided to go through Catonsville again, I would never act with men: it would be a women's action for me or I wouldn't act. The Vietnamese and Algerian women have provided me with a real inspiration.

I think men get into competition with each other, and I don't know what the hell everybody's trying to prove. We're all absurd when you come right down to it, but somehow all of us together add up to something that makes sense. And I don't think that any one person or any group of people makes any *more* sense; somehow it's a totality of making sense. The anarchism of the Movement, with the very different groups operating, makes sense. Out of all that is going to come a future that is a human society.

I was very excited by the Weatherpeople in the "Days of Rage" in Chicago. I was in Chicago for that, but I was with RYM-II people. [an antagonistic SDS faction]. I felt that Weatherman was raising questions that the Movement wasn't even dealing with. Unfortunately, RYM-II just so overreacted to Weatherman that they—RYM people—ended up in the bag of being "good guys" and they're not going to have any confrontations.

The day I arrived in Chicago, four Weathermen had been

picked off from the middle of a demonstration. The Panthers had had a demonstration in front of the courthouse, and then RYM had one, and these four Weatherpeople, two of whom were from Baltimore, were picked off: The cops just walked right into the crowd, picked up four people and walked out. The RYM people did nothing. I said, "Oh, wait a minute, I've reconsidered this whole thing; I ain't hitting the streets with you. It's insane." Our Baltimore group got together and we talked about it, and I said I couldn't see any political reason to hit the streets with people who were going to let their own people be picked off. And what the RYM people said to me, which freaked me out, was that the Weatherpeople were not "ours" to begin with, so they could be picked up. The proper response, they said, was to get the badge number of the arresting officer and find out what the charge was. I don't know too many police forces — pig forces — in the world that compare to Chicago, and I really didn't feel that there was going to be a big dialogue.

The Weatherpeople came to Chicago, and they said they were going to bring the war home. Maybe you don't think that's a good idea, but it's the first time I've ever known SDS to do what it said it was going to do. And I'm not sure that's a bad idea. I wasn't going to go out and *do* it with them, but I didn't think it was such a bad idea . . . car windows and apartment windows . . . I don't have any problem with that . . . or the Loop . . . that's all right. Weathermen are raising questions. They're continually going through these insane fits of theirs, but some of their basic questions still haven't been answered. I disagree with them. I don't think that Red China's going to come marching over here and save us. I really don't think the blacks are going to be able to "do it" without us. I think Rap Brown really believes in a colorless revolution, and I really believe in it too. But I think it means we've got to rethink our tactics: and one of those tactics is going to jail. At the time of Catonsville, going to jail made sense to me, partially because of the black scene — so many blacks forever filling the jails and the whites being "very concerned." Jail was not part of the scene for those whites. I don't think it's a valid tactic anymore, because of the change in the country itself. I don't want to see people marching off to jail with smiles on their faces. I just don't want them going. The seventies are going to be very difficult, and I don't want to waste the sisters and brothers we have by marching them off to jail and having mystical experiences or whatever they're going to have. We're trying to get Bobby Seale and the sisters *out* of jail in New Haven. We've got to start picking up again on our sisters and brothers who have been put away and who have been screwed royally by this society. I think you have to be serious and realize you could end up in jail, but I hope that people would not seek it, as we did.

I have no problem with my own jail sentence. I'll be at the Women's Federal Reformatory at Alderson, W. Va., and there's a whole bunch of sisters down there in that jail — sister criminals as a matter of fact. I think it will be interesting to see what the women's response will be to women's liberation and the whole Movement. I hate to make this confession, but I am really looking forward to two years of peace, two years of three meals a day, and a bed I can sleep in every night and count on. I don't know what their "solitary" or whatever they call it is like, but — two years: I can make it.

The idea of jail doesn't bother me that much; the idea of cooperating with the federal government in any way at all irritates the hell out of me. My alternatives are to go to jail, go aboveground with an assumed identity, stay underground, or leave the country. Any way I choose, the government is choosing for me. But what we're questioning is their right, and they lost that right because of the obscenity and insanity of their actions, which are growing more and more obscene and insane.

I'm not worried about getting parole, because I wouldn't know what to do with it if I did get it. Parole can really screw you. They demand that you have a nine-to-five job that's a fairly decent job, and it's very much like being on welfare: they have the right to inspect where you live; you can't move without their permission; you can't get married without their permission; you can't go out of town without their permission; you have to be careful whom you see and what activities you're involved in.

* * *

What's happening in the Movement now is a separation between so-called "good guys" and the dirty "bad guys." A lot of people say that Weathermen are for shit and we're not going to waste a lot of time helping them or defending them or trying in any way to deal with the issues they're raising. You know the line: the government is going to have to take care of them, and we're better off probably if they do because their tactics are terrible and their politics are worse. The Catonsville Nine have always been in most people's minds the good guys; we've been socially acceptable. Most people wouldn't be too upset to have us to their house. You know, "take-a-nigger-to-lunch." But if we think the establishment is illegal, then what are we doing making ourselves so legitimate and so acceptable? It seems to me that we're playing the establishment game. I think we should be saying that we identify with the two Kathys and with Ericka Huggins and the women in New Haven.

I very definitely see myself as a criminal. I don't even know what the hell "prisoner of conscience" means. I think if we're serious about changing the society that's how we have to see ourselves. That "prisoner of conscience"—if there is any such thing as conscience and if anybody has it—I guess all of us are prisoners of it, but it doesn't do anything politically to me at all. We're all out on bail, and let's all stay out.

April 20–27, 1970

America:
Honor or Off Her

Andrew Kopkind

On the eve of the Fourth of July in Washington, the airport was empty, the hotels untenanted, the taxis idle, the restaurants half-filled. The Upper Middle Americans who people such places must have been asleep, away or afraid. The action, such as it was, flowed along the freeways into the capital, spilled out from the highway Hot Shoppes and Howard Johnsons, and condensed on the avenues and parks in the monumental center of the city. There were no hardhats, stiffnecks or straightlaces in sight. The patriots gathering for Honor America Day were everything their founding mothers and fathers worried about: dirty, hairy and very stoned.

It was one of those dark and swampy Washington nights, when a stroll around town felt like a tour through someone's mouth. From certain fetid cavities, cops on horses rode out to meet the bands of freaks who splashed in the marble fountains and strung out on grassy knolls. The skirmish lines were rough and random. For their own reasons, the cops would decide to chase the kids off this or that strip of territory as the night wore on. "This area is closed," the loudspeakers atop the police cars blared. The cars would move along the grass and almost nudge the kids. Then the park police condottieri would trot up and push them further on. The kids would move along to occupy some other piece of turf. There was no moon at all, but a fume of marijuana hung over the Mall like gunsmoke over Lexington and Concord.

Straight Nation did not fall to Freak Nation on this Glorious Fourth. The most the kids could do to honor America was "mar" (the media's favorite verb) an otherwise inane celebration: by hassling police, splashing the horses, booing Bob Hope, and generally calculating to *épater les bourgeois.* There was a predictable complement of doping, nudity, vandalism, sex, cherry bombs and tear gas. But if it's true that the revolution is in our heads — or at least begins there — the weekend was not without its victories. This 194th anniversary of Independence was certainly different from the other 193. President Nixon and his plastic sub-cabinet of motel managers, franchise tycoons and Late Show producers "brought us together" as they had promised. Us and Them.

The day's adventures began with a pious demonstration by the Puritan Right at the Lincoln Memorial. Miss Teenage Runner-Up of 1967 declaimed "I Speak for Democracy." A baffled token Negro mastered the ceremonies. Kate Smith sang her song and waved her World War II salute, although it was unclear which side of that conflict she wanted to evoke. Finally, Billy Graham gave a short and rousing sermon, ending in a rhetorical cadenza cribbed from a George Wallace campaign button: "Never! Never! Never!"

While the straight people stuck American flags in paper cups forming a giant U.S.A. on the White House grounds, the freaks repaired to the Reflecting Pool and the Washington Monument slopes to toke up, rip off and tear down whatever wandered into their lines of sight. Orangeade dealers who raised their prices from an exorbitant quarter to an outrageous 30 cents were the first to feel the force of the revolutionary fist. Then three huge arc lights, one of them mounted on a truck, were hurled into the pool by the enraged masses.

Mounted policemen who dared interfere were swept into the dustbin of history under a blitzkrieg of firecrackers.

Those revels ended in a furious thunderstorm, but others began as the gala show of Hollywood stars performed before national "educational" television cameras and a large audience of Washington suburbanites. Bob Hope told his sad stale jokes once again — perhaps for the last time — and the crew of comedians and singers struggled to recall an Other America where racism, sexism and national pride were more universally appreciated. Then the freaks co-opted the fireworks display by getting stoned and digging them in dimensions unknown to the straights, and the whole expensive affair sputtered to an end in cop-baiting, tear-gassing and busts.

* * *

For half a year or more, the Yippies, the White Panthers and others on the anarcho-freak wing of the radical Movement had tried, without success, to organize a smoke-in for the Fourth of July in Washington. One thing did not lead to another, and organization dissolved in the different hang-ups of the various groups. Rumors that a hundred freaks were working nine-to-five in hippie pads all over Washington to roll 10,000 joints in stars-and-stripes cigarette papers gave some hope that underground organizers would emerge at the last minute, but nothing like that ever happened. (The flag papers were distributed during the day, but there was little free grass.) Instead, J. Willard Marriott, Nixon's favorite motelier, got it on as the Yippies never could. Hundreds of thousands of dollars were raised for Honor America Day from scores of corporate PR departments, among them: ALCOA, AT&T, Campbell Soup, Chemical Bank of New York, Eli Lilly & Co., General Mills, Gulf Oil, J. Walter Thompson, McCall Publishing, Newsweek, Owens-Corning, Pat Frawley Enterprises, Proctor & Gamble, RCA, Raytheon, Reader's Digest, Sears Roebuck, Scott Paper, Standard Oil of California, Indiana and New Jersey, Travelers Insurance, U.S. Steel, Walt Disney Studios, Young Americans for Freedom Inc. A letterhead was formed comprising a good cross section of the ruling-class Right, which was then expanded to include a select corps of their liberal lieutenants: Hubert Humphrey, Roy Wilkins, Jackie Robinson. On cue from the Administration, Sen. Mansfield enlisted a covey of doves to further legitimize the proceedings. George McGovern endorsed Honor America Day: "I believe that the flag should be held high above the debate on the war in Southeast Asia. We are passing through troubled times."

Like all the ideas of Nixonism, Honor America Day grew out of a sense of advertising and public relations and no sense of the social forces underlying press agentry. Like his "plan" to end the war in Indochina, Nixon's plan to end the war at home is not just useless but self-defeating: that is, it traps only those who set it. In the case of the foreign war, the Nixon plan to evade domestic criticism by withdrawing American foot soldiers—the while winning a military victory through Saigon—will founder on the reality of the Indochinese people's war against the United States. Nixon cannot understand that struggle, so he chooses not to believe it. So he must suffer political defeat himself, or oversee the destruction of the society he was elected to preserve.

Nixon's domestic plan, in the same way, does not bring people together, but creates the very situations which will tear them apart. Honor America Day—not a very significant project any way you look at it—is still a good example of that self-set trap. It gave a time and space dimension to all the values which much of young America finds most alienating, exploitative and repressive. A cleverer president would have held an enormous Fourth of July rock festival on the floor of the Grand Canyon or on top of Mount McKinley—and Columbia Records or Sara Lee would have rushed to bankroll it. But at bottom, Nixon is still a loser, and his tacky, third-rate festival provided one more opportunity for kids to liberate themselves, for the police to enrage themselves, and for Middle Americans to frighten themselves to death.

* * *

It should be clear by now to everybody except the blindest denizens of the White House that the social transformation of America cannot be stopped, at least without committing genocide upon the Black Nation and much of the white population under thirty-five. In the last few years the possibility of leading decent lives has occurred to so many people that it is inevitable that they will find ways to lead them. Visions of liberation proceed in no orderly way, but they travel with an iron logic of their own: from Birmingham to Woodstock, Peace Corps to Weatherman, red base to blue acid — and back again. There are a thousand ways to see the future, and they all work.

The disintegration of Bob Hope's America — in the same way — is disorderly and entirely logical. It is failing because its institutions cannot allow people to integrate the aspects of their lives in a way that makes sense. It will quite literally blow Nixon's mind when he realizes that many of his subjects find it more meaningful to die in a revolutionary collective than live in an anomic suburb.

What John Sinclair calls "death culture" is built into the social institutions and fundamental relationships of technological America. The best universities are authoritarian, the most liberal politicians are elitist, the most generous corporations are exploitative, the nicest families are repressive, the most tolerant people are racist, the wisest diplomats are imperialists. As America gets better and better, it gets worse and worse.

That essential contradiction eludes J. Willard Marriott, but it is simply and easily comprehended by the kids who grew up in his motels. At this moment in history, they are driven to oppose motel values and to destroy the institutions which express them. Dumbfounded editorialists and threatened politicians may call that nihilism, but it is the very opposite: the destruction of the worse America is in itself the construction of the better; the culture of opposition is the only culture of affirmation. Happy Independence Day!

July 13–20, 1970